ANA PERAICA
VICTIMS SYMPTOM (PTSD AND CULTURE)

ANA PERAICA
VICTIMS SYMPTOM (PTSD AND CULTURE)

Theory on Demand #3

Victims Symptom
PTSD and Culture

Editor: Ana Peraica
Copy editing: Vicky Anning and Michael Dieter
Texts: Sezgin Boynik, Adila Laidi Hanieh, Geert Lovink, Ana Peraica, Stevan Vukovi
Interviews by: Ana Peraica (with Enrique Arroyo, Noam Chomsky, Agricola da Cologne, Anur
Had iomerspahic, Joseph de Lappe) and Marko Stamenkovic (with Peter Fuchs, Jonas Staal,
Carlos Motta, Neery Melkonian and Tomas Tomlinas)
Artists' statements: Mauricio Arango, Alejandro Duque, Andreja Kuluncic, Marko Peljhan and
Martha Rosler
Glossary: Tihana Jendricko and Tina Peraica
Comissioned by: Lab for Culture, Amsterdam, 2008

Design: Katja van Stiphout
DTP: Margreet Riphagen
Printer: 'Print on Demand'
Publisher: Institute of Network Cultures, Amsterdam 2009
ISBN: 978-90-78146-11-7

Contact
Institute of Network Cultures
phone: +3120 5951863
fax: +3120 5951840
email: info@networkcultures.org
web: http://www.networkcultures.org

This publication is available through various print on demand services.
For more information, and a freely downloadable pdf:
http://networkcultures.org/theoryondemand.

CONTENTS

The project *Victims' Symptom (PTSD and Culture)* was commissioned by Lab for Culture in the occasion of their first anniversary and sponsored by European Cultural Foundation. The project itself was based on Nettime and Yasmin mailing list discussions entitled 'War Profiteers in Art', following up the Venice Biennial 2007 settlement. It was critical of the use of victims in cultural production, but necessarily found itself in the dangerous field of reusing them again.

The project consisted of commissioned texts, artworks and interviews as well as a glossary assisting with the transfer between different disciplines, grounding the research in clinical psychiatry. They were meant to verify our notions of victims in terms of cultural hyper-production that shifted from original clinical meanings some time ago.

According to contracts for maintenance, the site is going to be taken down following with conclusion of the commission period with artists in 2009. After this point, we'll no longer be able to access the essays and discussion live on the site. As a curator of online projects most of which disappeared for similar reasons (*Technology of Sounded Space* back from 1997 and *Machine_Philosopher* from 1999), I found myself in the problem of how to document media artworks that were not commissioned by art institutions, but rather for temporary events, anniversaries, symposia or festivals.

To lose hard work and great collaborations among clinical psychiatry professionals and cultural practitioners, as both artists, theorists and programmers, would be a great mistake, specifically for the reason that this type of academic interdisciplinary research demands a great deal more effort from all participants in crossing the boundaries of their own disciplines, as it begins with rechecking all terminologies and methods. But being not at the same time 'academic' in terms of production, it would be hard to squeeze an Internet project into official academic proceedings.

The new book series from the Institute of Network Cultures (INC) has provided a solution for the preservation of this work. Although there are some differences in the transfer from a dynamic Internet project to a static book, at the expense of artworks, the project will ultimately itself stay with its original public – the online communities for which it was meant, and from where it originally arrived.

Most importantly, it would also document a precise moment in which it was produced; Kosovo's fight for independence, Srebrenica's cries for acknowledgement and the problems of Palestine just prior to the last attacks in Gaza.

To document means not to commit a mistake – of reusing victims of the time for a mere event, be it an anniversary or festival.

Ana Peraica
Split, 2009

THE EXPLOITATION OF DEATH
ANA PERAICA

This introduction is one of the outcomes of the debate provoked by my email – 'War Profiteers in Art' – criticizing Robert Storr's set up at the 2007 Venice Bienniale.[1] The debate was held in parallel on two email lists/networks in September 2007 – Nettime and Yasmin – and ended up in a project called Victims' Symptom – Post Traumatic Stress Disorder (PTSD) and Culture (Lab-forCulture, European Cultural Foundation, 2008).[2] Problems of curating such art were presented separately at Continental Breakfast Meeting in Istanbul (2007), while methodological discussions were included at the Mutamorphosis Conference in Prague (Leonardo and CIANT, 2007). Critical input to the thesis has been injected by George Slavich, a researcher in psychology who has, after his public lecture in MediLS, claimed the possibility that, "whole cultures are suffering from PTSD", referring to the Croatian population.[3] The reason for introducing a clinical definition of PTSD into this discourse around a cultural project was its analytical and clinical testability.[4] As an indicator of trauma, it provides a clear definition based on practical evaluation via scientific methods, as opposed to the vaguely defined notion of trauma often used in cultural studies, especially trauma and Holocaust studies.[5] More specificially, the scientific definition includes a hormonal reaction, showing the level of cortisol hormone.[6]

Using scientific tools, continual strategic research would, therefore, open up more radical methods of distinguishing a report of the victim and a diary of a real or fake victim as well as its narratives, but also the dangers of evoking the original trauma and, therefore, re-victimizing the untreated or even unrecognized victim in a variety of ways, through political, but also cultural productions.

Bringing together artists, theoreticians and programmers, the project Victims' Symptom mapped an interdisciplinary field between cultural studies and clinical research that explored a variety of methods, frameworks and practices. Two young scholars, Tihana Jendri ko and Tina Peraica, from the Psycho-trauma Center in Zagreb, have carried out research working with PTSD patients in practice. A new critical glossary was introduced to help clarify the definition of symptoms.

One additional methodological and contextual task, provoked by the death of Joseph Weizen-baum, the author of the first software program dealing with contemporary (Rogerian) psychiatry – the ELIZA (1966) – was to examine the abuses of psychiatric knowledge, not only its possibili-

1.   52nd Venice Biannual had the concept/title: Pensi con i Sensi, Senti con la Mente, or Think With the Senses, Feel with the Mind: Art in the Present Tense.
2.   Project Victims Symptom (PTSD and Culture): http://victims.labforculture.org
3.   G. Slavich, Slobodna Dalmacija, 2006 (the newspaper's archive has been inaccessible since 01.01.2008).
4.   Glossary: 'Posttraumatic Stress Disorder (PTSD)', p. 143.
5.   Stevan Vukovi : Niemand zeugt für den Zeuge' p. 49.
6.   Glossary: 'PTSD', p. 143.

ties to cure.[7] Besides New Age self-help and the neoliberalist conceptions of the customer as the victim to be saved by a product, more radical examples emerge; for example, the engagement of psychiatrists in armed con ict and war in ex-Yugoslavia.

The negative outcome of psychiatry in the cases of Serbian war criminals Jovan Raškovi and Radovan Karad i , who obviously misused the psychological and social knowledge, inducing the social discourse of the 'victimisation' ("we are the victims") as a call for historical revenge ("do not forget"), was analyzed by artists, theorists and scientists to find ways of de-victimizing the dominant discourse that precedes and contributes to war itself.[8]

Toward this end, a need for mapping the intersection of various discourses (clinical, cultural and political) and finding its key elements was crucial. The central questions were: why are victims reported so frequently? How are they reported? In which specific discourses do they appear? What might these discourses indicate? What impact does the report have on the public when calling upon victims? Are there hidden intentions or goals implied? Are real victims' speeches present in the reports about them and how? Are they in any way helped or are they possibly used? What is the difference between the real victim's speech and a fake victim? How do we recognize a fake victim? Why are there fake victims? How does our culture institutionalize victims? What is the advantage gained by a fake victim?

Victims' Symptom Layout

The first phase of the Victims' Symptom project was to map the constantly recurring phenomena of victims in the media, using the Internet, which fortunately today includes other (older) media, such as newspapers, TV and radio via portals. We have used their RSS feeds to track, record and visualise this information.

The page, designed by Pieter van Kemenade (aka Pike) from LabforCulture, enabled a Google search in 12 languages that are thought to have news on victims, searching for up-to-date articles (i.e. "fresh victims"). Unfortunately, the outcome of a couple of months of analysing RSS news feeds has shown that victims of World War II are frequently included in the news. They have become, for their cultural institutionalisation, more important than contemporary fatalities. This shows a present cultural need for revenge in a historical context, behind the institutionalisation of a victim's narrative.

The mapping of these discourses was made possible through an artwork by Mauricio Arango (Colombia/USA) titled Day by Day.[9] This was a version of his earlier work, Vanishing Point, which demonstrated how certain countries appear and disappear from the world map of information on a daily basis; such as, for example, the relatively unknown phenomena of Myanmar or the sudden emergence of various ex-USSR countries after civil unrest or con ict. The map we produced, which curiously enough omitted Australia (having only four 'victims' in a period of a month, two

---

7.   "ELIZA is a computer program by Joseph Weizenbaum, designed in 1966, which parodied a Rogerian therapist, largely by rephrasing many of the patient's statements as questions and posing them to the patient. Thus, for example, the response to "My head hurts" might be "Why do you say your head hurts?" The response to "My mother hates me" might be "Who else in your family hates you?" ELIZA was named after Eliza Doolittle, a working-class character in George Bernard Shaw's play Pygmalion, who is taught to speak with an upper class accent". http://en.wikipedia.org/wiki/ELIZA

8.   Glossary: 'Necrophilia and Generals', p. 140.

9.   Mauricio Arango: 'Day after Day', p. 17. Original artwork at http://dayafterday.labforculture.org

of which were actually natural accidents, one a human accident and, finally, one arrested terrorist suspect), showed a totally strange picture. Paradoxically, the term 'victim', obviously re ected the discourse behind the mapping process, pushing up the USA, UK, Germany and France to the same level of intensity as the Myanmar/Burma tsunami and a fatal earthquake in China. In one month, the map had totally erased Tibet, which did not appear in any official media reports. Also, despite the huge number of 'victims' occurring in Africa, the whole continent was only slightly vis-ible on the map, revealing that victims were becoming what media theorists would call 'redundant old news'. The world is not interested in the serialised death of 'one by one', but rather, large-scale dying in distinguishable groups.

What happens when we receive this news through different media? This was the subject of detailed research entitled Bad News by Andreja Kulun i (Croatia) in collaboration with Tina Pera-ica.[10] The thesis was supported by research that a cortisol level may indicate trauma, even when a person is not directly affected audio-visually by a trauma, but the effect is mediated.[11] While inviting users to test their own stress levels and giving them solutions for a cure in terms of self-therapy, the Bad News online pool collected statistics about which news and victims are relevant to the user in terms of gender, age group, nationality and level of education, among other char-acteristics. The data can be filtered to show many interesting outcomes: post-war societies have developed social coping mechanisms while societies living in peace have not developed such coping techniques. Also there is a higher level of tolerance to stress, whereby some news does not appear as life threatening in countries that have experienced major shocking events such as combat, natural disaster and so on. A subsequent study of the media, as I have suggested in the debate No News – Good News, would include several layers of analysis on how media is not only used for broadcasting and reporting, but also for in icting trauma onto the public. Comparing news productions in different countries, one may notice a couple of important stress inducing presentations.[12]

How to deal with stress in terms of self-monitoring tips such as those offered by the Bad News project is also discussed in the text by Geert Lovink (The Netherlands), who is concerned with exploring people's journalism – or the blogging culture – as a self-management tool.[13] Un-fortunately, some cases have shown that bloggers have also produced a counter-culture of sorts; predatory psychiatrists leaving their advice in the comments section of blogs, producing a hybrid culture of 'taking care'.

Alejandro Duque (Colombia/Switzerland) in WDWTH? (Who did What to Whom?) has been

---

10. Andreja Kulun i , 'Bad News', p. 90. Original artwork at: http://badnews.labforculture.org
11. Glossary: 'Trauma from a Distance', p. 141.
12. As; (1) The speed of TV reports (news reporters talk much faster than other journalists) in combination with background music that has a rhythm comparable to high blood pressure or even bringing together the frequencies of voice and the background music close to the state of two coinciding pressures – creating 'a heart attack effect' that is used for increasing the public's adrenaline level; (2) The shock ef-fect of inducing the public into traumatic news – always starting with the most threatening reports and concluding with the least threatening news, ending with 'the least of adrenaline' in sports, instead of preparing us for the most shocking news that can be analyzed for the narrative oscillation. (3) Unclear reading of reasons, introducing a confusion about the possible threat, usually showing up the threat and with a delayed calming down, which is a known stress inducer; (4) The actual impossibility of doing, underlining media's declared helpless state of 'just seeing'.
13. Geert Lovink, 'Blogs as Self-Management Tools', p. 91.

working with an expert team to show the impossibility for the survivor to socialise, revealing our prejudices towards PTSD patients.[14] In doing this, he has made another version of a net.art classic, My Boyfriend Came Back from War by Olia Lialina (1997).[15] While Lialina presented a fictional story from the outside, as told from the girlfriend's angle, Duque shifts to the subjective speech of a survivor whose story is neglected, mixing it with ordinary Internet Relay Chats (IRC) and people's communication. A constant repetition of one's own story showed a total sense of disorientation, both in space and time, induced by a parallel coexistence of the world of the past (the recurring trauma) and a sense of 'being used' by society to fulfil the 'dirty job' of building another world, a future that ironically does not include one's own place within it.[16] While in Duque's work the narratives were individual, in the text of Sezgin Boynik (Kosovo) they were a cultural point of the meeting of the victim and the aggressor after the con ict that reached its peak with the destruction of the Kosovo art show Odstupanje in Belgrade.[17] The problem of the survivor's tale and the reconstruction of events was additionally analysed in the work in progress by Marko Peljhan (Slovenia), which uses the military maps of Srebrenica, showing up the objective and a series of subjective interpretations.[18] This, in the text of Stevan Vukovi (Serbia), has shown the problem of the survivor and the witness, as analysed in terms of reliability of witnessing real and oppressed memories.[19]

The possibility of reconstructing history from the memories of survivors, as claimed by clinical positions, is indeed impossible as the only clear picture of events are held by medical ethics or released only for special circumstances to courts.[20] As such, it is inaccessible to the public, which in turn romanticizes and fictionalizes the event. While real witnesses are unable to speak and become invisible, or their stories are kept off the official record and hidden, a cultural need for the proliferation of fake witnesses appears along with the generation of victims' discourses ("we are the victims").[21] This logic becomes an interpretative manoeuvre in the work of Martha Rosler (USA), which explored the significance of the stress function in the total conspiracy and madness of the post 9/11 world, inducing paranoia in the smallest details of existence, which in turn contextualizes and re-interprets everything.[22] This induction of the victims' discourse can be understood as emerging from a need to control, as victims are by definition helpless.

After mapping the discourse of victims, both diachronically and synchronically, analysing the reasons for their media coverage and abuse and the engineering of the discourse of victims, with the resulting clash between survivors and the public, and the impossibility of reporting the traumatic event without inducing further trauma, we analysed the memorial – a highly personal expression that excludes the world at large.[23] In the text by Adila Laidi Haineh (Palestine), the problem of the representation and dignity of death, and dealing with the grief of other people, is

---

14. Alejandro Duque: WDWTH', p. 30. The original artwork at http://wdwtw.labforculture.org
15. All versions of Olia Lialina's MBCBFW at http://myboyfriendcamebackfromth.ewar.ru
16. Glossary: 'Re-experiencing', p. 130; 'Regression', p. 131; 'Repression/Repressed', p. 131.
17. 'Force of trauma', p. 32.
18. Marko Peljhan: Landscape 1995', p. 48.
19. Stevan Vukovi : Niemand zeugt für den Zeuge', p. 49.
20. Glossary: 'Amnesia', p. 105; 'Avoidance', p. 107; 'Denial', p. 113; 'Dissociation', p. 114.
21. Glossary: 'Dependence Projective Identification', p. 113; 'Ingratation Projective Identification', p. 118; 'Martyr', p. 120; 'Victim Role or Posited Roleplaying', p. 142.
22. Martha Rosler, 'Dust of the Office', p. 66. The original artwork at http://dustoftheoffice.labforculture.org
23. Glossary: 'Memorial', p. 121; 'Mourning/Bereavement', p. 121.

examined using the example of building a memorial.[24] Memorials only serve survivors. The urban memorabilia that are present not only in monuments and graveyards, but also in practices of naming were researched as a starting point for introducing a politics of revenge in the discussion.

On the Institutionalisation of Revenge

Contrary to ordinary victims' narratives, clinical psychiatry offers us the definition of the stress of hope that includes the culturally oppressed desire for revenge.[25] The original drive for revenge has been politically institutionalised by systems of justice, as political philosophers like Hobbes would note, to end an originary state of chaos.[26] Revenge was abandoned by the social contract and handed to the justice system. But once the justice system fails, and it surely fails wherever there are victims of a human action involved (including victims of natural disasters induced by humans), the problem is – what happens to the social contract? Radically speaking, each victim is a failure of the social institutions that claim legitimacy through the anticipation of con ict. In other words, victims are caused by events such as wars, but are then produced by a failure of a social contract that should have prevented these con icts in the first place. When this happens, the original need for revenge that was given to society in exchange for peace and safety fails and the necessity for compensation increases; which is, of course, the state of war, the state of revenge. In this situation, is the original need for revenge or the institutionalised and instrumentalised form of revenge doing more harm? As I argue in this text: it is not problematic when the individual feels a need and manages to express the original revenge under moral restrictions. But it is a problem when society instrumentalizes the same need, instead of resolving the revenge in terms of justice.[27] It is especially problematic if the instrumentalisation has been done for other purposes, being the colonisation of territory or individual gains (as pensions, apartments, or even PhDs, Pulitzer Prizes or fame). But first – let's dive out of the dilemma of real and fake victims: ones that ask for revenge and others that ask for something induced by the feeling of remorse and helping.

Victims and Heroes

One of my students recently wrote on the 1994 Pulitzer Prize winner Kevin Carter's photo of a baby starving to death in front of a vulture, specifically by considering the shock of viewing a photograph in Barthesian terms.[28] He immediately deconstructed the image into a 'good baby' and an 'evil bird', applying the discourse we learn from childhood where there is a victim on the one side and an aggressor on the other. Even if the situation in the photo were different – a small baby killing a bird – he would have mostly likely concluded the reverse case scenario: a nasty child kills a bird. But the fact is that birds do not pass ethical and moral judgments. And in terms of survival, it is not even applicable legally in human terms, even in extreme cases such as starving on a boat. It is a fact that vultures eat corpses, including human corpses, which also includes babies. So even if a baby could kill a bird for fun, while a vulture waits for the death of a baby for survival, the outcome in either case cannot be easily differentiated. There must be some other

24. Adila Laïdi-Hanieh, 'Regarding One's Pain: The 100 Shaheed-100 Lives Memorial Exhibition', p. 68.
25. Glossary: 'Revenge', p. 131.
26. T. Hobbes, Leviathan, Oxford: Oxford University Press, 1996.
27. Glossary: 'Power Projective Identification', p. 128.
28. R. Barthes, 'The Photographic Message', A Barthes Reader, New York: Hill and Wang, 1991,. 15-31.

instance when the decision is made.

What is frightening when seeing this photo is that we are immediately constructing a learnt mechanism: victims are good; the opposite of victims are aggressors, and we cannot perceive an interpreter (the photographer is standing still). That is what is terrifying. It is the photographer who is the only moral adult present not in a helpless state and not in mere survival mode. He makes the decision to take a picture instead of throwing a stone at the vulture. He has another goal and only his goal applies outside this situation: the photography – the publicity – the award – the fame.

Well, the photographer killed himself, we learnt afterwards. But the problem is that many of us feel he should have been 'killed' for the photo, not been awarded a prize. Connecting the suicide of the photographer with the photography was disputable. One death can be drawn directly to the meaning of the other only in a murder, not suicide, as Mirbeau observed in his morbid writings.[29] The revenge of a viewer appears here as the decisive fact, a disguise. What makes me angry is that we have been deprived of our right to avenge the victim, if we cannot change the original circumstances, but we are oppressed to see them, to observe the indolence of the other. We may feel: the photographer should have been imprisoned; Miloševi should suffer a live trial; the Dutch army should be punished for their act towards Srebrenica, and the original meaning of the anger and thinking is actually our right to revenge.

From this point, we can already establish some clarifications: the victim is a person who has been found to be totally helpless, in a life-threatening situation, without her or his own will. In other words, the victim emerges from a totally passive condition and cannot be guilty. By the means of social interaction (the outer viewer) – the victim seeks our moral and ethical judgements, incorporated in the hero-victim narrative that is encapsulated in popular culture and family narratives, as well as religious stories, forming the first but also the most banal dichotomy deeply rooted in our conscience. There are no heroes without victims, but there are victims without heroes. The revenge comes from the hero, but is orientated to the public. If there is a hero, the public is satisfied. The inversion of a particular role into that of a victim can produce emotional blackmail, known as the 'victim role', where someone has positioned themselves as a victim for the sake of de-valuing the 'aggressor', asking for revenge or gaining something, and therefore, opening up a space for political speech, as inviting publicity, at the original site of revenge.[30] From this, it is possible to conclude that the public needs heroes and heroes rely on victims, but the other way around might be manipulation. So, if there are no victims, fake ones are invented or situations are constructed so that someone can be perceived as such. To clarify the difference between the victim and the fake victim in terms of instrumentalisation, one needs to analyse the subsequent narrative in terms of the dichotomy of victim-hero as survivor, discover who is telling the story according to the motive; deconstruct the motive of a hero (fame, profits) and survivor (blame, revenge).

In the case of Kevin Carter, it appears the survivor was not a hero, he had to victimise the baby. But what would happen if the baby survived and told a story about Carter? Or what could happen if there was anyone else who could take revenge in the name of the baby, being the proper hero?

Revenge and the Use Function

Comparing the posters of Anur Had iomerspahi and Ajna Zlatar using brands of clothes of

---

29.   O. Mirbeau, Torture Garden, trans. A. C. Bessie, New York: Claude Kendall, 1931.

30.   Glossary: 'Victim Role or Posited Roleplaying', p. 142.

people exhumed in the Srebrenica massacre with posters of Toscani made for the Benetton, we can see completely different goals.[31] They appear similar – but they are meant to say different things. Contrary to the purpose of Toscani's clothes, which were used for 'awareness raising' but with commercial ends, the posters of Had iomerspahi and Zlatar were fundamentally revolting or revengeful, with clearly con icted discourses. There is no visible gain behind them, as with the 'heroic' act of Toscani. This is easy to understand as soon as we know 'who speaks for whom', from which we can decide if that is the original discourse of victims; which is only the discourse of revenge.

Eye for an Eye, and an Eye for the Money and the Fame
Victims fill media space and art shows. Only a couple of days ago a new spectacle of a man dying in a gallery filled the headlines in the newspapers. The only difference between the Venice show and the more recent example is this: the former was dealing with massacres and genocides. Still, whether we are concerned with one death or millions, they change nothing, as in the art world they are not meant to change anything, but appear to have another goal justified by the 'right to the truth' and pseudo-activism. However, they soon get exhausted, informationally redundant or authorised by some artist – so hardly any other artist would dare to 'take up the topic again'. Walking through the Venice Biennale, as I noted in the curatorial statement, a colleague observed that strangely enough every massacre seemed to be represented except one – the massacre of Srebrenica, which was at that moment still in the process of becoming immaterial and uncapturable.
Srebrenica has unfortunately shown that numbers do not matter even when it comes to massacres. Dying one by one in the case of Africa, visible in the work of Arango, seemingly has no effect, while the sudden death of many also sometimes apparently changes nothing. There is a point from where Africa and Srebrenica seem similar: the aggressor cannot be easily identified, as we have already seen. The question – who is guilty? – is the matter of an anticipated responsibility, as with most wars, through chains of command from soldiers to generals. But the situation seems far more complex: it is not one person or one army or one state that is guilty in the case of Africa or Srebrenica, the problem is – who is subject to revenge? Srebrenica is the shame of NATO, the Netherlands, of the Hague court, our media society. But then who is excluded or beyond reproach? The event is impossible to interpret clearly.

The Exchange
The original need for revenge is expressed through evaluation, and most often by the problematic form of currency exchange, not the motivating desire itself. The mathematics of revenge as exchange value is usually directly expressed, though never by the archaic measure of 1:1. As with Iraq, a single US soldier seems to mean more than dozens of civilians. Here, the sophist paradox of a unique individual and the mass seems to have a strange resolution: a mass is defined by the discourse, not by the number. It is a value system, as Noam Chomsky observes.[32]

Positive and Negative Economies
The economy of original revenge is, moreover, something highly visible. Since Bataille's interest

---

31.   'Death and Advertising: An Interview with Anur Had iomerspahi ', p. 61.
32.   'Worthy and Unworthy Victims: Questions to Noam Chomsky', p. 64.

in potlatch, the cultural logic of the negative economy has been theorised as a key component of sociality.[33] While the regular economy is about positive exchange, wars are concerned with exchange for the purposes of revenge. Our (again, healthy) need to take revenge has been civilised in a variety of institutions that do not exist in war and encounter problems even in the post-war period, though the biggest issue for the institutionalisation of revenge is not related to justice, but the institutionalisation of the need for revenge in the history of other social institutions.

Postponing Revenge, Or, "Do Not Forget" – The Memorial
Comparing the way Anur Had iomerspahi and Ajna Zlatar deal with images of clothes from people exhumed in Srebrenica and the images Adila Laidi Hanieh has presented in her 100 Shaheed memorial, we can see different ways in which memorabilia function.[34] The distanced position of the curator of 100 Shaheed, which exhibits only the objects belonging to victims and photos taken during their lives, showing no signs of murder or blood, was a healthier way of dealing with the problem.[35] While the designed posters depict decayed clothes from the exhumation of victims in a morbid way, a psychiatrist at the show has noted that the images display other noteworthy aspects of the missing person.[36]
In neither of these cases has there been an image of the victim being victimised (the usual mass media image), but one of them shows something scarier than the corpse we are used to: the image of decaying without a body. It actually shows the total irrelevance of the victim, turning it against us with the question: what happened to the person wearing those clothes?[37] Have they been forgotten in the same way?

Horror Parks
This revengeful rhetoric of the guilty conscience, somehow isolated from the image of the same body, is different from the museum of mourning. Here there is nothing to avenge; it is the end of vengence.
With the proliferation of online memorials, one can still ask – what is the goal of heroes taking revenge instead of victims?[38] If made as part of an artistic project, we can read out goals in terms of the domain of art institutions. But if it is political, things can get much more complicated, as politics can mobilise a much larger form of reprisal, using another currency value. The institutionalisation of death in memorials, therefore, mobilises social revenge on a grand scale.
As Stevan Vukovi has nicely put it, "memory has no expiry date".[39] The tale of personal or family suffering may persist as an encapsulated narrative of victims and aggressors through generations, where, if more oppressed, it becomes more dangerous. The problem of society waiting for another con ict is the institutionalisation of traumatic memories through the morbid practice of

---

33. G. Bataille, The Accursed Share: An Essay on General Economy, trans. R. Hurley, New York: Zone, 1988.
34. Adila Laïdi-Hanieh, 'Regarding One's Pain: The 100 Shaheed-100 Lives Memorial Exhibition', p. 66.
35. Glossary: 'Memorial', p. 121; 'Mourning/Bereavement', p. 121; 'Grief', p. 117.
36. A comment by Tihana Jendri ko.
37. Glossary: 'Necrophilia', p. 122; 'Necrophobia', p. 123.
38. 'Iraqi Memorial Online: An interview with Joseph DeLappe', p. 76; 'Commemorating Victims: An Interview with Agricola de Cologne', p. 79.
39. Stevan Vukovi : Niemand zeugt für den Zeuge', p. 49.

oppressing the remembrance of victims, or even engineering them.[40]
At a certain point, they may find their way into a victims' discourse, as our war psychiatrists were using them in their speeches, asking for revenge going far further than the remuneration that could have been taken in the first place when it was censored and, therefore, escalating its algorhythm.

But the outcomes are clear: the need for a hero occurs where there is no guaranteed legal security for a victim, who is a signal of that failure. Heroes are the only ones who gain at the victims' expense (assuming the aggressor is going to be revenged). If there are no victims to enforce returns for the hero, the victims' narrative is invented. Un-revenged victims are encapsulated in narratives of revenge for the future. If the revenge is postponed, legal security considered, the state appears to be a hero and victims serve to illustrate the condition. But how can the narrative be so limited?

It is obvious; aggressors never admit what they have done, victims usually cannot talk, survivors have difficulties as PTSP. So we are left with heroes who take their place in history and culture, even if they are not authentic.

---

40. Glossary: 'Repression / Repressed', p. 131.

PART 1 - VICTIMS SYMPTOM

DAY AFTER DAY
MAURICIO ARANGO

Day After Day presents a world map based on coverage of 'victim '-related news. On this map, those countries whose victims produce the highest resonance in the news media appear the most prominent, while those that do not make the news gradually disappear from sight. The map operates on a custom made system that retrieves, chooses and classifies news items from several international newspapers on a daily basis.
As imperfect as this system may be, the resulting cartography, a map full of voids, is not meant to indicate that these empty areas are places free of con ict and, hence, free of victims. On the contrary, these empty spaces give faith to the many biases of news media because it seems that even when it comes to counting disgraces some victims are more worthy than others.

Illustration 1 – Mauricico Arango: Day After Day

VICTIMS SYMPTOM: POSTTRAMATIC STRESS DISORDER (PTSD) AND CULTURE
ANA PERAICA

What is a Victim?

The concept of the victim, usually in relation to the oppressor, has been analysed widely in literature on the subject, especially on its disciplinary intersection with studies on gender and sexual
identity (or queer studies). Major theorists of the twentieth century have attempted to decode literary texts that speak directly about victimhood – texts that were prohibited or forgotten because
of the prescriptive censorship of previous centuries, such as writings by the Marquis De Sade or
the nineteenth century Austrian writer Leopold von Sacher-Masoch, as well as twentieth century
French theorist Georges Bataille.[41] A wide interest in the obscure, perverse personal relationship
that actually symptomises political relationships – both totalitarian and oppressive – has found its
way into other interdisciplinary research. However, apart from examining the concepts of victim
and oppressor, other detailed concepts have rarely been considered.

Psychiatric (rather than psychoanalytic) diagnosis of neurosis, schizophrenia and psychosis has
found its way into cultural studies; these conditions are analysed as cultural symptoms disin-
fected of their clinical negative value directly in the writings of French psychotherapist Félix
Guattari.[42] They have become concepts that, on the one hand, have helped to prevent cultural
condemnation of mental illness, showing that whole cultures and societies (can) display the same
symptoms. But they have also opened the way to an exploration of the innovative, lucid or obscure
knowledge 'of madness' that was previously censored.

On the other hand, they have also shown the cultural participation of producing symptoms in
individuals. Whatever is defined as 'behaviourally' or 'mentally disturbed' and 'mentally ill' is
boomeranged back to society itself (minus some genetic predispositions), with the pressure of
society on fragile individuals returned to the source.

What is Posttraumatic Stress Disorder?

Although I am not a psychoanalyst but a media theorist and curator, I have dared to take a 'hot'
concept from the last few decades in the territories I come from (South Eastern Europe), a
concept that has political and economic implications and therefore opens up a discourse. The
concept, entitled Post Traumatic Stress Disorder – or PTSD – has been popularly named 'Vietnam

---

41.   Among the most crucial are writings of Roland Barthes, Jacques Derrida, Michel Foucault and Gilles
       Deleuze. See R. Barthes, Sade, Fourier, Loyola, trans. R. Miller, Berkeley: University of California Press,
       1989; G. Deleuze and L. v. Sacher-Masoch, Masochism: Coldness and Cruelty & Venus in Furs, trans.
       J. McNeil, New York: Zone, 1989; M. Foucault, The History of Sexuality, trans. R. Hurley, London: Allen
       Lane, 1978; M. Foucault, Discipline and Punish: the Birth of the Prison, trans. A. Sheridan, New York:
       Vintage Books, 1977.
42.   G. Deleuze and F. Guattari, 'The First Positive Task of Schizoanalysis', in G. Genosko (ed.) A Guattari
       Reader, Cambridge: Blackwell Publishers, pp. 77-95.

syndrome', or an event specific series of titles, 'torture syndrome', 'concentration camp syndrome', 'psychosexual torture syndrome' or 'Stockholm syndrome'.[43] It is a clinical diagnosis which describes a variety of symptoms that have one trigger in common: a trauma.[44]

Indeed, trauma has been examined widely in the field of cultural analysis, especially in literature studies, but also in film studies, predominantly analysing Holocaust-related literary and movie production. These include analysis of formative narratives that use ' ashbacks' to the traumatic event, with its specific oppressive time looping, but also symptoms of PTSD such as denial and unwillingness to talk about the traumatic event.[45] However, the clinical concept of PTSD has not been applied.

PTSD has a more specific, usually political, definition that may not be applicable in all cases mentioned in the previous analyses. First of all, it does not distinguish between the victim and the oppressor, but treats everyone with symptoms as patients.[46] Furthermore, PTSD is institutionally framed; it includes the political and also the social and economic aspect of victimhood. This depends on the interest of the state or international human rights organisations against torture, as well as interest in the effect of trauma on direct or collateral victims in terms of their social functioning. It also depends on the negative aspects of perceived danger for society, where danger to oneself is also subsumed. Often suicides or mass murders, combined with suicides as a result of PTSD, can continue terrorising the environment and re ect the trauma back to society after a traumatic event such as war has finished. The inversion of roles may happen almost at any time. Another part of the political and economic meaning of PTSD is, as forensic psychiatrists warn, the in uence of 'secondary gain', such as war pensions or taking advantage of the health system. This can produce exaggeration or even simulation of PTSD, which becomes a barrier for forensic evaluation, putting enormous pressure on the forensic psychiatrist. Fake PTSD has a different set of apparatuses to gain different profits.[47] In contemporary society, PTSD has become an 'institutionalised victim', something that society might be afraid of.

In this text, I intend to elaborate further on the possibility of applying the psycho-traumatic diagnosis of PTSD to the broader field of culture, especially to the realm of media theory, analysing the recipient or the public. In the first part of the text, I focus on the precise use of the concept of the 'victim' through the quite disturbing lens of queer studies, which is coming to terms with the topic of 'self-victimisation' and a cultural need for victimisation and institutionalisation of victims as mentioned by Beauvoir, who was referring to the behaviour of 'saints'.[48] From there, I will return to the original context of media studies.

---

43. Glossary: 'Stockholm Syndrome', p. 136; 'Vietnam Syndrome', p. 143.

44. "Post Traumatic Stress Disorder (PTSD) is a psychiatric disorder that can occur following the experience or witnessing life-threatening events such as war, military combat, terrorist attacks, serious accidents or violent personal physical assaults, rape, etc." D, Kozaric–Kova i and N. Pivac, 'Novel Approaches to the Treatment of Post-traumatic Stress Syndrome', in S. Begeç (ed.) The Integration and Management of Traumatized People After Terrorist Attacks, Amsterdam: IOS Press, 2007, p. 13..

45. Glossary: 'Amnesia', p. 105; 'Avoidance', p. 107; 'Denial', p. 113, 'Flashback', p. 116; 'Re-experiencing', p. 130.

46. Glossary: 'Posttraumatic Stress Disorder', p. 124.

47. Glossary: 'Vicarious Retribution', p. 143.

48. Glossary: 'Self-Victimisation', p. 135.

Empathy Quest

In her writings, the French feminist author Simone de Beauvoir drew attention to the socially accepted inverse victim-role.[49] A consecrated victim, she noted, could be a tyrant as well. By reading saints as exhibitionists who play upon our guilty conscience to divinise themselves, our notion of 'heroes' as 'moral paradigms' becomes destabilised.[50] This concept has actually been transferred to the field of performance studies. Bataille has also subversively elaborated on the political connotations of the role of the victim, analysing the perverse enjoyment of the role and its actual sadistic power principle.[51] Victims can engage in and even enjoy their passive aggression and the moral responsibility for their own pain, thus displacing the original source of pain, and victimising the other.[52]

What can be deduced from the writings of both authors is the rhetoric of the 'speech of the victim'.[53] Once we recognise this speech, we can interpret a variety of writings around us, using it as a matter of style rather than content. Victims have culturally replaced the role of heroes, they have started freelancing to become more anonymous and socially constituted. Victims have become whole nations, religions or social groups.[54] Still, it is only in media studies and political science that research of this discourse appeared, especially in regard to recent US politics. 'Victim's speech' is used for economic and military gain, becoming a simple pattern that shows itself easily inverted while emotionally direct; to justify attacking a country it is enough to state – "we are their victims" and ask for compassion rather than reason.

Collateral Victims

Since the concept of the victim has been disconnected of the real victim, it has almost become impossible to decide 'who is the victim of whom', and which is the original trauma.[55] This also applies to the radical trauma of PTSD.

One of main parameters of PTSD research has been focused on the assessment of the "prevalence of the trauma that ranges outside the normal experience in the population", producing a feeling of horror, fear or helplessness in the face of a traumatic event, or even if not – expressing anger and shame for not experiencing horror during the first encounter.[56] However, nothing has been said about the effect that media images or discussion can have on the population in general. Is the continuous drip feeding of war images in contemporary society creating the same levels of fear and paranoia on the general population? If so – trauma can be produced by media. But is that news? We were warned by education experts that violence on TV can in uence the

---

49.   Simone de Beauvoir, The Second Sex, trans. H.M. Parshley, London: Jonathan Cape, 1953.
50.   Glossary: 'Exhibitionism', p. 115.
51.   Glossary: 'Sadism', p. 134.
52.   Glossary: 'Passive Aggression', p. 124.
53.   Glossary: 'Vicarious Retribution', p. 143.
54.   "Epidemiological studies show a high prevalence of post traumatic stress disorder in the general population and specific groups exposed to traumatic events (survivors of war trauma, natural disasters, terrorist attacks, etc.)". D. Kozari –Kova i and N. Pivac, 'Novel Approaches to the Treatment of Post-traumatic Stress Syndrome', p. 13.
55.   Glossary: 'Vicarious Trauma', p. 142.
56.   D. Kozari –Kova i and N. Pivac, 'Novel Approaches to the Treatment of Posttraumatic Stress Syndrome', 13-40

behaviour of children, especially children exposed to "in your house, too" horror fiction.[57] And surely, we know the role-call of nightmares has been in uenced by the terrifying figures of media horrors, too. Fears and stress, paranoia, images of wars, death, corpses on TV – all these have an impact, slowly but surely mixing real and simulated disturbance, or more precisely, mixing the real and political speech.

Trauma at a Distance

If mediated images can produce symptoms of PTSD, the problem becomes: who is deciding to produce these images and why? Are the people who are providing us with such imagery as guilty as the people in non-simulated reality? Does this reality have the same effect? Phenomenologically, it would appear so. Wars can be conducted simultaneously in reality and on TV. Speaking about war then, immediately introduces its discourse, creating a meaning of war that it does not have in reality. It forces us to choose a side at least, even when we are not affected by the war in real life. By choosing sides, we are actually placing ourselves in the middle of the war itself.

Images of War

There is a difference between how the media reports on war are consumed in peaceful societies versus war-affected societies.[58] Usually denying the cruel reality of war images, citizens of countries that are affected by war do not have a need to watch footage of wars on TV. Some authors refer to these societies as 'erotic', for different reasons: these citizens are more inclined to live in the moment due to the direct threat of death and there is proof of higher birth rates during the period of con ict. At the same time, cultures that reside in peaceful societies, whether they enjoy that peace or not, are more compelled to watch images of war, and are accordingly identified as 'thanatic' – disengaged, less concerned with mortality, behaving as if they would live forever, but also having 'colder' social relationships.[59] Still, outside of poetic description, there might be a commonsense reason there – for some, it is a trauma that prevents a direct confrontation with such imagery.[60] Furthermore, traumatised memory tends to return, while consumption mimics the same repetition.[61]

But why is there a desire by societies not affected by war to integrate this war imagery into their lives? The algorithm of real and virtual seems to be out of proportion. As the Dutch media theorists Adilkno have noted, violence in the media increases as the media becomes more distant from the body.[62] So the more distant the danger is, the greater the need to be afraid, to feel alive

---

57. Glossary: 'Trauma and Media', p. 139.
58. Glossary: 'Trauma from a Distance', p. 141.
59. On the eroticisation of death and thanatisation of eros, see G. Bataille, The Tears of Eros, trans. by P. Connor, San Francisco: City Lights Books, 1989.
60. Also a dimension of PTSD, the major symptoms – anxiety, repeated nightmares, ashbacks, fear reactions, phobic avoiding of events that are connected with traumatic experience.
61. An interesting artwork from this perspective is Eduardo Kac's intravenous injecting of photographs, or Maria Grazio's destruction of his own face from the family album while in an asylum.
62. Adilkno, The Media Archive, New York: Autonomedia, 1998.

and separate from 'deathness'.[63] Still, are they safe from being traumatised? And what happens when the tolerance of such imagery increases?

Can our media society be affected by mediated PTSD?[64] And what is the relation to the real victim?

Numbers of Corpses

A discussion of my text 'War Profiteers in Art', which was held in parallel on two email lists/networks in September 2007, talked about the use of war imagery at the Venice Biennale exhibition curated by Robert Storr and has opened up a space for analysis of the media use of victims, or re-victimisation of the victim.[65] Namely, a great number of artworks displayed war images, although their authors had no original experience of the war itself. This 'war tourism', recognised by Susan Sontag, has grown into a kind of mass 'war postcards' consumption.[66]

The text was written as the Bosnian city of Srebrenica was fighting for victim status. Srebrenica, which fell under the media spotlight during the time of the massacre that was recognised as the largest genocide in Europe after the Holocaust, has lost its media attention now. Images of other conflicts have become more important,.[67]

There is no copyright on war imagery, of course. However, there is the original trauma of the victim, though it has nothing to do with the 'speech of the victim' and needs of contemporary society to enjoy these images on TV.[68] After all, it is not the event but the intensity and duration that produces PTSD, resulting eventually in a coherent refusal of such imagery, with this denial as a symptom.

---

63. A good description of the separation from deathness is given by feminist philosopher Julia Kristeva: "No, as it is true theater, without makeup or masks, refuse and corpses show me what I permanently thrust aside in order to live. These body fluids, this deathment, this shit is what life withstands, hardly and with difficulty, on the part of death. There, I am on the border of my condition as a living being. My body extricates itself, as being alive, from that border. Such wastes drop on that I might live, until, from loss to loss, nothing remains in me and my entire body falls beyond the limit – cadere, cadaver." J. Kristeva, Powers of Horror: An Essay on Abjection, trans. by Leon S. Roudiez, New York: Columbia University Press, 1982, p. 3.

64. G. Slavich, Slobodna Dalmacija, 2006.

65. Ana Peraica, 'War profiteers in art (Biennale di Venezia, 2007)', comments on Nettime, http://www.mail-archive.com/nettime-l@bbs.thing.net/msg04212.html; comments on Vlemma blog (in Greek), http://vlemma.wordpress.com/2007/06/11/biennale-venezia-07/

66. S. Sontag, Regarding the Pain of Others, New York: Farrar, Straus and Giroux, 2003.

67. 'Death and Advertising: An Interview with Anur Hadžiomerspahić', p. 61; Marko Peljhan, 'Landscape 1995', p. 48; Stevan Vuković, 'Niemand zeugt für den Zeuge', p. 49.

68. In a discussion about war images between a Sarajevo curator Asja Mandić, Suzana Milevska from Skopje and myself, an interesting argument was raised by Milevska, issuing from the copyright of images of death. On the 'unspeakable' trauma of war or 'the taboo' which by Freud's definition is on the one hand 'sacred', 'consecrated', and on the other 'uncanny', 'dangerous', 'forbidden' and 'unclean', S. Freud, Totem and Taboo: Some Points of Agreement Between the Mental Lives of Savages and Neurotics, trans. J. Strachey, London: Routledge and Kegan Paul, 1950. This formative aspect, of course, has nothing to do with the ethics of 'touching wounds' of others.

Internet: Medium for Therapy?

Contrary to state-owned media or international political agencies, the Internet is said to be an effective therapeutic tool for a variety of symptoms and disorders, for its displaced, non-personal, but direct connection. However, as has occurred since the early days of the Internet, fake identities are a part of this medium too. For example, one psychiatrist assumed the identity of a woman experiencing the trauma of a car crash with severe invalidity.[69]

Victims' Symptom

Victims' Symptom is produced online, in several phases/layers; including documentation, an online debate featuring theoretical texts (including this one as a starting point), and finally a series of commissioned artworks.

Between the 'confession of a victim' appearing in blogs and the 'role of the victim' appearing in the mass media that treats people not as individuals but as illustrations for mass daily war reporting, totally disinterested in their individuality, the project served as a shift (in the curatorial sense), tunneling through different information.

The project connected artists and theorists in online discussions on various platforms, as well as anyone else interested debating concepts of the victim, victimisation and the institutionalisation of victims. Its goal was, therefore, to de-construct and de-activate the emancipated 'third agent' construction of victims by the media, which acts as an intermediary between the different sides of war.

The project was organised around commissioned artworks that served as triggers and was accompanied by a chat space for discussion and writing by theorists, artists and other interested individuals. An open call was sent out inviting participation in the discussion, as well as inviting artists to contribute to a database of artworks dealing with some of the following topics: Why is an image of a dead body meaningful in some societies while in others it loses its capacity to provoke anger or compassion? Why does the mass media prefer to talk about numbers of corpses, calculating them morbidly, instead of the victim's status? Does the number of victims make any difference? Is there a sophist paradox between a number and a mass of victims? At what point can we start talking about genocide and mass murder?[70] And in what ways are we affected by these events?

---

69. See D. Timms, 'Identity, Community and the Internet',
http://www.odeluce.stir.ac.uk/docs/Identitypaper26Aug.pdf
70. Especially regarding the cases of Vukovar and Srebrenica.

ON SAINTS AND SNUFF
AN INTERVIEW WITH SUE GOLDING AKA JOHNNY DE PHILO

Ana Peraica (AP): What do you think of the concept of the institutional 'role of victims' suggested in the writings of Simone de Beauvoir on saints?

Sue Golding (SG): The role of the saint in de Beauvoir's work is, of course, complex and useful for this discussion – but I think not clarified as much as it could be, given the expansive growth of what constitutes 'media/technology' as both logic and structure/system, and what has shaped the political mass movements (around sexism, homophobias, ethnicities, religions etc.). Depending on a variety of factors, economic in the widest sense of the word: economy (to include libidinal, assemblages and not only 'exchange' – but also exchange, of course), the lens by which information is gathered, and 'kept alive' in the papers, radio and TV, not to mention the Net, have their own 'lifespans'.
Take for example the story of Madeleine McCann: who's the victim?[71] The child? The parents? The 'tapas 9', Murat and his girlfriend? The Portuguese police? This modern (or postmodern) tale shape-shifts the victimhood role on a continual basis. I am working on this kind of 'institutional sexism' or 'institutional racism' and how it controls/infiltrates the media – so I could speak on that.

AP: How does it happen, or by which maneuver, do victims turn out to be heroes?

SG: There is no 'one' maneuver, but there is a rhizomatic 'plane of immanence', which ip- ops (in more than binaric ways, i.e. more than just 'hero/victim/sadistic/accomplice'). Again, this could be discussed in detail.

AP: Somewhere there is a power-principle in the 'politics of self-victimisation' of saints' own decision to finish something that has no meaning (life) by giving a meaning, making it metaphysical?

SG: Not sure I understand this remark – but if you're suggesting that people 'need' to make sense of their own life, I'm not sure I agree with the sentiment. My guess is that people may or may not need to make sense of their life, but they absolutely need to be in environments that are not soul-destroying. This means there are certain kinds of ethics/morals and 'honours' that must be in place, otherwise a person will go mad (this theme is developed a lot in my long essay/book: Honour).[72]

AP: What makes those victims more important than ones getting killed daily?

---

71.   Read the case chronology,
http://en.wikipedia.org/wiki/Disappearance_of_Madeleine_McCann
72.   S. Golding, Honour, London: Taylor Francis, 1999. See also, S. Golding, The Eight Technologies of Otherness, London: Routledge, 1997.

SG: Nothing. Everything. Have you read Heinrich Böll's 'portrait of a lady' where he asks a similar question, though more crudely: 'what makes a vagina more expensive than any other one?'[73] The imperative 'do not forget' seems to me not functioning, as the meaning of a history lesson, which it suggests as the same events are re-appearing side-by-side even today.

AP: What is the role of a maxima 'do not forget'? Is it a ground for an inscribed revenge in culture, rather than a teaching of 'the lesson'?

SG: The battle-cry 'never forgot' is usually best placed as a rallying point for the present problems rather than an actual attempt at remembering. I am thinking of Shoa, and also of the excellent work of Jean-François Lyotard in this regard in his Heidegger and the jews where the word 'jews' is lower-cased to mark the utter 'forgetability' of the situation (called genocide).[74]

AP: If historical victims are discussed, there is a field mined with horror and warnings around the 'de-secration of victims', obviously making them taboos. Still, it is not a taboo to report on current victims in distant places in manners that do not give them enough respect? What do you think about this discussion?

SG: There is an online (web) network that shows 24/7 the beheading of people by various religious sects — with no horror or warning labels attached, and certainly no taboo. Are you pointing to the 'established' networks then? Like The New York Times? Or outwardly mercenary ones (I mean the ones that actually take pride in being mercenary)? My thinking is that people never give up power willingly, and certainly not if they are 'proved' to be racist/sexist/nationalist, etc. Power corrupts, as the old saying goes, whereas absolute power is kinda nice (slight shift in the motto). When discourses create forms of legitimacy as though there is no problem (or never was one, etc.) it has less to do with manners and a whole lot more to do with the way in which power as common sense gets established and reproduced.

(Interview conducted by Ana Peraica on 05 dec 2007)

---

73.   H. Böll, Group Portrait with Lady, trans. L. Vennewitz, Harmondsworth: Penguin, 1976.
74.   J.-F. Lyotard, Heidegger and "the jews", trans. A. Michel and M. S. Roberts, Minneapolis, University of Minnesota Press, 1990.

SNUFF AND ART
AN INTERVIEW WITH ENRIQUE ARROYO

Ana Peraica (AP): What do you think the production of snuff movies in contemporary culture indicates about our culture?[75] Namely, this type of movie has started to appear widely only when the equipment was made cheaper. Do you know it existed even before video times or it is rather a product of the contemporary society that has started to consume death?

Enrique Arroyo (EA): The first information about snuff films I found is from the 1920s in the United States, from Hollywood. It was shot on 16mm. I don't think snuff films are a product of video technology; I think video technology has made them accessible. They are easier to make and to distribute, and the Internet is a fertile medium for that purpose. Unfortunately, I don't think "societies need to consume death", as you put it, is a product of this era either. History shows that 'dead spectacles', have been popular in most societies. The Romans and their Coliseum could be an example. Do I think this says something about human kind? Yes I do, but that's an entirely different discussion.

AP: It seems that there were more snuff movies recorded in Mexico than discussions of these women who got killed? Has your film that actually enters into the genre and talks about the problem made some differences?

EA: The other American dream, the short film we made, talks about a problem in a town called Ciudad Juárez that is in the border of México and the United States. By the time we started production there had been more than 350 women murdered, and more than 500 disappeared. In México these women are known as "las muertas de Juárez", the dead women of Juárez – and the first one appeared in 1993. We started production in 2004, eleven years after the first murder. Our short is not specifically about snuff film-making, although that happens in the short. Our film wanted to address the bigger issue of "las muertas de Juárez".
By the time we had finished our investigation there were eight reasons for the murdered women: drug trade, human smuggling, violent sexual crimes, passion crimes, satanic religious cults, organ smuggling, snuff films, and I'm forgetting one. There are people in jail for committing all these sorts of crimes, and there are dead women who were victims of these crimes. When we were writing the script, we tried to include all the reasons for the "muertas de Juárez". To my knowledge, snuff films account for a very small percentage of the "muertas de Juárez". This is determined by the type of dead they had, and I had the chance to read the forensic reports, in which the doctors explained how they died.
When we finished the film, we sent it out to a lot of organisations based in Ciudad Juárez, and in Chihuahua, the state to which Ciudad Juárez belongs, at the request of one of the mothers who had lost her 16 year old girl to the crimes in Juárez. They had been trying to generate a social conscience in our country for years, against the crimes, and she, along with other mothers who

---

75.   A snuff film or snuff movie is a motion picture genre that depicts the actual death or murder of a person or people.

have an organisation for this purpose, thought our film could help in raising awareness of the problem. That is the reason why we made it, so we were happy to comply. And they achieved their goal: the crimes were recognised by all the society, there were lots of discussions about it, about the horrors, and the government had to take a hand in stopping them. Although the crimes of Juárez have not completely stopped, they have been almost eradicated.

AP: I've heard the jury went out on one of screenings. Somehow this makes me conclude that not only are there people consuming violent deaths for real, but also there are others that deny what happens, turning their heads away. What do you find worst?

EA: You are asking me to make a moral judgment, and to assign guilt, and that is something I'm not prepared to do. But we have a saying in México, I'll put it in Spanish and try to translate it: "Tanta culpa tiene el que mata la vaca, como el que le jala la pata". In English it means something like: "the one who holds the cow is just as guilty as the one who kills it". If you want to assign guilt, I think we are all guilty, as a society, for not stopping this sooner.

(Interview conducted by Ana Peraica on 08 dec 2007)

PART 2 - VICTIMS

WDWTH? (WHO DID WHAT TO WHO?)
ALEJANDRO DUQUE

The full story: Non-linear open narration is a common thread between both works, WTWTW? and MBCBFW. In our case, the story is not about love, but about war and related traumatic tensions, told by people chatting with each other.
WDWTW? is a place for lost memories, the buried facts that don't quite belong to a place that has once been an artists' playground and today seems more like a shopping mall (back in the 1990s the Internet had another face). If WDWTW? helps to open a space where people can re ect on human rights abuses and war, its purpose has been fulfilled.
WDWTW? gathers testimonies from anonymous Internet visitors to recreate the symptomatology of a victim via text that appears on screen in an attempt to connect so many people around the world that live under such conditions.
The original work of Olia Lialina was created in 1996 when web browsers and Internet technology was beginning to capture public attention.[76] At this time, interactivity was the magic word and the hyperlink was used to create a new kind of narrative and storytelling. This is where MBCBFW hit the nail on the head. Today (in 2008), interactivity in the sense of hyperlinks has been exhausted. We have shifted into the so-called 'social web' days (for me, the web has always been social and this new slogan obeys the rule of mass marketing strategies).
So, in the case of WDWTW?, the narrative is made up of two directives: inclusion of the main symptomatic PTSD categories; a database made up of sentences (10-20 per category). There are two categories: Re-experiencing Avoidance and Hyperarousal (feelings and sudden states of being). Sentences are short, a maximum of 20 words each.[77]
Access to the piece by anyone in the world and the ability to 're-code', according to life experience and the messages on the screen (considering the lack of visibility of documents that can enrich a world memory for future analysis and comprehension). In WDWTW?, user input plays a very important role since the piece is not closed to just click from the viewer/reader, he or she is invited to express, to tell the story, to answer the question: Who Did What to Who?
Such input (answers to the question) appears in the middle of the screen and is sent also to a chat room (#victims in irc.goto10.org <http://irc.goto10.org>) where everyone visiting the piece is assigned a name in the order of: victim_000933 (the number corresponds to the time when they join the piece). This also allows anonymity.
Who Did What To Who? is a question used by researchers in areas where they need to gather information related to human rights abuses. When the user accesses the website, he/she is invited to use an input line to answer this question, and given an explicit invitation to tell their story. In the background, every visitor to the page is default also joining a chat room (#victims in irc.

---

76. See Lialina's work and all references:
http://myboyfriendcamebackfromth.ewar.ru/
77. Glossary: 'Re-experiencing', p.130; 'Avoidance', p.107; 'Hyper-arousal', p. 118.

goto10.org http://irc.goto10.org). Users are assigned an automatic nickname under the sign of: 'victim_1053941'. The number is taken from the date/millisecond when the user joined the chat room.

This chat room is the meeting point for the piece and represents an extended space to develop social interaction that can also be accessed via web browser or via an IRC chat client.

The messages that come back from IRC lose their 'authorship' since not even the nickname appears on the interface of the web. They feed the interface that becomes a repository of stories. A two-way communication channel that goes from the underground of the Internet (IRC) to reach full visibility (on the main page of the LabforCulture site) and all the way round, since everyone logging into the website is also part of the chatroom under the name of victim as stated above. Thus messages cross from public to private, from unrepresented to represented and from silent to loud.

WDWTW? builds a social and open-ended narrative. Every visitor to the piece can tell their story within the context of victims of war and human rights abuses. Based on the work My Boyfriend Came Back From the War (MBCBFTW, Olia Lialina, 1996, a landmark in the history of net.art), it's a space to gather facts and stories that depict the socio-political unrest of this so-called 'expanded' and 'interconnected' world.

WDWTW? traces a parallel fictionality to that established by the Russian artist. Twelve years on, the atmosphere generated by such black and white contrasted space gets a revision to include the notion of interactivity, which involves not the mouse click but the user/visitor text input. Hence the title for this work complies to the premise often used by researchers who strive to find scarce victims' testimonies in places for freedom.

Illustration 2 - Alejandro Duque: WDWTH

FORCE OF TRAUMA
SEZGIN BOYNIK

Face-To-Face Encounter

The recent, failed attempt to bring two different but inter-connected 'traumatised' contemporary art scenes face-to-face will be the starting point for this article. The brave and courageous exhibition series, curated by Vida Kne evi , Kristian Luki , Ivana Marjanovi and Gordana Nikoli , with the title Odstupanje (Exception) aimed to bring "together with roundtables, presentations and publication in the forthcoming period, analyse certain facts that an average person from Serbia was not allowed or did not want to know [about Kosovo]".[78] Organisers of the exhibition wanted to create a platform for people in Serbia to think about Kosovo in a different way, rather than as a territory of their spiritual heritage and the roots of their national identity. And to accept and understand that Kosovo is populated with Albanians with their own exceptional history of recent parallel institutions, mass deportation and violence conducted by Serbian military and paramilitary forces. They wanted people to think about the trauma that the Albanian population in Kosovo lived through in the nineties.

What happened after the exhibition opening, which took place on January 22 2008 in the Museum of Contemporary Art Vojvodina in Novi Sad, is that members of the ultra-nationalist Radical Party condemned the Odstupanje exhibition as blasphemy. The second part of the project, which had been planned to open in the Kontekst Gallery in Belgrade on February 7 2008 was violently attacked by the organised ultra-nationalist group 'Obraz' during the exhibition opening; one work displayed in the exhibition got destroyed.

After the demonstration by this group, the police closed the exhibition to protect the security of organisers and participants. What happened in this exhibition was that the face-to-face encounter of Serbians with the trauma and experience of Albanians in general was impossible. This impossibility has one main reason, which is the language of pain and trauma that finds its home in silence. Particularly, in this case, it means that Serbian people who do not know anything, or are not allowed to know anything about the trauma of Kosovo Albanians (as organisers of the exhibition assume), will never be able to empathise with the situation because of the different language they speak. This different language must not be understood in ethnical philological terms, but rather as a different language, which the oppressor and the oppressed are speaking. The theory of George Bataille, according to which sadism is only possible when the torturer does not understand the language of the tortured, can be applied to this situation. For Serbian police, it is impossible to imagine how it hurts to be Albanian. The Serbian police (like all police of the world) are interpellated into an ideology that does not recognise the experience of the other as valid, human or even possible. For a Serbian citizen (and not to mention police) to be able to look at a contemporary artwork by a Kosovar Albanian, the most necessary fundamental need, or

---

78.   Artists participating in the exhibition were: Artan Balaj, Jakup Ferri, Driton Hajredini, Flaka Haliti, Fitore Isufi Koja, Dren Maliqi, Alban Muja, Vigan Nimani, Nurhan Qehaja, Alketa Xhafa, Lulzim Zeqiri, all of them born after 1980, with the exception of Hajredini. Quotations form the catalogue text by the curators of the exhibition.

minimum consensus, is to be open to the language of the Albanian experience.[79]
Even if it is not clearly mentioned, the Odstupanje exhibition is about the reconciliation of Serbs
and Albanians for a better future in better co-existence; it is an optimistic possibility for "remorse
as an ethical act activated in true face-to-face encounter", as Jill Bennett formulates in her famous book on trauma and contemporary art.[80] But as Bennett shows in her analysis of Deborah
Hoffman and Francis Reid's 2000 documentary film Long Night's Journey into Day, where they
want to show what happens when a police officer who killed black Africans has a face-to-face
encounter with the dead men's mothers, what happens is silence. Silence of the mothers towards
the policeman, who was begging for forgiveness for the crimes that he had committed years
ago.[81] But here forgiveness is impossible (as is any kind of empathy), not only because of the
unbearable pain and grief, but also because of the different language that the mothers and the
police officer are speaking.[82] That is why we cannot talk about reconciliation of those who don't
understand each other.
In order to show the impossibility of this kind of encounter, Bennett quotes Derrida's note on forgiveness where he says: "Even if I say 'I do not forgive you' to someone who asks my forgiveness,
but whom I understand and who understands me, then the process of reconciliation has begun".[83]
But in the case of the film of Hoffman and Reid, no reconciliation happened, as is the case with
the exhibition of Odstupanje.
In order to start the process of mutual understanding, for mutual co-existence in a safe future,
maybe the first step would be for the Serbs to accept the minimum consensus proposed by
Branimir Stojanovi ; then the experience of trauma and parallel institutions would be lessons that
the Serbs could learn for political emancipation.

Theorising the Trauma
Ironically, one of the most problematic artworks exhibited in Odstupanje was an installation titled
Face to Face by artist Dren Maliqi. The work, which Maliqi realised in 2003 in completely different
circumstances, consists of two photographs in an Andy Warhol style, facing each other with guns.
One of the photographs is of Elvis Presley, taken from a movie. Another one is of Adem Jashari,
a member of UÇK (KLA – Kosova Liberation Army), who was killed together with all of his family
in 1998 by the Serbian army, and who has become one of the most popular Albanian heroes of
its recent past. According to the artist and the curators, this confrontation between Presley and
Jashari in Warholian style deals with consumer society, which invests all the heroes of the modern
world with the same political economy, representational system and the rules of the society of

---

79. This minimum consensus is most radically formulated by Branimir Stojanovi in an email discussion
     in the aftermath of cancelling the Odstupanje exhibition: "contemporary art of Kosovo is the voice of
     political resistance against apartheid and democratic potential of the parallel institutions' politics of non-
     violent resistance, which Kosovo society produced during the nineties. Or more radically, we learned the
     politics of fighting against terrorist regime from Kosovar Albanians. Or even more radically to formulate,
     we learn democracy from Albanians".
80. J. Bennett, Emphatic Vision: Affect, Trauma and Contemporary Art, Stanford: Stanford University Press,
     2005.
81. Glossary: 'Commemorative Silence', p. 108.
82. Glossary: 'Forgiveness', p. 117.
83. Bennett, Emphatic Vision, p. 110; see J Derrida, On Cosmopolitanism and Forgiveness, trans. M. Dooley
     and M. Hughes, London: Routledge, 2001.

the spectacle. Apart from this general interpretation, we can also read this work as an attempt to look at UCK's Marxist past, which is in direct opposition to the American Elvis-style capitalism. In general, what I want to show here is that the work of Maliqi and of other contemporary artists from Kosovo have a complex relation with their ideological, economic and global formulations in relation to their recent trauma. As in the previous section, I tried to show how difficult it is for Serbs, because of language problems, to engage with Albanian traumatic experiences. Now, in the following two sections, I will try to show two different approaches to traumatic experience by Kosovo artists themselves. That would mean in practice that Face to Face is more than a simple provocation of face-to-face encounter of Serbs and Albanians.

In her book Jill Bennett wants to show that the fundamental error in many contemporary artworks dealing with trauma is "lying in the aesthetic reduction of trauma to the shock-inducing signifier", which de-politicises and a-historicises trauma as a psychological term by reducing art's function to catharsis or to sublimation effect.[84] This is largely consumed, for example, by the type of 'traumatic art' and rapid reconciliation programmes of the humanitarian organisations.[85] Bennett is interested in works of contemporary art that are trying to deal with trauma beyond the principle affect of original experience. Instead of categorising trauma to first-hand and second-hand experiences, she is more interested in how to talk about trauma so that it is not just understandable to those who had the misfortune to experience it. But at the same time, she is aware that we cannot only talk about trauma through a theoretical discourse, rationalising it (and indeed reducing it) to the extent of pure historical and mnemonic phenomenon. This is the reason why Bennett says that "there is something innately uncontainable about the phenomenon of pain [and trauma] within the representation", which means that with our everyday language and representational semantics we cannot understand the real effect of trauma.[86] Here Bennett, in order to understand trauma, uses the term that Deleuze coins as encountered sign to describe the sign that is felt, rather than recognised or perceived through cognition. This sensuality of theory then would enable theoreticians to discuss trauma and allow artists to work with it in a more critical way. In the end, she hopes this is the tool that would give élan to theory, which is lacking affectivity, and to visual art, which serves this theory.

---

84. Bennett, Emphatic Vision, p. 65.
85. Of course, here one must keep in mind that all the religion-based NGOs are dealing with trauma in a populist and 'humanitarian' way.
86. Bennett, Emphatic Vision, p. 50.

Illustration 3 - Sokol Bequiri, When Angels are Too late, 2002. (1)

Illustration 4 - Sokol Bequiri, When Angels are Too late, 2002. (2)

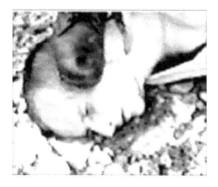

Illustration 5 - Sokol Bequiri, When Angels are Too late, 2002. (3)

Sokol Beqiri is one of the rare artists in Kosovo who deals with the experience of trauma in his entire opus. In his works, he deals with trauma as confession (Supermen), as metaphor to art history (The End of Expressionism [Painted by a Madman]), as banality of evil (Milka), and as impossibility to produce new art work (Everything You Wanted...). However, in each one of his pieces, trauma is something that transcends the personal experience of evil, banality or pain, and is conceptualised in more global and political terms. His work When Angels are Late (2001) is perfect for showing this global interconnection of tropes in traumatic experience. The work is a large reproduction of the painting by Caravaggio, with the religious theme of Abraham's sacrifice of his son Isaac being interrupted by an angel descending from heaven as saviour who is replacing the son with a sheep to be sacrificed. Approaching the panel we discover a peephole in the middle of the painting through which we see a very short, grainy and looped video of an unbearably shocking scene: a man lying on the ground, his head is pressed down with a military boot and his throat is being slit with a sword. This is a gorey video, which shows violence to Chechnyan fighters taken from Internet. In this work we can obviously see the association with NATO intervention, which was experienced in Kosovo almost as a messianic salvation. Western intervention, which brings freedom and saves Kosovars from trauma, is represented in the work of Beqiri as angels, which is actually an ironic nod to the NATO intervention, always represented within the religious discourse of war between the ultimate evil and good. This religious fight became even more obvious in the intervention in Iraq. Representation of the traumatic experience of Kosovars with the Biblical motifs is a way of showing that what happens in Kosovo has global interconnections, and it is not just about the illogical evil of what unfortunate Albanians have been through. Just the fact that the peephole video is from Chechnya is proof that trauma is a more global phenomenon than it is normally understood. But for some people, as for the Chechnyans, the angels are late in arriving. Bennett, in order to discuss the problem of global interconnections of trauma, analyses works of the Australian artist Gordon Bennett, who has a series of paintings in the style of Jean Michel Basquiat titled 911, related to the 11 September 2001 attacks on New York City. According to Jill Bennett, Gordon Bennett is someone who deals with his Australian aboriginal origins by performing as 'the other' in the official national visual representation. In his work 911, he chooses to perform within the frame of Basquiat's aesthetics in thinking about the trauma that happened to New Yorkers. Australians with aboriginal origins paint the 911 trauma in the style of artists with African origins. This is, according to Jill Bennett, an artistic strategy to make the general audience realise the global interconnection of the trauma, which happened, for example, in New York. This means that the 911 attacks have a connection with the American policy in the Middle East, traumatised asylum seekers in the West, military inequality, oil, and so on.[87] These interconnections of the experience of trauma are something that Bennett repeats again and again in her book; she is interested in an artwork of trauma that "finds its way to activate and realise connections. The question to ask of the artwork is thus, not 'What does it mean?' or 'What trauma is depicted?' but 'How does it work?' – how does it put insides and outsides into contact in order to establish a

---

87.   Even if Jill Bennett's book is useful for analysing the connection between contemporary art and trauma in terms of the importance of affect, it is not political enough in elaborating this into radical critical inquiry. For example, for her, this war is about "American trade versus Muslim militancy"! Another problem of her argumentation is the complete lack of an economical explanation to violence and to capitalist expansionism, which is one of the main reasons for many collective traumas.

basis for empathy?"[88] Even if Sokol Beqiri does not go so far as Gordon Bennett, for example, he is also very much interested in finding the ways in which trauma functions in an artwork.

Jakup Ferri's Silence

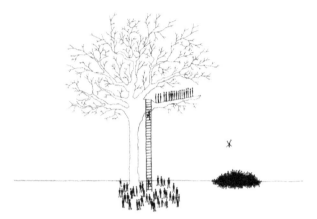

Illustration 6 - Jakup Ferri, untitled, drawing series, 2005-2006 (1)

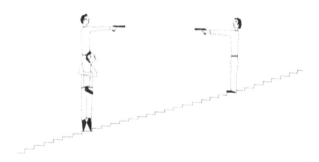

Illustration 7 - Jakup Ferri, untitled, drawing series, 2005-2006 (2)

---

88. Bennett, Emphatic Vision,, p. 45.

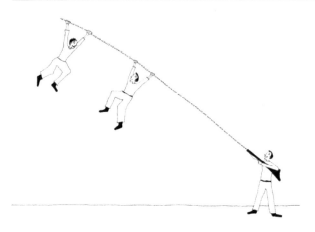

Illustration 8 - Jakup Ferri, untitled, drawing series, 2005-2006 (3)

All the artists participating in the Odstupanje exhibition, with the exception of Driton Hajredini, were born after 1980, after the period when Kosovo started its inevitable process of continu- ous de-Yugoslavisation in a sense of de-modernisation and vanishing from the political public space. Apart from the works of Lulezim Zeqiri and Flaka Haliti, none of the works exhibited in the Odstupanje exhibition are related to traumatic experience. This is something that is quite common in contemporary art production in Kosovo. The best example is artist Jakup Ferri, which I will focus on in this section. Ferri's work does not immediately manifest any traumatic experience. It is more about the history of contemporary art, which he is not part of, about rock'n'roll heroes, his childhood memories of life in a 'normal' world (clocks, father's shoes, father's art monographies), the lethargy and boredom of urban life, etc. In Ferri's silence on the issue of trauma we can in a way see that the new generation of contemporary artists in Kosovo are not interested in the works of their 'aesthetic' fathers.[89] No work of young Kosovo artists bears witness to any con- ict, irony, parody, or critique to the old generation of contemporary abstract painting of Kosovo modernism from the late 1960s to the late 1980s. All those are passé, fossils and dinosaurs from art academy curricula, representing the heavy national burden of ethnological and historical con- sciousness of being proud of being Albanian. These modernist painters, among the most prolific ones are Muslim Muliqi, Rexhep Ferri and Xhevdet Xhafa, were the ones who dealt with national representation as aesthetical mediators, ones who were canonising the political traumatised situ- ation of Kosovo with artistic values.

Jakup Ferri and his generation of artists now, in order to find some new way of expressing their everyday life politics, have totally rejected the aesthetic formulations of the old generation; first they changed their medium from painting to not-yet-discovered medium of video art, and then, instead of questioning the local and recent actual political history, they contextualised their art- works in the frame of international art history, referring to artists such as Damien Hirst, Yoko Ono,

---

89.   In Kosovo, these fathers are more than metaphors. Fathers of Jakup Ferri, Sislej Xhafa and Visar
      Muliqi, for example, were also very famous modern artists in Kosovo.

Bill Viola, Marina Abramovi , Christo, Baldessari, among others. These non site-specific artworks, which had the function of normalising the post Rambouillet situation in Kosovo, also created a lot of collateral damage. Damage such as silencing the collective trauma for the sake of normalisation, or de-politicising contemporary art for the sake of non site-specific formulations.

But is there a critical possibility in the silence of the trauma, as Shoshana Felman has discussed, especially in her text on Walter Benjamin. Here, one has to initially be aware of the silence of trauma and of silencing the trauma, even if they can overlap each other in many cases, even in very problematic way.

Felman's interpretation of Benjamin's silence is based on his two texts, 'The Storyteller' and 'Theses on History', but the real silence behind Benjamin lies in Port Beau, on the border between France and Spain where he died. Another death, which is supports the silence in Benjamin, is the death of his two best friends at the very beginning of the First World War, when they sent a letter to Benjamin prior to their suicide informing him where he could find their dead bodies. Felman argues that "their trauma must remain a private matter that cannot be symbolised collectively. It cannot be exchanged, it must fall silent."[90] This non-exchangeability of the experience of trauma is maybe the key in understanding the silence in Ferri's and many other artists' work. These kinds of works could also be described as an attitude against sociological quick interpretations, which want to hold critical distance toward the collectivisation of uneasy experience. Looking at Ferri's drawings, where he is using bullets and guns in the most productive, and in the most abstract, everyday life practices, like climbing the stairs, in Sisyphus-like games, we feel that anyway trauma is always there, but now silenced and closed from banal interpretations.

---

90.   S. Felman, 'Benjamin's Silence', Critical Inquiry 25.2 (1999): p. 207.

NEITHER VICTIMS NOR HEROES BUT SURVIVORS
AN INTERVIEW WITH JONAS STAAL

Marko Stamenkovi (MS): Jonas, you are best known for your series The Geert Wilders Works (2005-2007). This started with a series of public memorial works about the Dutch populist politician Geert Wilders, and ended up in a series of trials, in which you were prosecuted for "threatening a Dutch member of parliament with death". The notes and files resulting from these trials were recently published as the most recent chapter of the project, in which you approached the trials as a 'public debate' or 'happening' (finished with a trial in 2008). What is the whole fuss about this project (if you could explain it to an ignorant spectator coming from outside the Dutch scene), and – more specifically – how do you see the role of memorials in that context?

Jonas Stall (JS): To explain the reception of The Geert Wilders Works, it is important to be familiar with some key figures in what I call the 'Dutch populist movement'. Populism, as a political strategy, was actively introduced by the politician Pim Fortuyn in 2001. He participated in local elections in Rotterdam with his party 'Leefbaar Rotterdam' ('Liveable' or 'Endurable' Rotterdam), and then in national elections, with the Lijst Pim Fortuyn (List Pim Fortuyn). He won the local elections, but was shot by an animal rights activist before the national elections took place (after his death, his party still won 26 out of 150 seats in parliament). Fortuyn made use of a heavily 'sentimental', 'personalised' politics: his personal history was basically better known than his political points of view, except for his strong 'right-wing' position on immigration. The discussion on immigration had been a taboo in the Netherlands for decades, due to a strong sense of 'Colonial guilt' and the Holocaust. Fortuyn was one of the first – successful – politicians, who pleaded for a stop to immigration for so called 'profiteurs': immigrants who come to the Netherlands for 'purely' economic reasons.

Also, the re-implementation of secularism, the clear separation of church and state, was one of his spear points, pointing out that Muslim minorities were often living in excessively isolated and 'ghetto-like' conditions, not acknowledging fundamental 'western values', such as women and gay rights. Once the taboo on publicly criticising immigration and the Islamic religion in the Netherlands was removed, new figures arose after Fortuyn's death, such as Ayaan Hirsi Ali, and, most notoriously, Geert Wilders. Wilders used to be part of the liberal-conservative People's Party for Freedom and Democracy (VVD), but started his own party in 2004. He obtained nine seats in parliament during the 2006 elections, a representation of more than half a million Dutch voters. Wilders fights what he calls the 'Islamisation of society' to a much larger extent than Fortuyn. Like Fortuyn, the media form one of his main instruments. The media have spread his view on immigration and Islam, for which he is continuously threatened with death. He requires constant protection wherever he goes. This 'public martyrdom' has gained him much support, for he literally has sacrificed' himself to represent the 'average man's' vote. In that sense, even though he strongly opposes 'radical Islam', he himself is a radicalist per se.[91]

In the Geert Wilders works, I have drawn a direct relation between the 'public street memorials'

---

91.   Glossary: 'Martyr', p. 120; 'Self-Victimisation', p. 135.

that emerged after the death of publicly known figures, such as Pim Fortuyn and murdered film-maker Theo van Gogh, and victims of car accidents and the like, and the cult that has developed around populist politicians in the Netherlands. I refer to these memorial works as a phenomenon that can be traced back to Catholic rituals with clear elements concerned with 'death'. At the same time, they are a 'celebration' of the pop-status that certain politicians in the Netherlands have obtained.

It was this analysis that generated a fierce reaction in the public opinion: basically I acknowledged the fact that the taboo of publicly speculating on the potential death of politicians like Wilders has disappeared. I also pointed out the untouchable and irrational (sentimental) cult status that individuals like him have gained. Wilders, who felt threatened by the works, reported this to the police, which led to my temporary imprisonment and three trials, from which the last one was publicly accessible. My conviction is that these trials can only take place because of the same cult that I have emphasized with my memorial series. This forced me to present, document and integrate the trials as a fundamental part of my work. By sending out invitations to invite people to be present during the trial, I labelled the event as a 'public debate', in which my defense consisted of my artist's statement, in which I publicly claimed the trial as a work from my hand.

MS: In one of our last conversations in Amsterdam, you showed an interest in the aspects of recent history of former Yugoslavia, which generated a problematic context to distinguish the 'assassinator' from the 'victim' and the incapacity of international media, politics and general public opinion to make a clear point on this situation. Our conversation touched on the internationally criticised ceremony in 2006 in which the soldiers of Dutchbat III received medals from the former Minister of Defence Kamp (VVD), for having functioned 'up to their capabilities' in Srebrenica and afterwards had been "affected by a negative perception in the public opinion".[92] How do you personally relate to this issue?

JS: The ceremony played a central role in my attempts to approach Serbia as a context to develop a series of works, in cooperation with curator Marko Stamenkovi, in which I want to break through the status quo that surrounds Dutch art and politics, desperately holding on to a fiction of 'neutrality'. The Dutchbat III debacle resulted from the incapacity of the Dutch army to properly act to a direct threat, in this case coming from Mladi 's army. The Netherlands was only present there as a 'peace-keeping force', somehow only carrying weapons 'in case something would happen'. This is very typical for my country, which, as another example, did not initially participate on a practical level in the Iraq war, but did give 'political support' during the invasion.

Of course, neutrality, passivity, is a choice as well that demands as much responsibility as a concrete act of war, though this is not acknowledged as such. I think exactly the same problem is appropriate to describe the Dutch art scene: it is this strong will to keep 'our hands clean', not to have les mains sales. As if it would be possible to be 'politically involved', to take a critical position within society, without having to truly commit to a subject, and therefore inevitably be affected by it.

Just as our army and politics does, disturbing tactics are used in a continuous denial of the obvious within the Dutch art scene. Within the margins of the arts, one is allowed to re ect on populism, but not to be populistic; one is allowed to dream about a possible Utopia, but not to realise

---

92. See this collection, Marko Peljhan, 'Landscape 1995', p. 48.

it; one is allowed to make proposals for a memorial for Iraq, but not allowed to actually make it. Within these margins one is allowed to speak out, but prohibited from actually committing to a subject. To be brief: my interpretation of the Dutch art scene is one in which everything is done to keep up a myth of a de-politicised country, in which the greatest taboo is to actually penetrate the real, that is to say: to actually affect the structure and use of the public domain.

I see the military insignia ceremony performed by Kamp as being representative for the political (un)consciousness of the Dutch and their incapacity to seek true commitment and responsibility when entering in international con icts. Basically, it was an insignia given to the soldiers 'for being human, and having acted as such': having done everything to survive. In this respect, each and everyone in ex-Yugoslavia should have received the same medal, for they are all survivors.

It is impossible to determine which group or organisation or ethnic population of former Yugoslavia was 'right', was standing on the 'good side'. Bosnians, Serbs, Albanians, all having represented different religions, Catholic, Orthodox Christianity, Islam, etc. – it is impossible for an outsider (and probably for an 'insider' too) to define who was 'right'. In the end, the only thing that can be said is that the actors within the history of former Yugoslavia have all 'survived'. They were and still are humans, and have behaved as such (to refer again to my interpretation of the insignia ceremony). I think that, in that respect, the Dutch government, now that they have given these insignias to the Dutchbat III soldiers, should hand out medals to every citizen or former citizen of ex-Yugoslavia as well.

MS: In that regard, you seem to be specifically focused on the idea of the 'shared/collective guilt' and this could be seen as a main point of your approach to the aforementioned subject.[93] Could you please elaborate on this further?

JS: I think that the collective guilt in respect to the Srebrenica mass murder is representative for both countries: for Serbia as being an active victim and assasinator, and for the Netherlands, having employed the myth of neutrality once again as a weapon, with heavy consequences. For me as an artist, it has become more and more important to accept and allow the fact that, in respect to the subject matter that I am involved with, it is not possible to get away 'clean' or 'unharmed'. My impression is that in so-called socio-politically involved art, the exact opposite is actually the case. I want to permanently break the myth that any form of engagement can take place as a sort of 'neutral', 'formal' gesture, leaving all involved unharmed. I demand of art that it penetrates some form of 'reality'; that it accepts and demands actual consequences. It is for this reason that The Geert Wilders Works trials were of such importance for me: it forms my most fundamental statement in respect to the role of art within society's framework. 'Engagement' is not just one of the many things that you can 'do': it is inherent to the practice of art in the way that I commit myself to it. Approaching the collective guilt between the Netherlands and Serbia is in this respect a statement at hand, demanding full- and head-on confrontation from my side, to be able to generate meaningful projects in relation to both countries' histories.

MS: If we talk about 'survivors', what do you actually mean? Is it a position that goes beyond common dualisms between 'heroes' and victims', or what?

---

93.   Glossary: 'Collective Guilt', p. 110; 'Collective Unconscious', p. 112.

JS: I think that the term 'survivor', in respect to former Yugoslavia, acknowledges the fact that no one involved in its past con icts or wars can be labelled to be the 'assasinator' or victim all were involved, and in the end: all can be only survivors.

MS: The last thing: is it possible to detect and diagnose, within the contemporary Dutch society, any signs in everyday life that puts them in a position of those who suffer from a victim's symptom'? If yes, what are the reasons for such a conclusion? Does it also have to do with 'disrespectful and ungrateful' migrant-communities who were allowed to move and start living on Dutch territory or…?

JS: Before I can answer this, you'll have to explain to me what it is exactly that you interpret as the victim's symptom': what is it that you see as the 'symptomatic' aspect in the position of an individual who is victimised?

(Interview conducted by Marko Stamenkovi on 8 March 2008)

WE LEAVE NO ONE BEHIND! DE-VIC-
TIMISATION AND STEREOTYPES
AN INTERVIEW WITH PETER FUCHS

Marko Stamenkovi (MS): Jonas, you are best known for your series The Geert Wilders Works (2005-2007). This started with a series of public memorial works about the Dutch populist pol

We leave no one behind! – De-victimisation and stereotypes
An Interview with Peter Fuchs

Marko Stamenkovi (MS): So why does the mass media prefer to talk in terms of numbers of corpses, calculating them morbidly, with apparent disregard for the victims' status?

Peter Fuchs (PF): Let's make a quick overview on what 'victim status' is, who are stereotypical war crime victims? Defenseless, mostly rural inhabitants from a third world country, either eeing from some unknown menace in masses with makeshift carts (conjuring up visual experiences we obtained from the footages of Vietnam War) or in hiding in a devastated urban area from some supreme power. They possess no weapons (those who do immediately lose the status of the 'vic- tim' and become 'insurgents, freedom fighters, or even terrorists'), and staring into the objective of the camera with much innocence and sorrow on their faces.
These victims are people we don't know, so can't define with a proper form of identity. They are victims, maybe the same victims we saw in another con ict, maybe they are a tribe migrating from one con ict to another? They are not our friends, colleagues, but rather a faceless mass of people – please take note that victims, especially war crime victims, do not tend to dwell alone – since they have no identity, their main strength is in numbers, which somehow seems to re ect their magnitude of suffering. Lone victims tend to be overlooked by the media after the initial stage of the con ict. Take the 'San Francisco tiger attack', for example. We no longer care about the daily victims of violence in Iraq unless their number seem to beat some morbid stake the global media has, but the same media engine goes crazy on the unfortunate passing away of a San Francisco teenager.

MS: What you are describing is a serious stereotype, probably from Hollywood movies, but don't you think that we have a much more complex, re ective view on the subject?

PF: We could have, but since we have an extreme scarcity of actual, real life images taken of these people, either because they are hard to make or they are not as appealing to our idea of what it is to be a victim. Hence we accept those images that we think are the best representa- tions of what it is to be a victim of war, and these images exclusively come from the entertainment media, which are very well aware of this, and trying to produce even 'better' images from any imaginary or real con ict we might be interested in.

MS: But these movies are meant to be entertaining; they are not talking about genocide, mass murder, but rather giving a simplified version of some stereotypical events, like some kind of clichés. News channels are giving us facts, numbers, locations. Or is there no difference between imaginary genocides on the screen and real ones?

PF: Hollywood movies give really good, structured narratives in order to be easily understood by the audience. In these narratives, everything has its own place, as victims do. But there are not many of them: yes, there are genocides, but the victims of genocides are minor characters – and they are avenged; an important, statutory twist in the narrative structure.

In movies, all players have roles. The victim's role is to be victimised, later rescued, or avenged. Their number is only relevant for showing how large the effort was to save/avenge them, for this, they do not need to be counted, just shown that they are numerous.

I also have to add that those actors who have even a minor role in these movies, like the refugee father, his lost wife, or the nice old man slaughtered at the beginning of the movie to illustrate the cruelty of villains, are either becoming martyrs or 'rewards'. The same goes for friendly soldiers. They either die in glorious martyrdom (so allowing others to destroy the enemy encampment) or are sacrificed, just to show how skillful the enemy is.[94] Neither way are they considered to be victims, rather predestined beings fulfilling a given role. Their numbers are not for terrifying the viewers, but rather to strengthen the narrative.

A small band of highly professional Western country soldiers are evacuating a scientist/journalist/civic worker from a 'state of concern' in which mass killings are taking place: who are the victims in this stereotypical plot? The villains are definitely not. They are faceless, countless entities waving Kalashnikov assault ri es and dying like ies, like German soldiers in old Yugoslavian partisan movies. The innocent local people? They seem to be well seasoned to the circumstances. The western personnel, who happened to be in the middle of the con ict? Yes, in a way, but he/she will inevitably be rescued, by the soldiers. The lesser actor, who is shot at the end of the movie by the second lieutenant of the evil warlord? Hardly, he/she offers glorious martyrdom for the cause, and he/she will be not left behind.

MS: And what about the horror of images of victimisation? How are we affected by the mere sight of dead bodies? Why is an image of a dead body meaningful in some societies while in other societies it loses its capacity to provoke anger or compassion, but rather serves to produce attitudes?

PF: Actually, even the most realistic-looking action movies or war drama hides the dead bodies and casualities from our sight. Even if gruesome wounds are shown on the screen, they do not stay there for long, nor do the bodies of the deceased. Nevertheless, the dead bodies that remain on display only become sets, nice aesthetic objects that strengthen the realism of the movies and illustrate the noble efforts of the remaining fighters. That especially goes for contemporary war movies and video games, in which dead bodies become 'objects', which can no longer be touched, nor interacted with. These bodies have no identity as such, so they rely on numbers again. Unknown numbers. They are usually lying face down, becoming identical, unlike in reality, where victims retain their personality either displayed on images or on narrative structures – I mean we distinguish them from each other.

MS: Is it possible to 'return' the identity to these victims, to outwit the stereotypical images and

---

94. Glossary: 'Martyr', p. 120; 'Self-Victimisation', p. 135.

turn away from a neutral, aesthetic way of looking at victims?

PF: Imagine a situation in which you give identity to these people, victims not by the numbers, but faces: assume that they are your friends in a social networking site like MySpace or Facebook. You know these people, they are your friends, relatives, former schoolmates, ex-lovers, drinking buddies, whatever. Usually you have about 400 of them: an act of violence happens in your neighborhood, for example, in your university (perhaps the Baghdad Mustansiriya University attack in the January of 2007). Many people die. You had close connections with via six of them via social networks or direct and active friendships. Six faces, people, not numbers.
You might be well aware that MySpace users created a blog for other members who passed away – one of the most depressing things to browse for our generations. The entire life and deeds of the deceased are included with pictures, so we might feel that even our story could fit that sad list. What if the same would happen with war victims? What would happen if they all had faces, like the MySpace dead have? Would that change anything or they would remain as distant and as prone to be appropriated by Hollywood as before, or would we have to rethink how we perceive images of war, images of suffering?

(Interview conducted by Marko Stamenkovi on 28 jan 2008)

PART 3 - WITNESS

LANDSCAPE 1995 - OKRANJINA 1995
MARKO PELJHAN

The meta-archive Landscape 1995 examines the strategic and tactical situation on the battle-grounds and fronts of Bosnia and Herzegovina from 1992 on, with a special focus on the final events around the declared United Nations Safe Areas of Srebrenica and Zepa. Documents produced by an array of technological sensors, observers, lawyers and analysts are used in the structure that examines the military drive and logic that led to genocide by using a comparatively similar set of tools and systems as the observed processes.

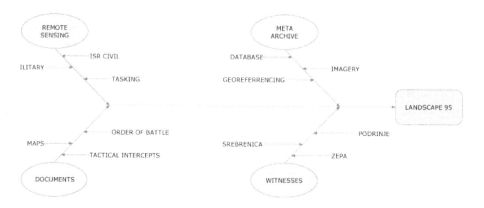

Illustration 9 - Marko Peljhan. landscape 1995

NIEMAND ZEUGT F R DEN ZEUGE (LEVI S PARADOX: CULTURAL AND POLITICAL REP-RESENTATIONS OF THE VICTIMS AND THE SECONDARY WITNESS PROB-LEM, FROM AUSCHWITZ TO SREBRENICA)
STEVAN VUKOVIC

Suicide of a Witness as Deferred Death

Suicide was the fate of many survivors of Nazi concentration camps; this was almost a kind of a deferred death, taking place right after accomplishing their testimonies, and thereby also resolving the so-called Levi paradox. Paul Celan, Jean Améry, Tadeusz Borowski and Primo Levi all testified in a literary form about the horrors they had witnessed, the horrors that they had stored in their mind's eye all the time of their post-camp lives.[95] They were waiting for an appropriate form to disclose these memories, so they could be conveyed to people who were unaware of them. Absolved of that task, after making their testimony, and getting rid of the 'burden of witnessing', they decided to put their lives to an end and join those innumerable ones in whose name the testimonies were made.

As Jean Amery, one of the death camp survivors who later committed suicide, once wrote in lines that Levi has subsequently quoted: "Anyone who has been tortured remains tortured". In the case of Levi, the everlasting torture was caused by the shame of surviving something that the others could not, which he considered as a kind of betrayal. He suspected that "each man is his brother's Cain" and that he "has usurped his neighbor's place and lived in his stead".[96] So, to justify his own survival in that situation, he took advice to "look carefully at everything around you, and conserve your strength", as Borowski has suggested, "for a day may come when it will be up to us to give an account of the fraud and mockery to the living – to speak up for the dead".[97]

But Levi's recurring nightmares were constantly casting doubts on the mere possibility of ever staying among the living, after giving a testimony. As one of his poems demonstrates, his wish to get back was realised in his dreams always with an internal time limitation. Therefore, it was fixed as a wish "to return; to eat; to tell the story / until the dawn command / sounded brief, low: / 'Wstawàch'!"[98] His persistently recurring dream of going back home kept on being interrupted by the capo's voice ordering 'Get up!' (Wstawàch!). Even when he really got back home, in 1962, he made notices of unceasing dreams in which everyday situations suddenly collapse, and he is back to the camp, right after hearing "a foreign word, feared and expected: get up, 'Wstawàch'".[99]

---

95. Glossary: 'Survivor Guilt', p. 137.
96. P. Levi, The Drowned and the Saved, trans. Raymond Rosenthal, New York: Summit Books, 1988, pp. 81-82.
97. T. Borowski, 'Auschwitz, Our Home (A Letter)', in This Way for the Gas, Ladies and Gentlemen, trans. by B. Vedder, Harmondsworth: Penguin, 1967, pp. 115-16, 122.
98. P. Levi, Collected Poems, trans. R. F. and Brian Swann, London: Faber & Faber, 1992, p. 11.
99. P. Levi, If This is a Man and The Truce, trans. Stuart Woolf, London: Abacus, 1987, p. 394.

The content of these two versions of the dream, the one prior to and the one after the return from the camp, was formally the same. But, as i ek argues, the way in which the stereotypical everyday situation is interrupted in them is significantly different. In the first place, "the dream is cruelly interrupted by the wake-up call, while in the second, reality is interrupted by the imagined command".[100] Responding to such a command, actually, to paraphrase Cathy Caruth, means responding to "a call that can only be heard within sleep"[101] – a call of the dead. Awakening within that dream was awakening into a situation of witnessing deaths again, in everyday life in the camp, so that, as Wiesel wrote, he finally "died at Auschwitz 40 years after returning home".[102] Cathy Caruth, in fact, refers to another case of awakening within the dream, the one Freud writes about at the beginning of his Interpretation of Dreams. That is the case of a father who had a dream that "his child was standing beside his bed, caught him by the arm and whispered to him reproachfully 'Father, don't you see I'm burning?'".[103] Interpreting the case of awakening in response to that call in the framework put forward by Lacan in his 'Seminar XI', she derives a theory of "a trauma of the necessity and impossibility of responding to another's death".[104] This is applicable as well, as i ek writes, to "the Holocaust survivor who, unable to save his son from the crematorium, is haunted afterwards by his reproach: Vater, siehst du nicht dass ich verbrenne?"[105]

Surviving to be a Witness

A father had been watching beside his child's sick-bed for days and nights on end. After the child had died, he went into the next room to lie down, but left the door open so that he could see from his bedroom the room in which his child's body was laid out, with tall candles standing round it. An old man had been engaged to keep watch over it, and sat beside the body murmuring prayers. After a few hours' sleep, the father had a dream that his child was standing beside his bed, caught him by the arm and whispered to him reproachfully: 'Father, don't you see I'm burning?' [Vater, siehst du denn nicht dass ich verbrenne?].[106]

The child had died prior to the fire, and there was a watchman failing react to it who could be blamed, but the father still felt responsible.

In relation to this dream, one could argue that Levi's dreams from the camp could fit into the frame that was proposed by Freud's interpretation of the dream about the burning child, but Levi's dreams upon his return call for a Lacanian reading. Namely, the Freudian reading is focused on the escape from the traumatic reality into a dream as a wish-fulfilling psychological device, while the Lacanian reading stresses the escape from the traumatic encounter with the Real – which happens in dreams – into the reality. In the Freudian reading, the father falls into sleep in order

100. S. i ek, 'Freud Lives!', London Review of Books, May 25, 2006: http://www.lrb.co.uk/v28/n10/zize01_.html
101. C. Caruth, Unclaimed Experience: Trauma, Narrative and History, Baltimore: The Johns Hopkins University Press, 1996, p. 99.
102. La Stampa, April 14, 1987.
103. S. Freud, 'The Interpretation of Dreams' in Standard Edition of the Complete Psychological Works of Sigmund Freud, London: Hogarth, 1953-74 Vol. 5, p. 509.
104. Caruth, Unclaimed Experience, p. 100.
105. i ek, 'Freud Lives!', http://www.lrb.co.uk/v28/n10/zize01_.html
106. Caruth, Unclaimed Experience, pp. 509-510.

to get back into the situation in which the child is still alive, and tries to stay there as long as possible, while in the Lacanian reading, he wakes up to avoid the accusing call from the child.[107] The accusation is very simple: the father has survived, the child has not, and that goes also for Levi's dream: he has survived, most of his fellow detainees did not. "His survival must no longer be understood," writes Caruth, "merely as an accidental living beyond the child, but rather as a mode of existence determined by the impossible structure of the response."[108] The father will never be in a position to really respond to the call of the dead child. Even more so as that very child did, by addressing him when the fire has begun, actually save him, while he couldn't save him at the time. "It is precisely the dead child", Cathy Caruth claims, "who says to the father: wake up, leave me, survive; survive to tell the story of my burning", and so makes sense of his survival.[109] Primo Levi has survived as a witness.[110] He has survived to tell the story of all those who could not make it, who were killed and burnt in the crematoriums of Auschwitz, who were addressing him and urging him to survive, to tell their story, and he saw them burning, even though he has never approached the crematorium. As long as he was writing, it was always the same story, even though he never considered himself a writer, but a chemist, he coped with responsibility. He felt like a dead man on parole, in the same way as Antigone, after the death of her brother, about which she was to give testimony, saw herself as ordained to "dwell not among the living, not among the dead",[111] because "her soul died long ago, and that she is destined to give help to the dead".[112]

But, there was another dream, quite similar to the first one, torturing him all the time. It also had a homely atmosphere as its milieu, and a traumatic turn – a failure to witness. "It is an intense pleasure, physical, inexpressible, to be at home, among friendly people, and to have so many things to recount: but I cannot help noticing that my listeners do not follow me", wrote Levi in Survival in Auschwitz, recalling the night on which he, while still in the camp, dreamed that he was back home. "I have dreamt it not once but many times since I arrived here", he continued then, "and I remember that I have recounted it to Alberto and that he confided to me, to my amazement, that it is also his dream and the dream of many others, perhaps of everyone".[113]

The Levi's Paradox: a Paradox of Witnessing
Giorgio Agamben, in his books titled Homo Sacer and Remnants of Auschwitz, argues for an ethical paradox, which he names after Primo Levi. He quotes from Levi, stating the following: "We, the survivors are not the true witnesses ... we survivors are not only an exiguous but also anomalous minority. We ... did not touch bottom. Those who did so, who saw the Gorgon, have not returned to tell about it or have returned mute, but they are the 'Muslims', the submerged,

---

107. Glossary: 'Survivor Guilt', p. 137.
108. Caruth, Unclaimed Experience, p. 100.
109. Caruth, Unclaimed Experience, p. 105.
110. Glossary: 'Witness', p. 144.
111. Sophocles, Antigone, trans. A. Brown, Wiltshire: Aris and Phillips, 1987, p. 91, lines 850-52.
112. J. Lacan, The Ethics of Psychoanalysis 1959-1960: The Seminar of Jacques Lacan: Book VII, trans. D. Porter, edited by J. Alain-Miller, New York and London: W.W. Norton & Company, 1997, p. 270.
113. P. Levi, Survival in Auschwitz: The Nazi Assault on Humanity, trans. S. Woolf, New York: Collier, 1993, p. 60.

the complete witnesses".[114] Primo Levi, in The Drowned and the Saved, as quoted in Agamben's Remnants of Auschwitz, doubted his ability to testify on behalf of the 'Muselmänner', the living dead who have crossed all human borders, becoming "too empty to really suffer".[115] Levi's biggest fear was that he will not only fail as a witness, but that he will finally discover that the whole issue of witnessing was a kind of a fantasy-construction that served just as a support for the reality of his selfish survival in the situation in which most of the others either did not survive at all, or have survived, but became 'Muselmänner'. He was afraid that he might at the time disclose that 'being a witness' had in fact for him an ideological function, in the sense in which Žižek defines it, as "not to offer us a point of escape from our reality but to offer us the social reality itself as an escape from some traumatic, real kernel".[116] As Dori Laub wrote of the Holocaust, it might just appear that it was an event without a witness, so not even Levi was one.[117]

As for his relation to the 'drowned', Ryn and Klodzinski wrote, that "no one felt compassion for the Muselmann, and no one felt sympathy for him either", that "other inmates, who continually feared for their lives, did not even judge him worthy of being looked at", and that, also, "for the prisoners who collaborated, the Muselmänner were a source of anger and worry; for the SS, they were merely useless garbage".[118] In that sense, we suddenly would not just have two parties at the camp, but at least three, of which one would be the Nazis, the other the Muselmänner, as the only true witnesses, who "carry an impossible history within them, or they become themselves the symptom of a history they cannot entirely possess", and Levi would belong to the third group. [119] What Agamben calls 'Levi's paradox' relates to the thesis that the Muselmann, as the 'drowned' victim who cannot bear witness for him- or herself, is the only complete witness. "The 'true witnesses' the 'complete witnesses' are those who did not bear witness and who could not bear witness", writes Agamben, stating that "the survivors speak in their stead, by proxy, as 'pseudo-witnesses'; they bear witness to a missing testimony".[120] The survivors are, for Agamben, who extensively cites Levi and Wiesel, only 'pseudo-witnesses', because, on the one hand, they could not experience everything the Muselmänner have and still survive and bear witness from their own experience, nor were they disinterested enough in that issue to legitimately play the third party. Agamben notes that, in Latin, the word 'witness' can be said in two different ways: 'testis', and 'superstes'. "The first word, 'testis', from which our word 'testimony' derives, etymologically signifies the person who, in a trial or a lawsuit between two rival parties, is in the position of a third party (terstis)", while "the second word, 'superstes', designates a person who has lived through something, who has experienced an event from beginning to end, and can therefore bear witness

---

114. Levi, The Drowned and the Saved, p. 63; G. Agamben, Remnants of Auschwitz, trans. D. Heller-Roazen, New York: Zone Books, 1999, p. 33.
115. Agamben, Remnants of Auschwitz, p. 44.
116. S. Žižek, The Sublime Object of Ideology, Verso, London, 1989, p. 45.
117. D. Laub, 'An Event Without a Witness: Truth, Testimony and Survival', in S. Felman and D. Laub (eds) Testimony: Crises of Witnessing in Literature, Psychoanalysis, and History, New York and London: Routledge, 1992, 75-92.
118. Z. Ryn and S. Klodzinski, 'An der Grenze zwischen Leben und Tod. Ein Studie über die Erscheinung des „Muselmann" in Konzentrationslager [At the Borderline between Life and Death: A Study of the phenomenon of the Muselmann in the Concentration Camp]', in Auschwitz-Hefte, Vol. 1, p. 127.
119. C. Caruth, 'Trauma and Experience: Introduction', in C. Caruth (ed.) Trauma: Explorations in Memory, London: John Hopkins University Press, 1995, p. 5.
120. Agamben, Remnants of Auschwitz, p. 34.

to it".[121] Primo Levi belongs to neither of the groups that could fit under these definitions, and that is the basic paradox, because the main goal in his post-camp life, the very core of his existence is in testifying. He can only testify on the impossibility of him being a witness.

Levi's 'Life-In-Death' and the Language of Witnessing

In Coleridge's Rime of the Ancient Mariner, it is Death and Life-in-Death that are gambling with dice for the Ancient Mariner's soul, and Life-in-Death wins. He survives the deaths of 200 of his shipmates, whose souls get to be set free of their bodies, and starts his wanderings from place to place. He has a strange power to single out the person who must hear his tale in each location he appears to get to. As he puts it: "I have strange power of speech; / That moment that his face I see, / I know the man that must hear me: / To him my tale I teach". Recalling his life after his return to Italy, Levi compares himself to the Ancient Mariner, as having the same urge to tell his story to everyone who would listen, and in a later book takes a rhyme from it as an epigraph. Levi's approach is immediate – he cannot help but telling everything at once in a plain language, the one he assumes to be comprehensible to everybody. Perhaps the most valuable thing about it is, in fact, not in the content of what is said, or written, but in his persistence, his dedication to follow the demand to tell, as the ultimate demand of his being. He simply cannot exist except in the role of constantly testifying. That is allegorised in his writing by the use of the tale of the Ancient Mariner. Levi dwells in the limbo between life and death, in a manner that is the exact reverse of the one of the Muselmänner. While they are symbolically dead, waiting for their proximate physical death, he cannot die without paying the symbolic debt for living after they have sized to.

In fact, when Agamben is quoting from Levi, and when he is dealing with his language of witnessing, it is never about Levi's standpoint and what he actually has to say. It is about what his approach to language and his position as a speaking being fails to take into account, but not just accidentally. This failure is exactly what keeps Levi going on, helps him in his attempts to provide a right testimony (even if he is not sure he could ever make it). While he was still in the camp, he was led by desire to get out and back to his lost 'normal' life, devoting himself to making sure that something like the Holocaust would never happen again. But after he came out, this desire turned into a drive, so the dignity that was lost appears as the dignity of the loss itself.

While writing, Levi reaches a conclusion that words from ordinary, everyday language fail to grasp the real experience of the Holocaust, and claims that only a "new, harsh language" could do that.[122] He turns then to the language he well masters, as a chemist working in a paint factory. In an interview with Phillip Roth, he discloses it as the idiom "of the 'weekly report' commonly used in factories", so that it has to be "precise, concise, and written in a language comprehensible to everybody in the industrial hierarchy".[123] But even though its role was to get away from the linguistic games of the Nazis, that idiom, as Cynthia Ozick points out, produced a "psychological oxymoron", and Levi as a "well-mannered cicerone of hell, mortal horror in a decorous voice".[124]

In fact, as it was repeatedly mentioned, Levi did not consider himself to be a writer, but a chemist who had to write, because he had to testify. He constantly feared that no one would notice what he had to say, that no one would even listen, as the reality of his nightmares was convincing

---

121. Agamben, Remnants of Auschwitz, p. 17.
122. Levi, Survival in Auschwitz, pp. 112-113.
123. P. Roth, 'A Man Saved By His Skills', The New York Times Book Review, October 12, 1986, p. 41.
124. C. Ozick, Metaphor and Memory: Essays, New York: Alfred Knopf, 1989, p. 40.

him. His words, which he knew would never accurately give voice to the 'drowned', were at least making the wrongness of their position, as the ultimate ethical 'wrong' of our civilisation, present in the narrative sense. By doing that, Levi was on his way to getting back his humanity that was stripped when he was turned into "Haftling number 174517". He has "become a man again ... neither a martyr, nor debased, nor a saint", in order to, finally be able to die in peace, as he did then.[125]

Levi and Celan

In July 1942, Paul Celan was sent to a labour camp in Tabaresti, in Wallachia, where he was detained until February 1944. His parents were taken to a concentration camp just one month before that. His father died of disease; his mother was shot. During the first year of his detention, Celan composed 'Chanson juive' ('Jewish Song'), whose title he soon changed to 'An den Wassern Babels' (By the Waters of Babylon), echoing Psalm 137. A few months later, he wrote 'Aus der Tiefe' (Out of the Depth), after Psalm 130, and in 1945 'Todesfuge' ('Deathfugue'), all of them dealing with the Shoah. When he committed suicide in 1970, Yves Bonnefoy concluded: *"I believe that Paul Celan chose to die as he did so that once, at least, words and what is might join"*. Primo Levi could not deal with Celan's treatment of language. He accused him of creating an 'atrocious chaos' and a 'darkness' that "grows from page to page until the last inarticulate babble consternates like the rattle of a dying man".[126] Even though he was treated better than the others in the camp for being a chemist, which was something quite useful for the Nazis, he could never forgive those who had a better treatment only for mastering the German language, and Celan was surely one of those. But Celan also found it very hard to deal with the fact that the language he was writing in was the language of his people's executioners, so he was constantly referring to the verbicide and genocide committed in the name of the Third Reich.

What Levi has seen only as the 'atrocious chaos', Celan has called "the inalienable complexity of expression",[127] "ambiguity without a mask [Mehrdeutigkeit ohne Maske]", and a "conceptual overlapping and multifacetedness".[128] This arose out of the responsibility in the articulation and transformation of post-Holocaust German poetry, which he could never consider to be the same as before. He dealt with the very materiality of the language, and he could never see himself in the position such as Levi's, writing 'for the judges', who were to learn from his testimonies and use them to legally sanction the people who were responsible for the atrocities. On the contrary, in the scope of Celan's work, only he was to be a judge, and the accused was the German language.

In Derrida's interpretation, Celan "wakes up language, and, in order to experience the awakening, the return to life of language, truly in the quick, the living esh, he must be very close to its corpse".[129] Celan does not have a nostalgic relation to the language as he experienced it before the camp, where all its 'normal' functions were suppressed. He is quite aware of the paradox that German, his mother tongue, is "indeed the language of his pride", but "it is also that of his

---

125. P. Levi, The Periodic Table, trans. R. Rosenthal, New York: Schocken Books, 1984, p. 151.

126. P. Levi, Other People's Trades, trans. R. Rosenthal, New York: Summit Books, 1989, p. 173.

127. P. Celan, 'Reply to a Questionnaire from the Flinker Bookstore, Paris, 1958', in Collected Prose, trans. Rosmarie Waldrop, New York: Routledge, 2003, p. 16.

128. H. Huppert, '»Spirituell«: Gespräch mit Paul Celan', in Werner Hamacher and Winfried Menninghaus (eds) Paul Celan, Frankfurt am Main: Suhrkamp, 1988, p. 321.

129. J. Derrida, 'Language Is Never Owned: An Interview', in Thomas Dutoit and Outi Pasanen (eds) Sovereignties in Question: The Poetics of Paul Celan, New York: Fordham University Press, 2005, p. 106.

humiliation".[130] His existence as a human being is inseparable from his existence in that language, which was mutilated the same way its speakers were. So, when he considers his task as a writer, it comes to digging "ashes of extinguished sense-giving ... and nothing else but that!"[131] Even though the Holocaust is always present in his writings, Celan does not confine his role of an author to the representation of atrocities and the people who have suffered them. In fact, the text he produces "no longer stands in the service of a predetermined reality, but rather is projecting itself, constituting itself as reality".[132] His standpoint is that "no one witnesses for the witness", and that silence is one of the characteristic modes of speech, not an anomaly. Perhaps the only way to deal with traumas sometimes is with a "mouthful of silence", for some things can never be told; only repeated. Or, even if they can be told, it could happen only in a language that is reconstructed, and in the manner that does not pretend to mirror things, events and situations that it deals with.

Photographic Testimonies on Atrocities as a Genre

Arguing historically, Allan Sekula wrote that the "photographic portraiture began to perform a role no painted portrait could have performed in the same thorough and rigorous fashion". That role was derived "not from any honorific tradition, but from the imperatives of medical and anatomical illustration".[133] Piles of bodies photographed by the photojournalists travelling with the Allied troops to document their progress at the end of World War II did look just like that. There was not much doubt on the part of the photographers about how those bodies, caught in their images that were immediately sent to major newspapers, would be represented. They were reduced to objects, whose representation was to serve the purpose of spreading the truth about the atrocities in camps.

George Rodger was one of those photographers, but surely not the most typical one. He did have more than serious doubts, even though after the fact. Namely, at the time, he was a correspondent for Life magazine. On April 20, 1945 he entered the concentration camp at Bergen-Belsen five days after the first British troops. He documented the situation they found there. His photos were consequently published in Life and Time, and the response they provoked made him a definite celebrity. But, as he confessed later on, when realising that in the midst of that horror he was mainly thinking about the composition, fully consumed with how the bodies were to be arranged to make the best photograph, he decided to quit war photography.

"This natural instinct as a photographer is always to take good pictures, at the right exposure, with a good composition," wrote Rodger later on, "but it shocked me that I was still trying to do this when my subjects were dead bodies ... I realized there must be something wrong with me... otherwise I would have recoiled from taking them at all ... I recoiled from photographing the so-called 'hospital', which was so horrific that pictures were not justified ... From that moment, I determined never ever to photograph war again or to make money from other people's misery ... If

130. P. Celan, Paul Celan: Selections, Berkeley: University of California Press, 2005, p. 217; see also, Edmond Jabès, La mémoire des mots, trans. P. Joris, Paris: Fourbis, 1990.

131. P. Celan, Gesammelte Werke, Vol. 3, Frankfurt am Main: Suhrkamp, 2000, p. 175.

132. P. Szondi, Celan Studies, Stanford: Stanford University Press, 2003, pp. 31-32.

133. A. Sekula, 'The Body and the Archive', October 39, (1986): p. 6.

I had my time again, I wouldn't do war photography".[134] After the war he did quit war photography and worked freelance for the National Geographic in Nubia, among other assignments. What has followed afterwards was a ood of images of atrocities, which, according to Joachim Paech, fully "re-arrange and often disfigure the phenomenon of the Holocaust",[135] as instant surrogates of its experience, without the ability to lead into to the "interior space" of the experience of the Holocaust.[136] Soon they also became mixed with the photographs taken by the Nazis. "It is now reckoned that Nazi photo albums, which occasionally turn up in auction houses, will fetch higher prices if they contain atrocity photographs", wrote Janina Struk in the final chapter of her book titled: Photographing the Holocaust: Interpretations of the Evidence, "predictably, 'extra atrocity photographs' are copied from books, aged and added to albums before being offered for sale".[137]
One of the reasons why Claude Lanzmann restrained from using Holocaust photographs in his nine and a half hour long documentary Shoah has was exactly this over ow of images, to which he was countering the singular authenticity of memories presented through interviews. "It was necessary to make this film from nothing, without archival documents", said Lanzmann in an interview, "to invent everything".[138] He has brought the experience of Shoah back from the obscene spectacle to the real story of human suffering, which made Shoshana Felman write that it was "the story of the liberation of the testimony through its desacralization; the story of the decanonization of the Holocaust for the sake of its previously impossible historicization?"[139]

Beyond the Immediate Visual Representation
In one of the typical scenes in Shoah, Lanzmann, who appears in the first person, asks a resident who works at the place where the concentration camp was: "Exactly where did the camp begin?" After he is shown where the fence was, he moves across the now non-existing barrier, asking again: "So I'm standing inside the camp perimeter, right?" and moving again: "So we're outside the camp, and back here we enter it … And at this point we are inside the camp" and finally: "So where we're standing is where 250,000 Jews were unloaded before being gassed?"[140] Instead of simply bombarding the viewer with images, he lets him/her imagine the horrors of passing that now non-existent and invisible barrier at the time when it stood there, and it is not less horrible. Here, Lanzmann is effectively reenacting the trauma, instead of representing it. He is not interested in showing a well-edited story of how things really were when the Shoah happened, but in finding out how we could today, as we are, in the times that we live, in spaces we inhabit, relate

---

134. C. Naggar, George Rodger: An Adventure in Photography – 1908-1995, Syracuse, New York: Syracuse University Press, 2003.
135. J. Paech, 'Ent/setzte Erinnerung', in Sven Kramer (ed.) Die Shoah im Bild. München: Boorberg, 2003, p. 13.
136. Paech, 'Ent/setzte Erinnerung', pp. 19-20.
137. J. Struk, Photographing the Holocaust: Interpretations of the Evidence, London and New York: I. B. Tauris, 2004, pp. 192-193.
138. Lanzmann in an interview to Le Matin de Paris, April 29, 1985, p. 12.
139. S. Felman, 'The Return of the Voice: Claude Lanzmann's Shoah' in S. Felman and D. Laub (eds) Testimony: Crises of Witnessing in Literature, Psychoanalysis, and History, New York and London: Routledge, 1992, p. 219.
140. C. Lanzmann, Shoah: The Complete Text of the Acclaimed Holocaust Film, New York: Da Capo Press, 1985, pp. 32-33.

ourselves to those impossible experiences, that no one could really convey to us. One could see this as a way of 'acting out' in which the author reproduces a repressed collective memory, "not as a memory, but as an action: he repeats it, without of course, knowing that he is repeating it".[141] But, in fact, this is a deliberate action of recollecting and reconstituting, or rewriting of the history, "in which conjectures about the past are balanced against promises of the future".[142]

Similar to Lanzmann's approach to the Shoah in film, are the approaches of Everlyn Nicodemus and Milica Tomi to different mass exterminations in visual art. Namely, in her work titled the "Reference Scroll on Genocide, Massacre and Ethnic Cleansing", made in 2004 on the basis of I. W. Charny's Encyclopedia of Genocide. Nicodemus produces an installation with no representative images, which simply lists the data from long centuries of genocides around the world. On the other hand, Milica Tomi , in her work titled 'XY Ungelöst', made in 1996/7, personally reenacts the traumatic events of mass killing of ethnic Albanians in Kosovo in March 1989, which led to all the other events in former Yugoslavia in 1990.

Israel W. Charny, whose work Nicodemus builds upon, defines genocide as, in a generic sense, "the mass killing of substantial numbers of human beings, when not in the course of military action against the military forces of an avowed enemy, under conditions of the essential defencelessness and helplessness of the victims".[143] That definition is very wide, and does not get entangled with identity politics, which leaves Nicodemus with quite a range of possibilities to simply put in public view a long list of massacres and ethnic cleansings, investigating the manners in which they become ideologically appropriated. Her work is, in its materiality, really an ordinary scroll, with inscriptions on it, presenting a 'politics of trauma'.

Milica Tomi appropriates the title of a German television programme broadcast on ZDF that aims to combat and solve crimes ("Aktenzeichen XY ... ungelöst", in translation "File XY ... Unsolved") to deal with a crime that was in icted upon her fellow citizens by the state apparatus, in the times of ethnic mobilisation and preparation for the civil war. The only traces of that event in the media were imprints of the bodies of the victims in the snow, which made a kind of an allegorical motive for the video work, featuring the artist herself, and the close circle of her friends, reenacting the falling of bodies of people shot down by the police, into the snow. At the same time, the other screen shows the process of redressing the same people as the very victims.

The Photographic Takeover

George Rodger left his personal involvement in war photography as a photographer, but still the effect of the wide publicity of and strong public response to these kinds of photographs created a whole new genre that exploited war, poverty and famine. The agency that he later founded with three other war photographers in 1947, namely Robert Capa, David 'Chim' Seymour and Henri Cartier-Bresson, did still take perhaps the biggest advantages of this scopophilic urge on the side of the audience to see images of the subhuman state that some people were caught in. So, there could be no major disaster or atrocity today, in any part of the world, without the presence of some of the photographers from Magnum.

For instance, when mentioning Srebrenica, or Vukovar, one cannot help but visualising those

141. S. Freud, 'Remembering, Repeating and Working Through', Standard Edition, Vol. 12, p. 150.
142. J. Lacan, Ecrits: A Selection, New York: Norton. 1981, p. 48.
143. I. W. Charny, 'Toward a Generic Definition of Genocide', in G. J. Andreopoulos (ed.) Genocide: Conceptual and Historical Dimensions, Philadelphia: University of Pennsylvania Press, 1994, p. 75.

places through the images of Gilles Peress and Josef Koudelka. They are strong and straight, and so massively reproduced that they reach and affect everyone interested in their topic. They are nowadays published in political magazines, shown at symposia dealing with various humanitarian issues, presented in gallery formats as art and circulated within the market and among private collectors as a commodity. There is absolutely no piece of writing, in any genre, that could get close to this publicity. It might happen that the atrocities in Srebrenica and Vukovar will be remembered from Peress' book The Graves, like Dachau from George Stevens' movie.

Undoubtedly the biggest star of Magnum in the last decade was James Nachtwey, who has fascinated the general audience, the humanitarians and the professional photographers alike with his extreme though quite stylised photo recordings of orphanages in Romania, civil wars in former Yugoslavia, street massacres in Rwanda and famine in Somalia. He has perfected the art of transforming the reality of heavily underprivileged people and those affected by war, disease or famine into a spectacle. While being a Magnum photographer (a couple of years ago he founded his own agency), he was really everywhere, at the smallest possible distance to the sources of catastrophic images, shooting symbolism and even the sublimity of universal victims.

One of the sources of his enormous popularity is the power of his images to evoke basic human empathy and instinctual solidarity with victims, who are pictured out of any context, so that the viewer, usually shocked by the explicitness of the content, can still elaborate around it. As one looks, for instance, at his photograph titled 'Indonesia, 1998 – A beggar washed his children in a polluted canal', presenting a person who has lost one of his arms and one of his legs, but still being able to take care of his family, one is at the same time visually embarrassed and emotionally pleased, for the scene is highly symbolic. But there is no context to it, no reason why it is so. We find out that context only when seeing the critical documentary on him by Christian Frei.

Or, one can also take as an example his photograph titled 'Croatian Militiaman Attacking Muslims. Mostar. Bosnia-Herzegovina. 1993'. It shows a gunman holding an AK ri e and firing through the window of a semi-destroyed bedroom, with blinds that shutter it for protection. There is absolutely no clue of what is going on outside, just an indication of complete chaos, in which a neighbor shoots a neighbor, for no obvious reason, while the face of the gunman is turned away from the viewer. For the photographer, he has no face, he has no name, and he just represents the madness of the region where it seems that wars happen as a kind of natural disaster. The task the photographer takes on appears to be just to freeze moments in which that becomes obvious.

Photography as 'Poornography' – On "Pure Beauty and Misery"

Commenting on his new war photographs straight from the battlefield in Iraq, Nachtwey articulated what he saw and what he wanted to present with a photo of a group of Iraqi women fully covered: "Pure Beauty and Misery – Women Praying in front of the Mosque". Of course, there is no word about how the troops that Nachtwey was following get to the point where they met these people, who are again without names and faces, reduced to their sex and confessional belonging, nor what happens to their surroundings and the local people around them, in the midst of the war. They are reduced to victims, paradoxically sublime in their misery.

Tirdad Zolghadr has called that approach 'poornography', a 'career-enhancing practice' by the 'representation of indignity', that functions in the context of "the market demand for quick-fix solidarity, living-room worldliness and that cushy sense of ideological superiority through critical consumption".[144] Nachtwey presents himself as a war photographer by profession, but an anti-war photographer by conviction, constantly stressing that his work is to bare both moral and political messages. He pictures things that are not happening anymore, but he does that in a manner in which a pornographer would constantly produce degrading porn in order to show how sexual abuse really looks in its obscenity and thereby elevate general moral and political consciousness. "There is something pornographic in the pejorative sense in Nachtwey's work", writes J. M. Bernstein on Nachtway's photographs published in a book titled Inferno, and it "derives not from what they depict, but from how that depiction occurs", which is "framing of devastation for the sake of the moral satisfaction of the liberal gaze".[145] His images are disconnected from any streams of lived experience, abstracted and fixed in their compositional perfection, made to provide a mix of disturbing elements, on the level of content, and pleasing elements, on the level of presenting that content. The strong aesthetic distance he has towards the presented, which is visually framed in a way that can be hung in any office, where these photos frequently end up, is to please that gaze.

Nachtwey presents himself as a witness, and his work comes out of an urge to witness, which is interpreted by Bernstein as being grounded in two principles. The first claims that "we must not avert our look from the face of extreme human suffering, at least when that extreme of suffering was perhaps preventable, that is, a suffering we have sufficient reason to believe was the product, finally, of conscious choices and actions", while the second that produced in specific Nachtwey style, "the photography of atrocity transforms each remnant, living or dead, into a 'mute witness', almost a moral conscience".[146] In this way, Nachtwey puts himself into a position of a secondary witness, who does not give voice to the victims, but makes visible their speechless numbness.

That finally brings us back to Levi and Agamben, and the paradoxes of the remnant as the only true witness, witnessing by simply living his dehumanised life. Bernstein analyses the proximity of Nachtwey's photography to Agamben's 'philosophic' camera.[147] He finds quite some analogies between them. He even utters that there is "something pornographic in Agamben's philosophic portrait of the Muselmann, the pure desire to bear witness," which fetishises the undignified.[148] The conclusion for Bernstein is that, "although there must indeed be an ethic of witnessing, witnessing is not ground of the ethical", so we need a new categorical imperative, for the "reconfiguration of culture and the structures of authority governing the everyday".[149]

144. T. Zolghadr, 'Them and Us', Frieze 96 (2006).
145. J.M. Bernstein, 'Bare Life, Bearing Witness', Parallax 10.1 (2004): 11.
146. Bernstein, 'Bare Life, Bearing Witness', p. 14.
147. Bernstein, 'Bare Life, Bearing Witness'p. 14.
148. Bernstein, 'Bare Life, Bearing Witness', p. 8.
149. Bernstein, 'Bare Life, Bearing Witness', p. 15.

DEATH AND ADVERTISING
AN INTERVIEW WITH ANUR HADŽIOMERSPAHI

Illustration 10 - Anur Hadžiomerspahic and Ajna Zlatar: Identify

Ana Peraica (AP): It's about the project with the exhumation... I've got to confess I couldn't look at these posters; somehow I know the world would not stay the same. A wo/man in media society can somehow get used to images of death, they are 'other bodies', but as soon as they appear with something in common (maybe even only this?) – the goods of the global society we usually face clean and new in shops, seems that world is, as Kristeva says 'contaminated' and we are faced with our own, not the death of the other.[150]

Anur Had iomerspahi (AH): So, the project was produced by Ajna Zlatar and me – it wasn't me alone. In the wish to make Bosnian people closer to the Western citizen, we made posters, on the tenth year of the genocide in Srebrenica, showing clothing of victims that were branded. Or, in a wish to make the Western citizen identify with usually far away victims, we have decided to make it via known brands/commercial trademarks, in which victims were slaughtered. Absurd, of course... But, if you say to a Western citizen that this and that number of people in Bosnia are being killed, it means little to him/her. If you show the victim was wearing sneakers (maybe s/he is wearing too) then, via the commercial trademark, becoming the common container a Western person may identify with the victim. That is how we have chosen (from the book of clothing of victims of genocide serving to families to recognise their relatives) clothing of the leading world commercial trademarks. So, on one poster there is Levis, on the other Adidas, on the third Lacoste, etc. We put posters up during the film festival in Sarajevo, when there were the most foreigners in the city, as this project was directly addressed to them. Later on the exhibition went to Italy (Milan) and some other cities outside of Bosnia. So we have tried to solve the problem of identification of Westerners with Bosnian victims, in a very efficient and absurd way – via commercial brands. Identification via big brands is at the same time sad and absurd and morbid in its efficiency.

AP: Though there is an obvious difference between the impossibility of falsifying the state of disintegration, not so familiar to this always 'hyper-new' society, did someone comment on the difference between your posters and Toscani's advertising for Benetton showing a Croatian soldier?

AH: As far Toscani is concerned, all respect, but I did not have that in mind, thinking on what would be needed that Europe is made closer to victims of genocide in Srebrenica.

AP: I've got to ask one more thing: do you think artworks speaking about Srebrenica – yours, Maja Bajevic, Sejla Kameric – have done something for Srebrenica?

AH: The answer on the question if artworks have done anything for Srebrenica – precisely that much art is capable of, in the society and time we live today, to act.

(Interview conducted by Ana Peraica on 16 dec 2007)

---

150. J. Kristeva, Powers of Horror: An Essay on Abjection, trans. by L. S. Roudiez, New York: Columbia University Press, 1982.

Illustration 11 - Toscani: Poster for Benetton

WORTHY AND UNWORTHY VICTIMS
QUESTIONS TO NOAM CHOMSKY

Ana Peraica (AP): Do you think victims of the past have more special status in media society than those happening today?

Noam Chomsky (NC): Economist and media analyst Edward Herman has made a distinction between 'worthy victims' and 'unworthy victims'.[151] Worthy victims, who merit lavish attention and concern, are those whose fate can be attributed to someone else, preferably an official enemy. Unworthy victims, whose fate is ignored or denied, are those for whose suffering or slaughter we are responsible. The criterion holds remarkably closely, past and present. He and others (myself included) have documented the matter quite extensively.

AP: What is, in your opinion, the reason why victims are measured in numbers and are those numbers making any difference?

NC: Some reasons are understandable. Slaughtering 1 million people is a worse crime than slaughtering 1,000. But this consideration is overwhelmed by the worthy-unworthy distinction, as again has been documented extensively.

AP: Where does the need of media society come from to confront distant trauma (both in time and space)?

NC: Sometimes it is real and genuine concern. All too often, however, traumas that are 'distant' – in the sense that crimes can be attributed to others – are quite popular for ugly reasons of power and prestige, while those that are 'close' – in that we share responsibility and can do a lot about them – are unwelcome. Again, very strong tendencies that are well documented.

(Interview conducted by Ana Peraica on 09 jan 2008)

---

151. E. S. Herman and N. Chomsky, Manufacturing Consent: The Political Economy of the Mass Media, New York: Pantheon Books, 1988.

PART 4 - MEMORIALS

DUST OF THE OFFICE
MARTHA ROSLER

Martha Rosler's Dust of the Office is a collection of HTML documents and supporting media focussed on the global biopolitics of control. The dominant themes are bodily confinement and surveillance in situations of highly rationalised, restricted office-cubicle life and battlefield terrain, and the concomitant internalisation of disciplinary strictures.

Dust of the Office evokes the bodily experiences of vast numbers of people around the world without suggesting that these experiences are equivalent: on the one hand, office or 'knowledge' workers – white-collar professionals, pink-collar secretarial workers, and those who y business – and on the other hand, the combatants and detainees, the individual actors on global stages of international con ict.

Philip K. Dick's futurist novel Vulcan's Hammer (1960), with its malevolent, post-apocalyptic, world-controlling computer that deploys death-dealing insect bots, appears alongside robotic ies and predator drones from the catalogues of modern-day war technology.[152] As with other writing by Dick, Vulcan's Hammer, as excerpted in Dust of the Office, also underscores the internalisation of disciplinary behaviours. Although the conditions of incarceration of Guantánamo and black-site detainees in the so-called Global War on Terror (GWOT) cannot be equated with the confinement and regimentation of office workers, they represent the same impulses of regulation applied to different subject populations.

Fun, leisure and entertainment as represented in Dust of the Office call to mind the eventful life imagined by the 'salaried masses' as the opposite of their stringent conditions of work: a sleek world of escapist glamour devoid – as Siegfried Kracauer explains – of the 'dust of the everyday'. (In Kracauer's analysis, industrial workers, at least in the Germany of the 1920s, still harboured hope for the transformation of work through communal labour struggles.)

It is part of the victim's symptomatology, perhaps, to fail to engender resistance or foment revolt; that would require an active renunciation of the status of victim a choice often confronted by Philip K. Dick's hapless protagonists. Those imprisoned under the expanded reach of GWOT cannot be expected to bring about 'regime change'. It is incumbent upon the rest of us to engineer that change.

---

152. P. K. Dick, Vulcan's Hammer, London, Arrow Books, 1976.

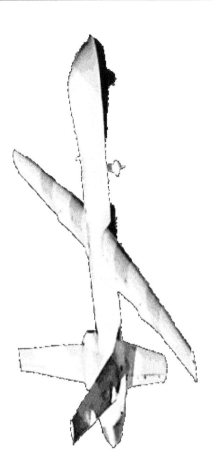

Illustration 12 - Martha Rosler, dust of the office

REGARDING ONE S PAIN: THE 100 SHAHEED-100 LIVES EXHIBITION
ADILA LAIDI HANIEH

This is a re ective testimony about conceptualising and curating the (100 Shaheed-100 Lives) art memorial exhibition (2001-2003).[153] I attempted to present an art project with the essence of the concepts of two unalienable human attributes often denied to Palestinians: dignity and freedom. The project became a crucible of perceptions and projections about self representation and politics.

Context

Art and culture practitioners in Palestine live a unique situation of being part of a post-colonial hybrid world, under an enduringly anachronistic brutal and dehumanising occupation; forcing the constant construction of a quasi-essentialist narrative of resistance, perpetually engaging in what Michel Foucault called a 'practice of liberty'.

September 1993 saw the signature of the Oslo interim peace accords, which established a national Palestinian Authority in Palestine, preceded by the withdrawal of Israeli troops from Palestinian towns. The brief interlude that lasted until the failure of the Camp David peace talks in the summer of 2000 saw the continuation of occupation and its repression in the countryside, but a short-lived economic recovery in the main towns. The failure of Camp David brought about the second Intifada on September 29, 2000, and its repression in an unprecedented manner with shootings at demonstrators, shellings of urban agglomerations, military incursions, and a fully edged multi-month siege and curfew on all West Bank towns, and the ongoing construction of the separation Wall.

For the first time in the history of the occupation, the phenomenon of the Shaheed appeared in force. The Palestinian liberation movement often modeled itself on Algeria's struggle for independence. However, where Algeria's grand narrative put its million Shaheed at the forefront, Palestinian Shuhada (plural of Shaheed) had numbered much less. The principal individual symbol of the occupation had been the prisoner and the Fedaee (freedom fighter). But now, the repression of the Intifada introduced the Shaheed concept in Palestine. With the daily shootings of demonstrators at checkpoints, the shellings of built-up areas, the intentional or 'collateral' damage of targeted assassinations, dozens of people were dying in the early days of the Intifada. Unlike earlier Shuhada, these were non-combatant young men, children, or the elderly. The term of the Shaheed that had been understood to be a person dying for a cause now also designated unarmed or unwitting victims of violence.

Whereas the dead in the Middle East are usually eulogised and mourned in the public space by newspaper announcements placed by family and friends, these Shuhada were mourned and celebrated in posters appearing a few hours after their deaths in the streets of their hometowns.

---

153. An extended version of this essay was first published in 2006 as 'Occupation, Death, Art & Remembrance: The 100 Shaheed-100 Lives Memorial Exhibition', in B. Madra (ed.) Maidan: Perspectives on Contemporary Art & Culture from Caucasus, Central & Middle East, Istanbul: BM Contemporary Art Center.

If they stood out by their actions, or by the gruesome circumstances of their death, their posters crossed the fragmented territory of Palestine to appear in other towns. Some, like Mohammed al Durra[154] and Fares Odeh,[155] were immortalised in iconic visuals that travelled across borders. In a country without a conventional army or a state apparatus to institutionalise the memorialisation of conventional war dead, street posters were the ephemeral memorials of Shuhada. And the incredible tales of dashed hopes and might-have-beens of these dead young men that circulated everywhere were becoming new building blocks of the Palestinian collective consciousness.

The Memorial

I was at the time running the Khalil Sakakini Cultural Centre in Ramallah, which had what was at that time the only art gallery in the West Bank, and ran a programme of art workshops for artists and children.

At the same time, my 1998 work on Palestinian narrative recovery through collecting testimonies of survivors of the Palestinian Nakba of 1948 made me realise the relative dearth of available work at the time on Palestinian oral history and micro history.[156] Caught since 1948 in a cycle of resistance, dispersal, exile and survival, Palestinians had had scant time to gather and archive their past. In addition, Palestinians were now labouring under a new accusation, that of instrumentalising death, and of disregarding the death of their own children.

Personally, it had also been ten years since one of my brothers was killed in an accident at the age of 23. I started comparing the outpouring of solidarity and affection that surrounded my family then with the fate of those killed now every day, and the ones who would be killed in the next few weeks. I knew how their families would be crushed by their loss like ours was ten years ago. But I also felt that their grief might be relativised, for what community would have the time and the emotional fortitude to devote to consoling the bereaved mother, father or siblings of a young man in their midst, when there were ten others every day whose life stories might be more moving, and whose circumstances of death might be more gruesome? Wouldn't this grief be relativised by the death of so many, at the same time, and in the same circumstances?

I thought of a kind of art project that would dignify the families' grief, provide a space where these interrupted lives would unfold and archive them in words and images, instead of surrendering to the death machine that cut them short.[157]

An art project would enable the unfolding of narratives of ordinary lives within the interstices of opposing political reifying discourses: Inside Palestine: victimhood or hero-isation, and outside Palestine: altering dehumanisation. The project also challenged the logic of art exploited for the political mobilisation or the generation of pity, in favour of a basic need to fashion a narrative out of silence, that of the absence of narrative about the lives of those who are economically and politically disenfranchised: the 'subaltern'.

In terms of space articulation, there was a path in the Sakakini gallery, beginning at the older Shuhada's room, through the young ones', ending with the children's room. This would be a journey

---

154. His killing by Israeli army bullets while crouching beside his father was captured by France 2 TV news cameras on 30 September 2000.
155. He was immortalised in a 29 October 2000 AP photo, standing alone in front an Israeli tank, throwing stones at it.
156. Khalil Sakakini Cultural Center: Nakba: http://www.alnakba.org.
157. Glossary: 'Grief', p. 117.

with 100 stations, for each Shaheed's name, photograph and personal object.
These two mediating devices would draw the contours of the life, and the companion book would sketch out each one's reality and aspirations. These mediating devices would stand alone, uncluttered by reductive, exploitative, maudlin, or otherwise reifying framing discourses or presentational displays.

As for the photographs, we received mostly formal portraits taken during happy occasions such as religious feasts, graduations, weddings or engagements. The vanity usually exuded by formal portraits was absent here, starkly illustrating Palestinian historian Elias Sanbar's observation about the presence of "those hunted out of time … who have succeeded anew to be visible … anxious to integrate photographic time, of not being left out of the image".[158] The exception was Alaa, a teenager who had been too young and too poor to be photographed in life, and whose only photograph was that of the points of entry and exit of bullets into his dead body. I did not use the photograph, but kept him in the Memorial since his lack of visual representation did not negate the reality of his existence.

As for the objects, I asked the families to provide an intimate possession. Since many of them were poor, they were mostly clothes, not the consumer society accoutrements of youth elsewhere. We also received some toys, work tools, copy books, schoolbags, and of course two roughly hewn slingshots, fragile tools of defiance and resistance for their owners, but also the 'weapon of the crime'. These owner-less objects were now useless. The rupture created by this newly acquired uselessness transformed them into objects that could find a new identity, and a new use in an art space.

After I developed the concept and selected the objects and photographs, painter Samir Salameh designed transparent boxes to display each object, wrapped and tied with a ribbon of twine. Lights were dimmed to direct the gaze onto the objects and photographs.

As I discarded bloodstained objects from the exhibit, I avoided the use of the colours red and black from the companion book that had a unifying beige colour scheme to deal with the heterogeneity of the objects, and featured Isabel de la Cruz's sepia photographs of the objects, again to sidestep the black signifier of mourning.[159]

Even though my intention at the start was to focus on each Shaheed's individuality, after working on the Memorial for five months, from selecting the objects received for display, to reading the accounts of the lives of the Shuhada, and then writing them and cross checking their facts, the end of the process was different. This was re ected in the curatorial statement. Each Shaheeds' biography retold elements of the same tale a 100 times: as etymologically, a Shaheed is a 'faithful witness', each of the 100 biographies in the companion book bore witness to a whole greater than their sum.[160] Michel de Certeau wrote of city walkers in "an urban text they write without being able to read". But in this case, these young men's lives and deaths wrote of a trans-historical, cross gender, a-religious, and cross class Palestinian condition of a reality shackled by occupation.

---

158. E. Sanbar, Les Palestiniens: Images d'une terre et de son peuple de 1839 à nos jours. Paris: Editions Hazan, 2004.
159. Glossary: 'Mourning/Bereavement' p. 121.
160. Glossary: 'Witness', p. 144.

Their lives painted a condition beginning with a family's loss and uprooting in the Nakba, continuing with the subsequent denied opportunities, and miseries of the refugee's condition. It progressed with a litany of deprivation, servitude, interrupted childhoods, Odysseus-like wanderings, house demolitions, killings, injuries and imprisonments. Even those whose lives appeared removed from the yoke of occupation, finally succumbed to its reach, with the circumstances of their premature passing. Yet, these lives also portrayed an irrepressible longing for freedom and spirit of struggle, illustrating Homi Bhabha's observation that: "it is from those who have suffered the sentence of history − subjugation, domination, Diaspora, displacement - that we learn our most enduring lessons for living and thinking".[161]

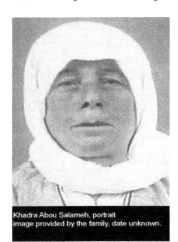

Khadra Abou Salameh, portrait
image provided by the family, date unknown.

Illustration 13 - Khadra Abu Salameh[162]

This story was told repeatedly: Mahmoud, a survivor of collaborators' denunciations, killed three days after his marriage, and after two of his friends had been killed in the same place where he was to die. Salameh, shot while returning to his refugee camp home after ending his shift at the Jericho Casino. Jihad, the well-to-do returning exile, and Ahmed, the security chief's nephew, killed at checkpoints. Omar, whose family's ancestral lands are now Ariel Sharon's farm, Mansour,

---

161. H. Bhabha, The Location of Culture, London: Routledge, 1994, p. 172.
162. Khadra Abu Salameh - 56 years old. Khadra leaves behind eight children. Widowed fifteen years ago, Khadra lived with her 24-year-old mentally disabled daughter Muntaha, her 28-year-old son and her daughter-in-law, in the village of Faqqoua'. One of her nephews was arrested and detained in an Israeli jail at the age of 17, and was subsequently sentenced to 15 years imprisonment, ending in 1990. Khadra owned some land where she raised cattle and planted crops. She had just returned from Mecca where she completed the Umrah pilgrimage. On September 29th, she traveled to Jerusalem to pray at the Aqsa Mosque, to sanctify her pilgrimage according to custom. Clashes broke out between worshippers and the Israeli border police. Khadra, who already suffered from a heart condition, died from tear gas inhalation. She was at first hospitalized in Jerusalem's Maqassed Hospital. Feeling her life slowly slip away, Khadra asked to be taken home to say her last farewells to her children and family. She died on October 3rd 2000.

killed on his way to buying a falafel sandwich for forming a V sign in the face of soldiers. Rahma and Aziza, two matronly friends waiting for a cab the day of the first helicopter-targeted assassination. Abdulhamid, the returning playwright and painter whose body was found riddled with bullets. Hussam, shot on his daily commute between his divorced parents' homes. Aseel, the teenage peace militant beaten to death with a ri e butt, and so on.

Bird's Cage, 20x30 cm
photo by Isabel de la Cruz, 2001

Illustration 14 - Birds Cage[163]

---

163. Full caption reads: On the morning of September 30th, Nizar left for school in a good mood. When his mother asked where he was going after school, he told her that he was going to the checkpoint. She begged him not to go, but he went nevertheless. His mother was sick with worry, and when it was time for her son to be back, she went looking for him. She thought she saw Bird's cage. Nizar Eideh, 15 years old. Nizar leaves behind his family, including two sisters and two brothers. Nizar was an excellent student in the ninth grade at Ramallah's UNRWA school. His family originally came from Ramleh, now inside Israel, from which they were expelled during the Nakba. He was an active young boy, who kept himself busy with aquaculture, swimming, horse riding, and breeding birds and pigeons. He bought a new bird three days before he died. On the following day, a Friday, Nizar went to pray at Al-Aqsa where this picture was taken. His favorite sport was playing basketball. After school he would grab the ball and play with friends on a nearby court. Friends say that his peers would turn to him whenever they needed advice. One of his favorite things to do was repairing electrical appliances, and he hoped to one day become an electrical engineer him in the distance and asked some of the young men to get him, but they told her that he wasn't there. She wasn't convinced, but when she couldn't find him, she returned home. Not having enough money, a taxi driver offered her a free ride. As she returned home, she was devastated to learn that her Nizar had been hospitalized. Surgeons were unable to save his life. Birdcage. He released the bird the morning of the day he was killed, saying he did not want the bird's mother to miss him.

Reception

The Memorial art exhibit opened in Ramallah on February 20, 2001. Dealing with the families' pain over the past months had been a trying experience. Out of respect for their grief, a special visiting day was set aside for them. They told us more stories about their children, some bringing more objects, and newer photographs. Later, some families whose children had died after work on the Memorial started asking for their inclusion.

The Memorial was thronged with visitors everywhere it travelled until 2003, to the Palestinian cities of Nablus and Nazareth only due to the siege, and then on to ten other Arab and Japanese cities.[164]

Working on the Memorial itself and then listening to audience reactions showed the visceral need for society to grieve, and to express its anger at what was being done. While working on the Memorial, we received countless unsolicited suggestions, from artists, academics, politicians, ordinary people, in Palestine and the Diaspora, about the best way they thought the Memorial ought to be set up. This was certainly no ordinary art project, receiving scant popular attention or interest: because of the immediacy of the political situation, and given the fact that the Memorial dealt with the hyper-sensitive issue of self representation, everyone wanted to contribute. This continued after the opening, when we received in Palestine and in some Arab countries, further suggestions about how the Memorial should be modified, usually in an expository mapping direction. My concern throughout was to reaffirm the artistic nature and purpose of the endeavour, and the subjectivity of curatorial choices.

In terms of the reception of the work itself – an alternative representation of mourning in the context of occupation: secular, humanistic, minimalist, and non factional – we were gratified to find scores of people, from all age groups and both genders thronging the gallery. I had been used to the scant popular appeal of the high-modernity templates of arts and culture structures that me and my colleagues operated. Like we who had worked on the Memorial, people needed to work through their grief, to give a face to the spiraling numbers, and a story to a name they had heard. Another reason why the project may have found this resonance in Palestine was that it revolved around life stories of people who came to bear the brunt of the Israeli repression, the economically and politically disenfranchised. The Memorial could not give them a voice, but it restored part of their presence and reaffirmed their human dignity denied by the circumstances of their death. Sometimes visitors came more than once, bringing acquaintances with them the second time. The companion book was given away in Palestine, and quickly ran out. A waiting list was opened to distribute the second printing. In some parts of historical Palestine, the Memorial had another resonance, for among the 100 Shaheed were 12 Israeli citizens who had been killed in October 2000 by Israeli police, in demonstrations of solidarity with West Bank and Gaza Palestinians. The Memorial blended them seamlessly with the others coming from the fragmented Palestinian territory made up of the West Bank, the Gaza Strip and Jerusalem.

As the potential for political decoding and exploitation of the Memorial always had to be side-

---

164. In addition, the memorial was exhibited in 2001 at Darat al Funun in Amman, Jordan; at the Abu Dhabi Cultural Complex in the United Arab Emirates and at the Manama Arts Center in Bahrain. It travelled in 2002 to Dubai and to the Sharjah Museum in the UAE, to the UNESCO Hall in Beirut, Lebanon. From June to September 2003, it was exhibited at the Kid Ailack gallery in Tokyo, at the Kyoto Museum for Peace, at the Sakima Museum in Okinawa, the Central Gallery in Matsumoto and the Osaka Human Rights Museum:Shaheed: http://www.shaheed.jp.

stepped in terms of public reception or in media coverage, it also had to be sidestepped in its display outside its original installation site.

The Post 9/11 World

In terms of the project's reception by Western audiences, the Memorial had received wide and favourable coverage in the major print media of Europe and Northern America, through their local correspondents looking for something different, and the human interest angle. We also received requests to host the Memorial in galleries and museums in Western Europe and North America. Then came the 9/11 terrorist attacks in New York and Washington in 2001. One consequence was that the word Shaheed acquired a new, ominous meaning. In Arabic etymology the word has three meanings: a faithful witness, one of the 99 names of God, and a person dying for a cause, connoting bearing witness in one's esh. There are in Islam Shuhada, people killed or tortured in the early days of Islam, but who do not have saintly status. With the development of anti-colonial struggles in Arab countries, anyone killed by colonial forces became a Shaheed, without religious connotations attached to the term. Indeed, Israel uses the word Shaheed to name its own war dead in official Arabic language broadcasts, and also on the memorials to its Arab collaborators. This was the main reason why I eschewed using the term 'martyr' in English or French, to avoid the historically religious Christian connotations.

But Shaheed became in the West synonymous with suicide bombers, hinting at some quasi-religious cult of death, and thus becoming a new tool of demonisation. This paranoia affected the 100 Shaheed-100 Lives project through the withdrawal of some invitations from European galleries, and also with a failed lobbying to have the Memorial close in Japan.

Process

The Memorial was not a finished art product, but was itself a conceptual process, part of a changing political context. I selected only 100 Shaheed to underscore the symbolic and artistic nature of the project, but also to symbolically mediate the thousands of others who were dying continuously.

Further violence continued through 2001, and the repression took many forms: with the curfews and siege of 2002, hundreds of thousands throughout the West Bank were imprisoned at home, helpless and terrorised, lives suspended out of time and place while their places of work were often vandalised and looted by the Israeli army.[165]

The Memorial continued to exercise an unexpected formal in uence, as the format of the Memorial was copied in various towns in Palestine to honour the most recent dead who had not been part of the memorial. Its design was echoed in a 2005 exhibition on Palestinian prisoners, displaying their letters in glass cases. The Memorial was also featured in two Palestinian films: Alia Arasoughly's 2001 This is Not Living and Liana Bader's 2002 The Green Bird. Even in 2004 Tehran, an Iranian artist used the format for a photo exhibition about earthquake victims, but focused on 100 photos of unidentified corpses. In 2005, a Dutch artist and an Israeli artist mounted projects featuring objects of Israeli and Palestinian victims of terror.

This instinct to protest the wrongful and premature disappearance of the Palestinian Shuhada was also part of a universal need to create meaning out of death, to erase silence by naming and

---

165. The Sakakini was one such place, ransacked, vandalised and looted by the Israeli army on April 13, 2002.

identifying, as evidenced by two very different projects: The New York Times 'Portraits in Grief' section, which documented the lives of those murdered on 9/11, and which were later gathered in a bestselling book; and the 2005 'Disappeared in America' art project, which sought to identify and document the men who disappeared in security dragnets in the US in the aftermath of 9/11. This process was an instance of gazing at one's own pain, during not after the traumatic shock that is very much enduring. The primary motivation being narrative recovery and affirmation, directed at the very community experiencing this pain.

IRAQI MEMORIAL ONLINE
AN INTERVIEW WITH JOSEPH DELAPPE

Ana Peraica (AP): What is the difference between your project and other projects of the kind, like governmental memorials? And the other Iraqi Memorial?[166]

Joseph Delappe (JD): I realise this is a very problematic and messy undertaking. We (particularly US citizens) bear implicit responsibility for the deaths of many thousands of people in a country we know very little about on the other side of the globe. The primary question I am asking through this project is essentially – how do we respond as artists (is it possible to respond) – to the deaths of Iraqi civilians that are occurring as the result of the actions of our government? I first conceptualised Iraqimemorial.org in reaction to the publication online of the 5,201 proposals for the official World Trade Center Memorial Competition in the fall of 2003. Even though the War in Iraq was still in its first year, civilian and military casualties already far exceeded the nearly 3,000 victims of the terrorist attack of 9/11. I thought, at the time, that there would never be an official call for proposals for a memorial to the innocent civilians killed in this war – a war that was, sadly, politically predicated by a propagandistic build up that, in the United States, sought to create a link between Iraq and the attacks of 9/11.
As the project idea evolved, I moved away from my first instinct, which was to purely mimic the design of the WTC site towards a more thoughtful and serious attempt at creating a project that would seek to honour and memorialise the civilian victims of the War in Iraq through an open call for proposed, imagined memorials. Iraqimemorial.org is very similar to, and in fact uses standard methods of any typical 'Call for Proposals' for a memorial or other public art or architecture competition. From my research prior to launching this project, the vast majority of memorials online to the Iraq war are primarily focused on the military dead – either en masse or individually. There are a few projects and websites dedicated to 'the victims of terrorism' as such, but few that are solely focused on recognising the civilian casualties in Iraq.
In the end, it was the importance of creating a forum for artists to focus on the issue of civilian casualties in the war that moved me to get beyond any coincidental and likely unavoidable similarities between this project and others. As a practising artist, one is always concerned about originality – yet in this context, I was troubled to think that other projects variously addressing the human toll of this war would cause me to abandon the effort and concept behind Iraqimemorial. org: the issue at hand is too important and deserving of further examination by artists.
I have put this project out there, in large part, as a memorial in and of itself – perhaps a futile gesture in light of the very real suffering by the Iraqi people – a suffering I can only imagine yet cannot disconnect from my level of comfort and complicity. I am hopeful that artists might respond to this project by creating ideas that seek to recognise the complicated nature of memorials and to question the social/political role of artists in such a difficult and very real context of death.

AP: What is the main motive for making such projects on the Internet as the medium?

---

166. Joseph de Lappe:Iraqi Memorial http://www.Iraqimemorial.org

JD: Functioning as an individual artist with minimal grant or institutional support, the web serves as a logical context for the viral distribution of media content. Iraqimemorial.org is, first and fore-most, a call for participation – a 'user content generated site' that requires the involvement of others in order to succeed. I am a media artist – I have been working with electronic art forms for much of the past 20+ years – much of my recent work involves using the Internet for inter-ventionist protest in computer game spaces. I suppose if I were a gallery owner or publisher or worked at a museum, this project could exist as a call for proposals for those contexts (exhibition or book). That said, the potential for the Internet to reach many thousands of people both in terms of participation and visitors to the site, presents an attractive and useful venue/medium to me as an artist/activist.

AP: Many Iraqi people cannot connect to the Internet. For whom are these pages done?

JD: Since the launch of the project this past December, there has been exactly one visit from Iraq to the Iraqimemorial.org project as recorded using Google Analytics. Persons in other countries in the Middle East, however, have visited the site in larger numbers. The project is still in its early stages, both in terms of participation and hopefully exposure to the viewing public who would have access to the Internet. As the project is ongoing I would hope over time that more Iraqis could have the opportunity to view the project.
To specifically answer the second part of your question, I would say that my first audience is per-haps my fellow countrymen here in the United States. Part of the impetus behind this project has been my frustration with the absence of serious consideration of the issue of civilian casualties. Through the US media, we have been constantly reminded of the sacrifice in American military deaths and the incredible monetary cost of the war, with the occasional mention of the deaths of innocents – although this most often reads as an afterthought. The deaths of civilians, estimated between 80,000 and 655,000 to now over 1 million by some sources, barely seems to register with the American media or the public.
Secondly would be the international community – a project such as this that simply suggests the validity of recognising the deaths of others due to the actions of our military communicates something positive and contrite. I accept my culpability and seek to express my frustration with the current state of affairs that led to this wholly avoidable con ict and its horrid results. The project perhaps allows others to take part in what is symbolically a collective gesture of memory and recognition.

AP: I find it interesting that you are American and you don't speak about Americans or journalists getting killed in Iraq. Why is this?

JD: American soldiers, contractors and journalists have been remembered constantly through the American media – there are any number of projects, both online and in the real world, that have been put in place to remember our own losses as a result of the war in Iraq. Iraqimemorial.org is precisely not about remembering 'our own' but recognising the humanity and suffering of others as a result of our actions.

AP: Have you been yourself in war or do you think you have been a part of it in a discursive way?

JD: I have not been in war. Yet I live in a country that has the largest, most powerful military force ever to exist. I pay taxes to the government – some of my money goes towards funding the United States military industrial complex. Part of my thinking surrounding this project is that it could be considered an attempt to conceptually close a loop in regard to what is essentially the logical result of having such a powerful military – that people, innocents by the thousands, get killed, we are told, 'to protect our freedom', or 'to fight them over there so we don't have to fight them here'. So yes, there is definitely a discursive manner in which I have come to personally consider this issue – it is this disconnect that we suffer from in regard to the consequences of our complicity in this war.

As I noted previously, Iraqimemorial.org is perhaps a futile gesture in the context of the magnitude of the suffering being wrought on the Iraqi people. I am very sensitive to the notion that this project is just another example of outsiders in a position of power and comfort defining or speaking for the experience of suffering 'others'. It is my hope that artists might be able to cut through these barriers to understanding and sincerely work to collectively take a risk – that it might be ok to say that one cares about what happens to Iraqi civilians and to do so through the expressive possibilities of their creative ideas.

(Interview conducted by Ana Peraica on 16 jan 2008)

COMMEMORATING VICTIMS
AN INTERVIEW WITH AGRICOLA DE COLOGNE

Ana Peraica (AP): Most of your projects have a commemorative character.[167] What is the difference between your project and other projects of the kind, like governmental projects?

Agricola de Cologne (AC): In a democracy, governmental or public projects mostly have the intention of dealing with history in a most objective way and turn the spotlight on the most thinkable
aspects from the most different point of views, by using a variety of sources in order to underline
this objectivity. Statistics play an important role, since they are said to represent the most objective way to tell facts. Even if this is not completely true, in statistics the human factor is nearly
completely eliminated. They often become this way rather an expression of inhumanity.
On the other hand, the view of history and the way people deal with history is not a static or constant value, but is different in each generation and different periods of history. So even if people
have the best intentions, even under the most ideal circumstances, just a kind of relative objectivity remains, since it is always man made. In a totalitarian system, governmental or official projects
are made to justify and underline the position of the current political ideology, and in nearly all
cases they more or less neglect humanity completely. An art work, no matter what type of subject
is used, whether commemorative or not, never has the intention to be objective, but the contrary
to express the (most subjective) artistic ideas of an artist.
So do I, and my personal point of view, the way I face things generally – and it's not different
from my position as an artist, whether I deal with commemorative aspects or not – my measure
is always humanity. It determines the way I approach such projects that have never any ambition
to cover all thinkable aspects, but reduced as they are, they go down to the essence of being
and a level that has the potential to touch people and motivate them to re ect on what has been
sensually experienced.

AP: What is the main motive for making such projects on the Internet? Is there a certain extropian
practice inscribed in making people that have gone, for any reason, constantly present online, an
effect of balsaming a memory?

AC: The first part of the question cannot be answered just in a few words. In the family I grew up,
humanity had always been the basic measure for all. At school the idea of humanism had further
lasting in uence on my view on life. So when I started dealing with art at the age of 15, there was
already the focus on the essential of human life, but I got the awareness for history and historical
contexts only when I was about 35.
When in 1989, the wall in Berlin fell, this forced my life into a new direction. While travelling in the
East of Europe, especially Poland, I was continuously confronted with Nazi history and the Holocaust. The following eight years I dedicated completely to a (physical) artistic memorial project
dealing with this thematic context, a period that was on the one hand extraordinarily touchable,

---

167. Glossary: 'Commemoration' p. 108.

since I was confronted with the personal history of countless victims. But this represented also a most violent period, since I became a victim myself, highly traumatised, not just once, but over a longer period and on different levels.[168] That was all highlighted by a panic attack, which did not only destroy a part of my artistic work, but it finished my life and my artistic career at that time. As a result I fell for some time in a kind of coma, but when I woke up, nothing was the way it had been before. I had to learn the essentials of life again, eating drinking, walking, everything was blocked. It returned after some time again, but it was really frightening that I had lost the sense of the material and physical. In this sense I was also not able to work any more physically as an artist the way I did before.

In order to train my brain and intellectual skills again, I started a kind of therapy by learning computer programming languages. When in 1999, the war and genocide in Kosovo was escalating, I felt motivated again to become active as an artist, but I did not know how.

At that time also the Internet became really popular and I got the idea to find out whether I could use the new knowledge of programming languages for something completely new related to creating art. And soon the virtual artist was born!

On 1 January 2000, I started a new life from point zero without any money and without any idea what eventually might come. My big life experiment had started, which still is running, by publishing online the mother of all future projects.

A Virtual Memorial as a kind of continuation of my previous physical memorial project, A Living Memorial Space of Art, which was by the way installed at 43 places in Poland, Germany and the Czech Republic between 1995 and 1998, among them Auschwitz, Majdanek, Dachau and Theresienstadt, but also Krakow, Berlin, Cologne, Hamburg, etc.[169]

So, actually one can really not speak, at all, of a motive that was driving me to work as an artist on the Internet and/or one who is executing commemorative projects online. For me there was no alternative to becoming active as an artist again, and without being dramatic, without the Internet I would not have survived, since over a longer period I was highly at risk of committing suicide. The second part of the question sounds a bit polemic, but the first part is actually also answering the second one, since I did not open a kind of funeral for balsaming memory.

AP: What is the difference between those memorials and pages of daily newspapers that daily announce who has died on the Internet? What do you think of the concept 'collective trauma'?[170]

AC: We learned already about the difference between my type of (art) working and public commemorative contexts and governmental memorials. Your question is mentioning a third party, i.e. the families or relatives of died victims.

These memorial announcements in a newspaper or Internet have another goal: they follow the need of the affected families. They represent forums for collective mourning, and this way a tool for overcoming an individual and also collective trauma, for instance. A collective trauma comes up, when many persons who are, and/or others who are not affected identify themselves with the victims. There were already collective nationwide traumata, because the charismatic leader of a political party was killed, or simply dying.

---

168. Glossary: 'Trauma', p. 137.
169. Agricola da Cologne: Virtual Memorial http://www.a-virtual-memorial.org/
170. Glossary: 'Collective Trauma', p. 109.

The massacre of Srebrenica, and the mass-rape of Muslim women for instance, had the goal to produce such a collective trauma, to paralyse people, to throw people into despair, to destroy living structures, social contexts, the consensus among nationalities and ethnical groups, etc. They represented highly symbolic acts for the perpetrators, as well as much more for the affected families.

By making announcements on such forums, the families and relatives demonstrate also, the victims are not forgotten; in fact the goal of the perpetrators failed in the end.

AP: Somehow the tone of each project doesn't appear shocking, but rather peaceful. What do you think, from the perspective of your work, of works by Tarik Samarak, who has recorded a journey to Srebrenica taking photographs of parts of people's lives on the way? Or posters by Anur Had iomerspahic of branded clothes from the exhumation of the Srebrenica massacre?

AC: Those artists who were dealing with the Holocaust thematically, know that it is not possible to visualise something that is blasting human imagination, something that the human brain is principally refusing.

The massacre of Srebrenica, for instance, belongs also to a dimension that is blasting human imagination in its own way, like war, violence on children and women, and much more, is blasting the mind of those who are not affected, and those who are affected even more.

An artwork dealing with such exceptional human experience has to go other ways than repeating the horrifying curios we all see daily in the news on TV or in the newspaper. Some people are continuously consuming such visualised pornographic violence, which becomes a part of their perception of life. Others principally refuse the continuously escalating visualisation of violence.

Massacres like Srebrenica have a very difficult position, since they stand in direct competition with other horrifying events, from the past, as well as the present. As long as they are in the news, people pay attention, but as soon as the matter is through it becomes more and more a problem to motivate people.

It is the best certainly to document such event scenarios the best way possible, at best by erecting types of multi-purpose documentation centres, so that they can be valued and interpreted by the coming generations from the distance of time and affection.

Artists like you mentioned above can help to give the public also another point of view, but like in the case of the Holocaust, time will show which is the best way to approach it, since whether artistic or not, it has to be one goal of all projects to initiate a better understanding for the dimensions (human, cultural, etc.) of such events.

Like the photos documenting war in all parts of the world, the aesthetics of the images incorporate the big danger of romanticising the situation. People who did not experience the situation of war, for instance, have generally no idea of it, and such aesthetical views give a completely wrong idea.

It makes a difference whether people see reproductions of horrifying curios of the Holocaust or they visit Auschwitz or Majdanek, the same is true for Srebrenica. My personal position is, by presenting the audience a variety of projects, approaches, events, etc. to motivate them to become active via re ecting, the projects I was creating stand in a common context.

If it was ever my intention to produce the impact of a shock, at all, then certainly not a 'horror vacui' lasting just the second until it is replaced by a next following shock, but a long lasting shock through re ecting.

AP: What do you think is the impact of those projects on victims of the same events you are focusing your attention on (tsunami, violence against women, holocaust) that have survived these events? Do you think forgetting these events would be better for them? And do you think that remembering violence can produce another kind of violence?

AC: I never made a survey among the visitors who were victims, and what kind of impact my projects might have made on them. As art projects, all projects are made for the art community and this may include victims potentially, as well. All these memorial projects you mention above, were active for a certain period, but are now completed and/or are not updated any longer.

All projects have a lot of good feedback; sometimes one gets the idea that deeply affected people write. Many of the projects are used for educational purposes, by universities or schools. The site statistics give evidence, but there is one special project that gives evidence of an enormous impact on survived victims: Women. Memory of Repressing in Argentina.[171]

The project is about the 'disappeared' people in Argentina during the military dictatorships in the 1970s and 1980, which were leading a war against their own people by terrorising the families of so-called different-minded people. Sons and daughters, but also husbands of families, were kidnapped and disappeared mostly without leaving any trace. From the 300,000s of disappeared, just a few survived in the end. The remaining mothers and grandmothers, better known as Mothers of Plaza de Mayo, do not only belong to the surviving victims, but they eliminated also these dictatorships in the end through the ritual of weekly demonstrations that were going on until the day after the political system changed. I had the privilege to collaborate with one of these mothers who is also co-curator. Her daughter and son-in-law and her son were kidnapped; her son died, while the daughter survived and collaborated also in this and other projects.

Realised in 2004, this project had a strange deep impact on the Argentinian activists, i.e. the mothers and associated organisations, since it was created and produced outside of Argentina. In 2005, I was invited to Argentina to present my project at museums, cultural centres and universities, and I met many of the still living initiators of Mothers of Plaza de Mayo, which was an extraordinarily touching experience.

Even if it is not possible that an art project causes revolutionary changes, my project was understood as a signal for all those who never gave up fighting for the research and recovery in the matter of the disappeared, which resulted in the Argentinian president Kirchner ordering the exhumation of countless mass graves. Many of the disappeared could be identified by name meanwhile. The process of overcoming this national trauma after so many decades is still going on, and the horrible dimensions of this 'state affair' becomes really visual over just these days. I am happy and most satisfied that my activities were able to have such a kind of impact on people, at all.

AP: And do you think that remembering of violence can produce another violence?

AC: It is said, that violence produces violence. And it is also known that people who became a victim of violence can become violent as a direct result of the violence. Personally I doubt that just the remembering of violence can cause violence, and for a better understanding it is good to know, actually, what happens to a victim of violence.

Physical injuries can be cured, but psychological injuries are not visible. Healing a psychological

---

171. See: Women: Memory and Repression in Argentina: http://argentina.engad.org/

trauma needs much more than the self-healing powers of the human vital system or therapy. If we understand that a psychological immune system exists as a genetic survival strategy, the destructive powers of a trauma do not only destroy this immune system in part or as a whole, but the personal, social, cultural, political or religious circumstances or living conditions can potentially cause that victim to become a victim again and again, resulting even in the collapse of the immune system.

My personal experience of the described traumatisation led to such a collapse in the form of a coma, but when it was over, I became aware that my psychological immune system did not exist any longer, since my vital systems identified words or reactions of other people as direct attacks I had to fight against.

One result was that my physical immune system went crazy, since it reacted against anything directly with high fever, and at the same time my direct re-'action' became very aggressive towards other people, basically verbally, since I do not tend to be physically aggressive, but also aggressive against myself.

In the first place, these 'reactions' happened automatically, without a chance to take immediate in uence; only afterwards I became aware what happened.

Of course, also the memory of violence plays a certain role. I hated the fact that there had been people who dared to take such a disastrous in uence on my life and made me a victim while I had been never a victim before. Then I hated myself, my inability to understand properly what actually is going on inside of me. I hated my helplessness. I think such personal situations have the potential to drive people completely crazy, and depending on the individual personality, dealing with oneself and the situation can lead to general violent behaviour and the use of violence on other people, I am sure.

AP: Do you think forgetting these events would be better for them?

AC: It would be better if the traumatisation would not have happened at all. But it did. It is just hypothetical to dream people could simply forget everything. Fortunately, there exists a kind of genetic emergency strategy, causing a kind of sleeping state of the trauma.

The outside world might even get the idea as if the trauma of a victim would be healed, but in fact it is just that the human vital system is developing individual survival strategies. From time to time, and mostly in the most inappropriate situations the memory is reactivated, showing a victim that the trauma is as fresh as on its first day.

In my case, the traumatic course of events caused a complete change and direction of my life, I would have never started working with electronic media and art the way I do, I am sure. I would never stand where I stand currently. Forgetting the events is not possible, but also not desirable, since they are part of my history. This fact is manifesting itself in my answers to your questions.
.

AP: Do you think that victims of the past have a special treatment, being institutionalised by history, than those of the present time in our culture?

AC: My projects refer actually to different types of victims, so it is really a question of which kind of victim you mean. Perceiving the victim as a person of relevance was a development of the 20th century, when the mass media came up and human rights entered the general awareness. This caused also a kind of revision of ancient views on history. In the public perception, of course, such mass phenomena of victims like from World War I, World War II or the Holocaust received a highly symbolical status, also because these events are and were the expression of unimaginable inhumanity. If certain groups of victims are and were institutionalised it is/was not caused by history, but those people who deal with history.

It does not actually matter in which time or society people live. In contrast to the perpetrator, the victim who is always identified as being a loser gets hardly any sympathy. In the end, it is the victim himself who is to blame for his situation. But society separates also good from bad, privileged and less privileged victims, depending on their social, political, cultural or religious position and context.

There are dozens of reasons why people institutionalise victims from the past or present, but since the view of history is changing from generation to generation, also the view of victims and perpetrators and values generally change.

(Interview conducted by Ana Peraica 01 feb 2008)

NOT A JOY RIDE (OR: DON T USE THE G WORD)
AN INTERVIEW WITH NEERY MELKONIAN

Marko Stamenkovi (MS): I am aware of the fact that you are neither a genocide scholar nor a trauma specialist. But your curatorial projects and art-writing have shown a considerable interest in migratory cultural geographies, the diasporic citizen or the transnational artist, and the nuanced effects of displacement to artistic production. Given that you were born and raised in the Middle East and have been living and working in the United States for sometime now, this seems like a natural predisposition. More recently though, you began to explore the historical facts and documentation as they relate to your own imaginary homeland – Armenia. Could you please elaborate on this interest and the way your professional engagement has been intertwined with this phenomenon?

Neery Melkonian (NM): As a third generation diasporan descendant of a genocide survivor, who grew up with plenty of horror stories and sufficient nationalist indoctrination – typical of threatened groups as a defense or survivor mechanism – I've had to put considerable energy to sort things out, to wonder off from my tribe, to separate myths from realities, to salvage love/compassion from the prongs of hatred/blindness/ignorance, to believe in justice and seek truth, sustain hope for a better humanity, to shed traces of victimhood and have agency, it's a never ending work and journey!

Fifteen years ago, and after several years of giving cultural space to other marginalised groups (called official minorities in the US, i.e. African Americans, Hispanics, American Indians, women, homosexuals, etc.), I began to articulate a framework to 'locate' the work of artists from the Middle East who lived in the West. Definitely both of those interests were related to my own historical background and were done at a time when such groups had little representation in the American cultural scene. My recent return to the difficult task of making sense of my own culture's artistic production in post-genocide context was something I first attempted in graduate school back in the 1980s. I did not go too far because the methodologies did not exist then, nor was it regarded as a legitimate subject of inquiry since, as an Armenian you existed only in the Medieval Art context, at least according to Western art historical canons. This is what preoccupies me these days, even if temporarily. I want to thread or take a pause from cultural 'space-less-ness'. Thanks to the multicultural movement, considerable progress has been made in the US in terms of having a more balanced minority representation within institutional spaces. But when it comes to sub-marginal groups like the Armenians, much of the mainstream art world's radar, for instance, still begins and ends with the renowned abstract expressionist Arshile Gorky. As you might know, he was a genocide survivor himself and despite his relative success in New York's cosmopolitan art scene of the 30s and 40s, tragically ended his life by hanging. So yes, when it comes to narrating or contextualising transnational Armenian artistic identity, across time and geography, there is a lot to be done to change such fixed perceptions.

MS: Sure, but could you remind us – what is the Armenian 'story' actually about?

NM: The 1915 Genocide of Armenians, which began towards the end/fall of the Ottoman Empire, culminated in the systematic cleansing of an entire minority-ethnic population from their ancestral homeland of 2,000 years (eight provinces in eastern Anatolia) through a number of means, which included: mass killings, starvation, death marches, labor camps, disarming the male population, sweeping arrests/loots of towns/villages, separating the elderly, women and children, forceful conversions of faith especially of young women, taking them as brides/slaves etc. to enable the formation of modern Turkey.

The current number games, as it gets played out in the mainstream international media, echoes the reluctant position of geopolitical power brokers (i.e. the US government as a strategic ally of Turkey and Israel since WWII). So in the last decades the battle has been combating denial, which follows a particular pattern or logic, with its corresponding 'official' rhetoric that involves numbers, and goes something like this: a) was it a million or million and a half lives that perished? b) it was wartime, we/Turks lost as many lives or suffered as much, they were all unfortunate, natural casualties of war. c) it's ok to call it massacres or atrocities but not enough to qualify labeling it as 'Genocide'. Don't use the 'G' word, while the truth of the matter is, if you have the material resources, you are occasionally allowed to buy/use the term 'genocide' in the public sphere. This has happened to me personally on several curatorial projects! d) it's been almost a hundred years, why don't you forget about it and move on? e) look, you finally have an independent Armenia that desperately needs to normalise relations with its neighbors; put an end to the economic blockade, open the borders etc. so count your blessings. Give back Karabagh to Azerbeijan otherwise... f) there is no sufficient scholarly proof to your claims anyway, so let's form a 'neutral-unbiased-independent' commission to investigate such allegations. g) the nationalist Armenian Diaspora and their lobby groups are to be blamed for pressuring US Congress through the Genocide Resolution #316 h) if the above passes, who knows what might come next? Maybe demands for reparations, return of lost lands, compensation for properties left behind etc. Keep on dreaming Armenians... hence Turkish Penal Code article # 301 to prevent insulting Turkishness, might be too severe, but we are working on reforming it, especially if we want entry into EU.

As a result of the above battle of numbers, in the last four or five decades much of diaspora Armenian resources, attention or investment have been directed towards proving that the genocide actually happened. Some would argue that they have been consumed even obsessed by this burden of proof.

MS: Beside that, what is to be said with regard to the power-game, and especially the media-articulation of the facts, as experienced through these specific historical data?

NM: Up until the late 1930s, plenty of evidence, combined with impressive headlines and graphic imagery, circulated in the international press regarding the atrocities. These also affirm that it was in the US's interest at the time to play a major role in saving 'the Starving Armenians' as the first Christian nation and/or from the 'hands of the evil Muslim Turks', etc. They did this through philanthropy and missionary groups who were instrumental in the survival of the remnants of the genocide, i.e. my grandmother through orphanages and rehabilitation programs, etc. These groups, of course, had direct ties with the state department and in uenced the Hollywood film industry to make a feature film at the time called Ravished Armenia! Other Western powers (i.e. England and France) were sympathetic too but more indifferent. They kept making promises to help but cared less to deliver and often changed their mind on signed treaties, depending on the geopolitical climate of the day. Anyway, there is plenty of this stuff in archives throughout the world but the resistance or denial has created, on the one hand (especially among Diaspora Armenians led by transnational institutions/schools/organisations, etc.) a level of distrust and insularity, which manifests into demands for recognition, justice, etc. On the other hand (this is more prevalent in Armenia), isolation yet also a dependence on foreign powers to mediate change.

MS: Beyond official rhetoric, paranoia and monolithic perceptions, what has been done towards re-humanising the victim and the perpetrator?

NM: There are some Armenians, me among them at times, who feel that we don't need more proof. For those truly interested, there is ample quality/dignified scholarship on the topic out there by non-Armenians, including Turkish and Western academics. How much proof is enough or does a culture need to prove its own death?
Also, some of us share a certain ambivalence towards the term genocide. We prefer using the word Catastrophe, which was used initially by those who actually experienced it and is the equivalent of the Jewish term Shoah versus, say, holocaust. One uses more physical/vocal cords when uttering the word Ca-tas-trophe, which resonates more somehow. In any case, it's warmer/closer in comparison to the more clinical/legal naming of it as 'genocide', a term coined in the 1940s to bring to justice Nazi perpetrators. But in the Armenian case, the term has so far and paradoxically distanced us from exploring the topic and its effects within multiple layers or more nuanced subtexts.
Some intellectuals have argued that this has led to the impossibility of mourning, that since the subsequent generations were not 'there' when 'it' happened, since we are not witnesses, the continued denial is repeatedly prolonging an unfulfilled mourning, a closure of sorts that in turn is necessary to come to terms with the memories, legacies, and the narratives passed on.

MS: Are we talking about mere terminological obstacles here, or...?

NM: Maybe the challenge at least for some of us is not to get stuck in labeling or number games, which could lead to perversions of sorts on both sides. And that the critical work at hand is not in 'illustrating' but mediating the blockages, looking into the cracks or slippages that might hold other possibilities without which transcendence becomes difficult, complex and less attainable.
Since among the first group of victims were approximately 150 leading Armenian intellectuals, writers, etc. who were beheaded in a public square of Istanbul in 1915 – graphic photographs/ narratives of which have passed on from generation to generation – overcoming the effects of such an immense loss of intellectual and creative potential is something the Armenian transnation is yet to recover from especially in dispersion. This is one of the reasons I find it hard to accept 'nomadism' as a strictly positive construct or as a preferred way of existence.
Displacement is not a joy ride. In their polycentric pockets of existence Armenian artists/writers etc. have suffered immeasurable losses, both in production and reception, despite considerable creative output. Add to this complications related to multiple diasporic experience because of wars, ideologies etc. of regimes they have lived in since the genocide. So how to 'thread space-less-ness' at this transnational moment, how to register continuity despite discontinuity, and without eliminating one's 'accent' is in many ways my, humble, work/role.
Tying it back to the issues of numbers, when you are not large in numbers then you are not considered an 'official' minority of adopted countries or host cultures. This means you are in the mar-

gins of margins with little or no representation to speak of, especially if you are not a member of a wealthy trans-nation. You tend to not 'register' or often 'miss' and not 'fit', and consequently find yourself in the cul de sac (bottom of the sack) of dominant narratives, both within and without, including those coming from the so-called avant garde. One option to bypass this predicament of perpetual displacement is to live in disguise, as someone else, as Gorky did. Or, get rid of accents, deny yourself, erase your own memory, etc. But if for some reason you refuse to 'disappear' then the other option is to mobilise and gain agency.

(interview conducted by Marko Stamenkovi on 23 feb 2008)

PART 5 - MEDIA AND THERAPY

BAD NEWS
ANDREJA KULUNCIC

There are numerous factors that have an everyday psychological in uence on humans. Some factors may have a stressful impact.[172] Personal vulnerability, exposure to different types of stress and intensity, as well as support from the environment, define the consequences of that impact. According to scientific research, exposure to a stressful event via media may cause increased stress even to the people living far from a specific stressful event. Increased stress can lead, among other things, to post-traumatic stress disorder – a psychiatric condition that requires professional intervention.[173]

This project is constructed with the intention of measuring the stressful intensity of bad news from the media on the participants. The project starts with a questionnaire that measures the stressful impact of media news on them. According to the results, participants are divided into four types of media consumers. When the participant finds his/her type, they can also discover their own symptoms, intensity of stress impact, and coping strategies with educational and practical materials about stress for personal use.[174]

Participants can compare their own scores in areas of symptoms, intensity of stress impact, and coping strategies related to stress with the scores of other participants. Our intention for displaying the results of all participants was to get a better insight into how bad news in media can in uence specific participants as well as others as a group.

The main aim of the project is the sensitisation of participants to the stressful impact of bad news. The additional aim is to help participants to improve their coping mechanisms.[175] For the realisation of that aim, we provide them with educational materials.

No means we are dead; too much stress can kill us.

---

172. Glossary: 'Stress' p. 136.
173. Glossary: 'Trauma and Media', p. 139.
174. Glossary: 'Coping Strategies', p. 113.
175. Glossary: 'Coping Mechanism/Coping Skills', p. 112.

Illustration 15 - Andreja Kulun i : Bad News

BLOG AS SELF-MANAGEMENT TOOLS
GEERT LOVINK

Dedicated to Joseph Weizenbaum, computer critic and inventor of the ELIZA programme (1966) in which the user talked to the world's first computer therapist. Weizenbaum died on 5 March, 2008 in Berlin.

I am tempted to say that we must return to the subject – though not a purely rational Cartesian one. My idea is that the subject is inherently political, in the sense that 'subject', to me, denotes a piece of freedom – where you are no longer rooted in some firm substance, you are in an open situation. Today we can no longer simply apply old rules. We are engaged in paradoxes, which offer no immediate way out. In this sense, subjectivity is political.
Slavoj i ek[176]

In Cold Intimacies, Eva Illouz states that capitalism has created an emotional culture.[177] Against the commonly held view that commodification, wage labour and profit-driven activities create 'cold' and calculated relationships, Illouz describes the rise of 'emotional capitalism'. The public sphere is saturated with the exposure of private life (and vice versa, the 'hot distance'). Affect is becoming an essential aspect of economic behaviour – and a fashionable object of contemporary theory. According to Illouz, "it is virtually impossible to distinguish the rationalization and com-modification of selfhood from the capacity of the self to shape and help itself and to engage in deliberation and communication with others". There is a narrative in the making, says Illouz, which combines the aspiration of self-realisation with the claim to emotional suffering:

The prevalence and persistence of this narrative, which we may call as shorthand a narrative of recognition, is related to the interests of social groups operating within the market, in civil society, and within the institutional boundaries of the state.[178]

We all know that media do not merely report. They play a key role in the circulation of senti-ments. We do not sit down and passively read and write but we are caught in a web of stimuli and feelings that are channelled in specific ways. Some platforms are better at capturing, storing and sorting the human sensory output than others. Email, for instance, is considered to be more personal and direct, if not impolite, compared to letters written on paper. Once, typewriters were considered a precondition for inspiration, provided the writer had access to a typewriter girl to dictate his streams of the unconscious. Today, the Internet creates an endless ow nervous re-sponses that become accessible for everyone.
It is not enough to study the impact of the new media output. We need to develop an awareness

---

176. S. Reul and T. Deichmann, 'The One Measure of True Love Is: You Can Insult the Other – Inter-view with Slavoj i ek', Spiked Online, 15 November 15 (2001): http://www.spiked-online.com/Articles/00000002D2C4.htm
177. E. Illouz, Cold Intimacies: the Making of Emotional Capitalism, Cambridge: Polity Press, 2007.
178. Illouz, Cold Intimacies, p. 4.

about which emotional responses are addressed by which software. What social networking sites such as Orkut, MySpace and Facebook, MSN, Twitter, blogs, IRC chats, email, Usenet and web forums all have in common is that they are not taming the beast. Instead of explicitly 'civilising' its users, the Internet lures users into an informal, grey space, in between public and private. The applications inform us, addressing specific emotional registers. They form us to say this, and not that. Each and every Internet application is provoking, shaping and packaging these sentiments in different ways. Building on Nietzsche, who once noticed that "our writing tools are also working on our thoughts", we can witness that each Internet application is addressing its very own set of human qualities.

This essay is part of a larger project to develop a blog theory. As we write this, in early 2008, there are anywhere between 100-150 million blogs, worldwide. Weblogs are successors of the 1990s Internet homepage. They create mix of the private (online diary) and the public (PR-management of the self). Blogs have been the software vehicle that turned the Internet into a mass media culture, way beyond the eccentric cyberculture of the 1990s. Blogs, and the social networking sites that they are becoming part of in the Web 2.0 wave, have made 'new' media mainstream.

Instead of looking into the emancipatory potential of blogs, or emphasizing its counter-cultural folklore, I see blogs as part of an unfolding process of 'massification' of the Internet after its successive academic and speculative phases. The void after the dotcom crash made way for large-scale, interlinked conversations through freely available automated software with user-friendly interfaces. Blogging in the post 9/11-period closed the gap between Internet and society. Whereas dotcom suits dreamed of mobbing customers ooding their sites, blogs were the actual catalysts that realised democratisation, worldwide, of the Net. As much as 'democratisation' means 'engaged citizens', it also implies normalisation (as in setting of norms) and banalisation. We can't separate these elements and only enjoy the interesting bits. Blogs ought to be positioned in the midst of the whirlpool. The abundance of blogs, the similarity of opinions and 'pimped' material go to the core of the Capitalist Project and should not be pushed aside as irrelevant info noise. It is exactly the 'secondary' status of blogs that makes the posted material so ruthlessly honest.

What Makes a Blog a Blog?

The entries often are hastily written personal musings, sculptured around a link or event. In most cases bloggers simply do not have the time, skills and the financial means for proper research. Blogs are not anonymous news sites, they are deeply personal. The blog software does a wonderful trick: it constitutes subjectivity. When we blog, we become an individual (again). Even if we blog together, we still answer to the Call of the Code to tell something about ourselves as a unique person.

Blog pioneer and RSS feed inventor Dave Winer defines a blog as "the unedited voice of a person". It isn't so much the form or the content, rather it is 'the voice' of an individual that characterises the blog as a distinctive media form. "If it was one voice, unedited, not determined by group-think – then it was a blog, no matter what form it took. If it was the result of group-think, with lots of ass-covering and offense avoiding, then it's not".[179] Winer does not believe that blogs are defined by comments of others. "The cool thing about blogs is that while they may be quiet, and it may be hard to find what you're looking for, at least you can say what you think without being shouted down. This makes it possible for unpopular ideas to be expressed. And if you

---

179. D. Winer, 'Scripting News': http://www.scripting.com/2007/01/01.html.

know history, the most important ideas often are the unpopular ones". Whereas social network-ing sites and email-based mailing list culture are focussed on social networking and (discursive) exchanges, blogging, according to Dave Winer, is primarily an act of an introspective individual that re ects on his or her thoughts and impressions.

For this techno-libertarian Californian, blogs are expressions of free speech, of an individualism that says each is entitled to their own opinion and should be brave enough to say it. Dave Winer's definition is a good example of a raw, Western, heroic individualism. "Me, I like diversity of opinion. I learn from the extremes". The blogger is portrayed as a Western dissident: the person who begs to differ. But there is nothing particularly courageous about expressing what one thinks on a blog. The medium knows this: what is encouraged and applauded, what gets the comments stirred up and starts a bunch of cross-posting, is the outrageous, the beyond the pale, the extreme. It doesn't matter whether anyone actually thinks the extreme view – it can be said just for jokes or kicks, just for hits or attention.

Playing the Language Game

Why is this language game about definitions so important? Winer's description leads us back to an original experience at the very beginning of this medium in the late 1990s. It is the initial arousement of the developers and early adaptors, to go where others haven't gone before, seek-ing the edges of ethics, of freedom of expression, of language and publishing and what is com-monly excepted, that informs blogging. There is a perceived challenge of the empty web form, to write whatever is on your mind. Users who arrive a decade later rarely have this sensation. They see themselves confronted with an extremely busy social environment and are puzzled how to fit in. Their challenge is not what to scream in the well but how to find their way through the busy ant farm called the 'blogosphere'.

Despite the short time it needs to set up a blog and the easy-to-use interfaces, users need time to get accustomed to the rules of the game called blogging. Here it is not so much the self-refer-ential moment of sitting down and writing up a story that matters. In Winer's ontology the essence of the blog experience is the very start of the blog itself. It's not the software or the social buzz, but the thrill of creating an account, naming your blog and choosing a template, and there you go. "What's important about blogs is not that people can comment on your ideas. As long as they can start their own blog, there will be no shortage of places to comment. What there is always a shortage of, however, is courage to say the exceptional thing, to be an individual, to stand up for your beliefs, even if they aren't popular".[180]

For Winer, blogging is a brave act because he associates writing with authenticity – with the unedited, the unin uenced by a group. Somehow, writing is a pure expression of an individual (comments just dilute the purity and risk pushing the author to conform to group think). Winer's emphasis on authenticity goes back to an old Romantic idea. In postmodern society this notion has lost its currency in favor of repetition, mimesis, and, everyone's favorite, the big Other. Most of what we say and think is a repetition of what we've read or heard (and we are aware of this). We are spoken through (rather than autonomous subjects creatively producing the new). This isn't bad or negative or something to worry about – we can get over the fetishism of the new and leave that to consumer capitalism. Shifts and alterations, changes in ideas and thinking, occur more accidentally and retroactively.

---

180. Winer, 'Scripting News': http://www.scripting.com/2007/01/01.html.

There is something in Winer's point about voice that he uses in a sense that is different from the Lacanian Mladen Dolar, author of A Voice and Nothing More.[181] The blog voice can emerge as an effect, accidentally; it can seep through the writing and not be produced deliberately via the author's intention. We could think of this as the subjectivity of the blog or the persona of the blog (which has the benefit of bleeding toward impersonation). Winer's error is to associate this voice or persona with authenticity and with courage. It is more convincing to associate it with the art of creating a figure. Blogging is a masquerade, impersonation, presentation and a drive to be seen, present, acknowledge, recognised, perhaps a drive just to be at all – period.

A Digital Extension of Oral Traditions

It's important to dig further into another aspect of Winer's blog definition. The voice also points at the verbal aspect that is gaining importance in new media. Blogging could be read as a digital extension of oral traditions more than a new form of writing.[182] Through blogging, news is being transformed from a lecture into a conversation. Blogs echo rumour and gossip, conversations in cafes and bars, on squares and in corridors. They record "the events of the day" (Jay Rosen). Today's 'recordability' of situations is such that we are no longer upset that computers 'read' all our moves and expressions (sound, image, text) and 'write' them into strings of zeros and ones. In that sense, blogs fit into the wider trend in which all our movements and activities are being monitored and stored.

In the case of blogs, this is carried out not by some invisible and abstract authority but the sub-jects themselves who record their everyday life.[183] Much like the SMS language used in mobile phones, blogs 'capture' the spoken word of the everyday, rather than being judged as a de-generated version of the official written languages as represented in literature, journalism and academic texts. At first hand, this is a confusing observation. Aren't blogs all about the return of quality writing amongst the ordinary citizens? Still we need to see the informal, unfinished style of blogging within a technological trend in which more and more devices are capturing speech. Paradoxically, at the moment this is (also) done through keyboards. As a secondary nota-tion system blogs have to be positioned between the officially sanctioned writing of books and newspapers, using automatic spell checking and the informal communication of email and text messaging. The example of chatting on MSN and other chat rooms is even more clear. Chatting is talking using the written word.

The blog is one step further towards sanctioned writing in that it is a form of publishing: we add a file to a database once we press the 'submit' button. At the same time, this text-based talk-ing to a screen is a personal way of storing a communication we have with ourselves (and the Machine). Whereas chats and emails have a person attached who we talk to, the addressed in blogs is often less clear. If the blog part of an (existing) social network, they are not more than nodes, created to store material (text, picture, profile). If the link list is absent or indicates that there are standard 'elective affinities' with A-list bloggers and news media, we can guess that the

181. M. Dolar, A Voice and Nothing More, Cambridge: MIT Press, 2006.
182. N. Gall: "a lot of the media are thinking about blogs as a new form of publishing but it's really a new form of conversation and a new form of community", cited in D. Kline and D. Burstein, blog!, New York: CDS Books, 2005, p. 150.
183. Source: Telepolis, December 27, 2005. Wolf-Dieter Roth, 'Mein blog liest ja sowieso kein Schwein': http://www.heise.de/tp/r4/artikel/21/21643/1.html.

blog experiment has a dominant re ective, introspective element. In both cases blogs express a 'distributed subjectivity', in the first case one that is positioned within a clouds of 'friends', in the latter it is pop media.

"Blogs are so 2004"

Let's face it: the novelty of blog studies that mapped the early terrain is over. The many millions of weblogs that currently exist can no longer be explained by those who pioneered the field. The masses of blogs appearing and disappearing at ever increasing rates easily exceed the terms introduced to describe the A-list of US-American pundits, the disaster and event blogs, and the political swarms. Given the enormity of the blogosphere, the variety of uses, engagements, attachments, performances, networks, and content produced through the practice of blogging, the lack of adequate theorisation is palpable. The concern here is not with the (potential) relation to the news industry but with the long tail of personal blogs. How does the unedited voice of the individual relate to the growing tendency, facilitated in software, to position the blogging subject in a web of users and links to documents and multimedia objects? For this, we suggest describing the blogger as a 'distributed subjectivity'. As blog culture progresses into its second decade, we see an increased pressure of the underlying software architecture to move away from the culture of insular retrospection towards a technical positioning of the blogger inside networks, mainly facilitated by search engines (read: Google). From now on the Machine automatically creates social relationships for us, we don't even have to do it ourselves, provided we feed the search engine with (personal) data. What we perceive as personal, the system has redefined as Working for the Engine.

Blogs validate and celebrate the personal, individual, singular. They mobilise the personal as celebrity, championing the individual even as good old liberal bourgeois rights are overwritten by neo-liberal capital and undermined, at least in the US, by enthusiasm for torture, security, and surveillance. In a way, blogs document a change in the status of the personal wherein the personal is mobilised and erased/ attened at the same time (erased insofar as blogging prioritises display over introspection, documentation without re ection, archiving without internalisation). At the same time, the personal that is produced for display uncouples from any supposition of a true or underlying self – that question simply isn't relevant. What matters is what appears. Communicative capitalism is not an identity provider. Rather, people produce their identities through networked communications media. The Internet is a medium for mass experience, but a highly differentiated and singularised mass experience. And this is where blogging comes in as the technology of that experience.

Technology of The Self

It could be useful to formulate a theory of blogging as a 'technology of the self,' a concept developed by Michel Foucault. Blogs experiment with the 'public diary' format, a term that expresses the productive contradiction between public and private that bloggers find themselves in. Until recently most diaries have been 'secret'. They may have been written to be published at a later stage, often after the author passed away, but were nonetheless 'of ine' in the sense of being not accessible. Despite obvious differences, there are also communalities, as we can read in Thomas Mallon's A Book of One's Own, People and Their Diaries from 1984.

Bloggers will recognise themselves in what Mallon writes: "I'm always behind. I try to write each night, but I often don't get around to writing up a day until several more days have gone by. But

I manage to keep them all separate. I suppose it's a compulsion, but I hesitate to call it that, because it's gotten pretty easy. There comes a point when, like a marathon runner, you get through
some sort of 'wall' and start running on automatic. Of course, there are days when I hate writing
the thing. Who needs it? I'll ask myself; but I'll do it anyway".[184]
After reading hundreds of diaries, Mallon concludes that no one ever kept a diary for just himself:
"In fact, I don't believe one can write to oneself for many words more than get used in a note
tacked to the refrigerator, saying, 'buy bread'".[185] Keeping a diary provokes re ection about the
activity itself. For Mallon, Virginia Woolf is the greatest critic of the genre: "The activity is, after all,
so queer, so ad hoc, and supposedly so private, that it doesn't seem amiss for the diarist to stop
every so often and ask himself just what he thinks he's doing". Her fundamental motive is to "hold
on to it all, to cheat the clock and death of all the things that she had lived". What intrigues me
here are the 'time folds' that we so often find in blogs as well. Many of Virginia Woolf's entries,
says Mallon, are provoked by her neglect of regular dairy writing. "The journals are frequently interrupted by physical illness, madness, the press of work or social life. And sheer disinclination".[186]
Sound familiar?
Situating blogging between 'online publishing' and the intimate sphere of diary keeping brings
into question the already disturbed separation between what is public and what is left of privacy.
It is remarkable that many participants do not perceive blogs and social networking sites such as
Orkut or MySpace as a part of public life. Online conversations between friends are so intense
that the (mainly young and often naive) users do not realise, or care, that they are under constant
observation. Yahoo! researcher danah boyd explains: "teens are growing up in a constant state of
surveillance because parents, teachers, school administrators and others who hold direct power
over youth are surveilling them. Governments and corporations are beyond their consideration
because the people who directly affect their lives have created a more encompassing panopticon
than any external structure could ever do. The personal panopticon they live in is far more men-
acing, far more direct, far more traumatic. As a result, youth are pretty blasé about their privacy
in relation to government and corporate".[187] boyd therefore advises: "unless we figure out how to
give youth privacy in their personal lives, they are not going to expect privacy in their public lives".
Until further notice the festive documentation of the private will continue – and it's up to family,
social workers and clergy to reconcile with this potlatch. Instead of raising concerns, one might
better start harvesting human feelings from weblogs, as wefeelfine.org has been doing.

Inside or Outside Media?

Because of its 'public diary' character, the question of whether blogs operate inside or outside
'the media' is not easy to answer. To position the blog medium inside could be seen as opportunis-
tic, whereas others see this as a clever move. There is also a 'tactical' aspect. The blogger-equals-
journalist might find protection under such a label in case of censorship and repression. Despite
countless attempts to feature blogs as alternatives to the mainstream media, they are often, more
precisely described as 'feedback channels'. The act of gatewatching mainstream media outlets

---

184. T. Mallon, A Book of One's Own, New York: Ticknor & Fields, 1984, p. xiii
185. Mallon, A Book of One's Own, p. xvii.
186. Mallon, A Book of One's Own, pp. 31, 34.
187. d. boyd, 'erosion of youth privacy - the local panopticon', apophenia, http://www.zephoria.org/thoughts/
    archives/2006/05/20/erosion_of_yout.html.

does not necessarily result in reasonable comments that will then be taken into account by any internal review by the media. In the category 'insensitive' we have a wide range, from hilarious to mad, sad and sick. What CNN, newspapers and radio stations the world over have failed to do, namely to integrate open and interactive messages from their constituencies, blogs do for them. To 'blog' a news report doesn't mean that the blogger sits down and thoroughly analyses the discourse and circumstances, let alone check the facts on the ground. To blog merely means to quickly point to news fact through a link and a few sentences that explain why the blogger found this or that factoid interesting, remarkable or is in disagreement with it.

It is a misjudgement to disregard blog culture as part of the larger self-marketing trend. What cultural pessimism is doing in such a case is blasting the perverse pleasure of narcissist and praising the hard-thinking intellectual who goes through the critical issues. Blogs are not the perfect media machine to express the laziness of self-centred ego. What ordinary blogs create is a scattered cloud of 'impressions' around a topic. Blogs will tell you if your audience is still awake and receptive. Blogs test.

Blogs express personal fear, insecurity and disillusion, anxieties looking for partners-in-crime. We seldom find passion, except for the act of blogging itself. The overall situation remains laid back and cool, if not indifferent. Often blogs unveil doubt and insecurity about what to feel, what to think, believe and like. In that sense they divert from the polished PR image. The blog confessions carefully compare magazines, and review traffic signs, nightclubs and t-shirts. This stylised uncertainty circles around the general assumption that blogs ought to be biographical while simultaneously reporting about the world outside. Their emotional scope is much wider compared to other media due to the informal atmosphere. Mixing public and private is constitutional here. What blogs play with is the emotional register, varying from hate to boredom, passionate engagement, sexual outrage and back to everyday boredom.

VICTIMS DIGNITY
AN INTERVIEW WITH CARLOS MOTTA

Marko Stamenkovi (MS): Could you please describe the video that was released at the end of 2007 and distributed via media all over the world, which is the main reason for this conversation?

Carlos Motta (CM): The video shows a woman sitting on a wooden bench facing – although never looking at – the camera in a 3/4 angle. She has very long hair, is extremely thin, and her hands are held together softly yet tied by a chain. She is wearing beige linen clothing and tall rain boots. To her back is a lush, green jungle, overwhelmingly alive, wet, green, spilling sounds of insects, animals and wind. The cameraperson holds the camera steadily, though it slightly shakes. He consistently zooms in and out to show her eyes. Although there are no words, he seems to be forcing the woman to stare at us, onlookers of an intimate scene of muted pain and transgression that lasts 55 seconds. He fails as she silently denies her gaze.

MS: What is so strange about it? Who is the woman? Could you put it into a context that explains it better?

CM: The woman is Ingrid Betancourt, a former presidential candidate from Colombia held captive by the FARC guerrillas. The video is part of recent proofs of the survival of several kidnapped persons seized from the abductors by Colombian authorities during a recent failed humanitarian exchange plan.

MS: What was actually the most striking point for you in that gesture of 'recognition'?

CM: This video has had a profound impact on me. I will try to brie y explain why. Ms. Betancourt currently stands as an emblematic figure of kidnapping in Colombia. She has been kidnapped for more than five years and, given her political background and double nationality (half French), her case has been consistently reported. Although the specifics of her case and kidnapping in Co-lombia deserve ample re ection, I want to concentrate here on what this recent video represents to me, which is an image of 'the victim's dignity'.

MS: What do you mean by 'the victim's dignity'? Is it a kind of public invigilation of private emotion, or...?

CM: The purpose of such a proof of survival is to prove that the victim is alive and thus encour-age continuing the negotiations. It is made to be public, to be distributed by the media and commented upon. It is an image of pain, an inherently political game meant to show off power. It instrumentalises the victim's lack of freedom doubly since it exposes his/her most vulnerable state without shame or respect. These proofs however are a way of communication – the only one – between the victims and their families and also they might be ways of temporal escape.

MS: Could you be more precise in terms of re ecting on the actual status of such a victim? How do you see it (between life and death, she says 'we have been living like the dead'), who is the victim here?

CM: Ms. Betancourt's video is devastating in all aspects I can think of. It primarily confronts us with her suffering, the impact of time on her seemingly ill body, the inhumane conditions in which her days go by. At the same time it showed me the jungle in its rawness, that impenetrable space of the Colombian south, which I don't dare to enter, not even in my dreams. That super-natural landscape of lawless piranhas and pink dolphins; home to the disappeared, the dead, the victims of the 50-year-old civil war.

MS: That is an interesting point, as you try to re ect through your artwork about political conditions in Latin America from an aesthetic perspective?

CM: Something that struck me about this video is it made me think of representation, of the indexical and symbolic nature of images, of composition and framing. Along these lines I can't escape to view this document from an aesthetic perspective, perhaps as a work of art. I recognise in the video a bit of Caravaggio's Saint Thomas Putting his Finger on Christ's Wound, or Robert Capa's Death of a Loyalist Soldier. These are iconic and aesthetic representations of pain. The cameraman carefully insisted on framing with 'correct' camera angles and consistently presented Ms. Betancourt dead-center on the frame. The cameraman victimised her again. As if her kidnapping wasn't enough, he attacked her with his gaze, to show us her grief. But Ms. Betancourt remained still. Although she sees us looking at her, although she sees the world reproducing her image in posters and banners, although she embodies her experiential and our empathetic pain, she chose to remain still, silent, to deny us her gaze. By doing so she reclaimed her dignity, she demanded respect, she freed herself from the chains, she claimed her autonomy. She pronounced her freedom.

(interview conducted by Marko Stamenkovi on 23 jan 2008)

SOFT GENOCIDES, ADMINISTRATIVE ETHNIC CLEANSING AND CIVIL DEATH IN POST-SOCIALIST EUROPE
AN INTERVIEW WITH TOMAS TOMILINAS

Marko Stamenkovi (MS): A seminar Translocal Express Jubilee Edition that was held this Feb- ruary at the Museum of Occupation in Tallinn (Estonia) addressed the growing tendencies of nationalism on the Eastern borders of Europe and their re ections in contemporary art. Your per- sonal and professional perspective – from the specific context of the Baltic region – coincides, to a certain extent, with the aforementioned subject. What is the link?

Tomas Tomilinas (TT): After the fall of communism in Europe it was radical nationalism that filled the free ideological space in most of the transition countries. In the Balkans the war was a solu- tion to the tensions that followed when leaders got rid of the Soviet political anti-fascistic 'correct- ness' and started to define the new enemy – the ethnic minority (instead of 'the West'). The idea was easy and effectively supported by the masses – all social problems would be solved if real national majority rule would prevail. But in countries like Bosnia, Latvia and Estonia – there were extremely serious problems regarding national 'majority' definition. Bosnia paid a bloody price for not being a typical nation-state. Baltic countries did not face violent ethnic con icts, but deep social con ict is still preserved and cultivated by national populists, who still lead these countries.

MS: During our conversation in Tallinn, we touched upon the issue of 'erased citizens' as expe- rienced, for example, in the recent history of Slovenia (in 1992), when "the newly independent state of Slovenia deleted the names of some 30,000 residents from the nation's civil registries", as reported by Jim Fussell.[188] What was your immediate reaction regarding your regional context?

TT: Just like in any nation state, ethnic minorities are always an 'obstacle' to comfortable develop- ment. Almost half of the population in Latvia and more than one third in Estonia do not belong to the ethnic group that defines the name of the country. Most of the 'strangers' are former Soviet citizens and their children, who immigrated to the Baltic during the second half of the twentieth century. When Latvians and Estonians gained independence in 1991 they refused to provide citizenship to the Russian-speaking people, even to those who were born in these countries. It was not the case in Lithuania, which provided new passports to all legal residents. The Latvian and Estonian (not Baltic) invention was two types of passports: passports for citizens and so- called 'grey' passports (passports for non-citizens or aliens). Non-citizens have no voting rights, limited pension rights, they are not allowed to work in government, police and civil services. This legal segregation was implemented by the last elected Soviet parliaments in Latvia and Estonia just after the proclamation of independence. The paradox is that people who are now non-citi- zens elected this parliament too. People voted for the deputies, who implemented administrative

---

188. Read News Monitor for Slovenia, 1998 to 2004: Izbrisani: (Erased Citizens) on:http://www.prevent-genocide.org/europe/slovenia/

'cleansing' on them afterwards, taking away their basic political rights and some specific social rights. The victims had chosen their butchers.

Having so many 'frozen' immigrants pushed two Baltic states into the development of integration strategies. The naturalisation and integration policy of the last 18 years failed, because the numbers say that there are still about 500,000 'grey passport aliens' in Latvia and Estonia (there are about 3 million citizens). Last year's Bronze soldier riots in Tallinn, although manipulated well by Russia, still demonstrate the absolute failure of Estonia's integration policies. Anger, deprivation and unequal treatment are not producing conditions for successful integration but violence and instability. Just as democracy cannot be built on oil-war, integration is not a must per se for a minority human being.

MS: And the position of the EU, in that regard?

TT: The history of the EU position towards the non-citizen issue in Latvia and Estonia reveals many interesting points about EU immigration policy development. The EU never officially supported the discrimination policies, but the official comments on the issue have always been modest and calm. The EU is not active in reducing the most obvious discrimination: non-citizens in Latvia, who lived all their life in the country, for instance, are still not able to vote (this is no longer the case in Estonia) in the local elections (and of course not in general elections). However, the right to elect Latvian local councils is provided to all EU residents by EU law. The problem of 'aliens' didn't cause many barriers for Latvia and Estonia to enter the EU. To say more – it looks like the EU is using similar methods on immigrants as Baltic nationalists did on their minorities. Despite the declarations and growing budgets of human rights institutions, the EU is still about defending the nationals.

Half a century ago, Hannah Arendt warned that being only a human being is not enough to survive, because 'human rights' will always be specific, second-hand rights. This is exactly the case in post 9/11 Western thinking, which is obsessed with the idea of diminishing the number of immigrants and implementing aggressive integration policies on them for security reasons. An absolute minority of politicians realises that it is almost impossible to regulate migration, especially by hard measures such as border control. Instead of concentrating upon migration limitations, mass deportations, 'border-walls', active migrant detention and assimilation, the EU has to examine other possible alternatives of police measures to provide better and more effective aid directed towards the reasons for migration. Unfortunately, instead of using soft and alternative policies, the EU is making efforts to legalise the old-fashioned and expensive system of migrant detention by European law. The growing number of migrant detention centres across Europe and in neighbouring countries symbolises a conservative approach to the solution of the illegal migration problem. European 'nationalism' makes those in power in Brussels blind and they don't see that it is not possible to solve the problem of illegal migration, except by making it legal.

(Interview conducted by Marko Stamenkovi on 7 March 2008)

GLOSSARY

Anniversary reactions

Rekindled grief, when the trigger for an acute grief reaction is a special occasion such as a holiday or birthday. It usually occurs each year on the day the person died, or in sometimes when the bereaved individual becomes the same age the deceased was at the time of death. Anniversary reactions tend to become relatively mild and brief over time, but sometimes they can be experienced as the reliving of one's original grief and can last for hours and days.[189] It is often found with persons with PTSD related to the day of someone's death or an important action. (T.J.) See also: memorial, commemoration

Amnesia

Partial or total inability to recall past experiences; may be organic or emotional origin.[190] Amnesia could be anterograde and retrograde depending upon whether the lack of memory relates to events occurring after or before the trauma.

In anterograde amnesia the individual is impaired in learning new information. Memories for events that occurred before the injury may be largely spared, but events that occurred since the injury may be lost. In retrograde amnesia loss of memory occurs for events and experiences prior to an illness, accident, injury, or traumatic experience. With improvement, patients may experience a gradual shrinking of the time for which memory has been lost, although some patients experience a gradual improvement in memory for the entire period.[191]

In amnesia memory is affected far more than any other function, sometimes to the extent that patients will forget conversations that took place only a few minutes earlier. Patients generally have some disorientation for time, and often for place. Some patients are apathetic to the memory problem; others try to hide it by confabulating. Confabulation is uncounscious filling of gaps in memory by imagined or untrue experiences that a person believes but that have no basis in fact.[192]

There are several types of amnestic disorders: due to general medical condition (e.g. head trauma, stroke, etc.), substance-induced amnestic disorder (most often in alcoholic patients), and with unknown underlying cause. Some causes of cognitive symptoms are also: age-related cognitive decline, dissociative disorders, and pseudodementia (from apathy and slowed responses, some patients look as if the have symptoms of dementia).[193]

Among different features of amnesia it is important to point out dissociative amnesia (formerly called Psychogenic Amnesia). It's central feature is the inability to remember significant events. It is more extensive than could be explained by common forgetfulness. It begins suddenly, usually

189. H. Kaplan and B. Sadock, Kaplan & Sadock's Synopsis of Psychiatry, Ninth Edition, Philadelphia: Lippincott Williams & Wilkins, 2003.
190. Kaplan and Sadock, Kaplan & Sadock's Synopsis of Psychiatry.
191. Kaplan and Sadock, Kaplan & Sadock's Synopsis of Psychiatry.
192. Kaplan and Sadock, Kaplan & Sadock's Synopsis of Psychiatry.
193. J. Morrison, DSM-IV Made Easy: The Clinician's Guide to Diagnosis, New York: The Guilford Press, 1995.

following severe stress such as physical injury, abandonment by a spouse, or internal con ict over sexual issues. Sometimes, the patient wanders aimlessly near home. After a variable time, the amnesia suddenly ends with complete recovery of memory. It is rare for Dissociative Amnesia to occur again in the same individual.[194] (T.J) See also: forgetting, dissociation

Art therapy, Art as therapy

Art therapy is a human service profession that utilizes art media, images, the creative process, and patient/client responses to art productions as re ections of an individual's development, abilities, personality, interests, concerns, and con icts. Art therapy practice is based on knowledge of human developmental and psychological theories, which are implemented in the full spectrum of models of assessment and treatment.[195]

Art therapy is an effective treatment for the developmentally, medically, educationally, socially, or psychologically impaired. It is practiced in mental health, rehabilitations, medical, educational, and forensic institutions. Art therapy emerged as a distinct profession in the 1930s. Since that time art therapy has grown into an effective and important method of communication, assessment, and treatment. Sound theoretical principles and therapeutic practices govern the modality. The theoretical orientation of art therapy includes psychoanalytic theory as well as art education.

Two schools of thought are fundamental to the profession of art therapy: Art Psychotherapy and Art as Therapy. Both have contributed to the progressive development of the field. Often basic tenets associated with both schools of thought are integrated in the practice of art therapy. Psychoanalytic tenets provide the basis for both methods of practice. Important persons in the development of this art as a therapeutic techniques are Margaret Naumburg, Edith Kramer and Myra Levick.[196]

Art therapists are skilled in the therapeutic use of art. Art therapists use their backgrounds as artists and their knowledge of art materials in conjunction with clinical skills. The art therapist treats clients/patients through the use of therapeutic art tasks. While the art therapy process uses art making as a means of nonverbal communication and expression, the art therapist makes use of verbal explorations and interventions. Art therapists do not own art or the healing that comes from its use.[197]

Professional qualification for entry into the field requires a master's degree from an accredited academic institution or a certificate of completion from an accredited institute or clinical program. Specialised training programs include didactic instruction and practicum experience. Graduate art therapy training programs are commonly associated with medical colleges or universities. The designation art therapist registered, ATR, is granted to individuals who have successfully completed the required educational and professional experience.[198] (T.P.)

Avoidance

---

194. Morrison, DSM-IV Made Easy.
195. M. S. Cohen-Liebman, 'Art Therapy', in Michel Hersen and William Sledge (eds) Encyclopedia of Psychotherapy, New York: Elsevier Science, 2002, 113-116.
196. Cohen-Liebman, 'Art Therapy'.
197. Cohen-Liebman, 'Art Therapy'.
198. Cohen-Liebman, 'Art Therapy'.

Sadock: "The principal clinical features of PTSD are painful reexperiencing the event, a pattern of avoidance and emotional numbing, and fairly constant hyperarousal".[199] According to DSM-IV criteria stimuli associated with the trauma and numbing of general responsiveness include: 1) efforts to avoid thoughts, feelings, or conversations associated with the trauma; 2) efforts to avoid activities, places, or people that arouse recollections of the trauma; 3) inability to recall an important aspect of the trauma; 4) diminished interest or participation in significant activities; 5) feeling of detachment or estrangement from others; 6) restricted range of affect; 7) sense of foreshortened future.[200] (T.J.) See also – PTSD, reexperiencing, hyperarousal

Behavioral disorders (and war)

General term used to denote mental illness or psychological dysfunction, specifically those mental, emotional, or behavioral subclasses for which organic correlates do not exist. The DSM-IV does not have the diagnostic category of 'behavior disorder', although it is included in the ICD-10. Although there is no clear definition of 'behavior disorder', it is usually meant to refer to a behavioral problem that is severe enough to warrant intervention, but which is not a part of diagnosable mental disorder.[201] (T.P.)

Behavioral Disorders and War

In wartime people particularly exhibit pathological behaviour patterns and other kinds of otherwise hidden negativities. In war, death and life are at their closest – and most terribly distant. Everything that transpires in the areas of destruction, violence, aggression and other kinds of human con ict is almost always based on the intimate needs of the individual. The more powerful, the more terrifying they are, and the weaker, they are more vicious, and prone to radically bizarre crimes. Having that in mind crime should be prevented, which is possible if necrophiliac tendencies of the leaders are seen as such ahead of time.[202]

Marx and Freud thought that deviant forms of behavior may anticipate the alienation of the individual from both society and himself/herself. Khan thinks that person with deviant sexual behavior places an impersonal object or phantasy between the desire and object that again leads to alienation of a person from himself/herself and from object of desire. Sexual deviation is hard to accept, it is condemned, and it provokes great curiosity. There is a difference between compulsive symptoms and sexual deviation. Such deviations are exclusively connected with sexual behavior. Their characteristic is that they disable experiencing of the genital orgasm through the obstacles that could be overcome with the deviant act. Individuals with sexual deviations use repression as a defensive mechanism. Sexual deviations are connected with fixations from a childhood. Such individuals do not experience greater or more potent pleasure than normal individuals, but it is harder for them to control their impulses.[203] (T.J) See also: necrophilia, sexual deviations (para-

---

199. H. Kaplan and B. Sadock, Kaplan & Sadock's Synopsis of Psychiatry, Ninth Edition, Philadelphia: Lippincott Williams & Wilkins, 2003.
200. American Psychiatric Association, Diagnostic and Statistical Manual of Mental Disorders, revised edition, Washington, DC: American Association Press, 1999.
201. J. Kay and A. Tasman, Essentials of Psychiatry, Hoboken, NJ: Wiley, 2006.
202. M. Kulenovi , 'Necrophilia and Generals', Polemos: Journal of Interdisciplinary Research on War and Peace, 2.03/04 (1999): 73-94.
203. M. Kulenovi , Metapsihologija, nastranosti, osobitosti, Zagreb: Naprijed, 1986.

philia), repression.

Commemoration

Commemoration is a ceremony to honor the memory of someone or something. Commemoration is at the heart of oral culture and ritualised societies; it underlines the very mechanism of memory. As the etymology points out, commemoration is a sort of joint 'memorisation' of things, a 'holistic' event.[204] Commemorative ritual gives wholeness and structure (relationships) to community. Commemoration has a psychological and sociological meaning. In the psychological meaning, it is a self-care strategy for a trauma survivor. It provides an opportunity for the person to finishing incomplete psychological processes. (T.P) See also: rituals and mourning, mourning, grief, bereavement

Commemorative silence

A common way to remember a tragic accident and to remember the victims or casualties of such an event is a commemorative silence. This usually means one or more 'minutes of silence', in which one is supposed to not speak, but instead remember and re ect on the event. A commemorative silence may be held at a workplace, a school, or similar institutions. Sometimes a government will advertise a commemorative silence for a specific period at a specific time, which everybody is encouraged (but not forced) to honor. One such example is after the events of 9/11, and on its anniversery several years afterward, when many governments around the world announced 3 minutes of silence in respect of the victims of the event.

Comorbid diagnosis or comorbidity

Comorbid diagnosis or comorbidity is the condition of having two or more diseases at the same time. It means that sometimes in psychiatry one diagnosis alone cannot be sufficient in accounting for all the symptoms. It can also imply the coexistence of physical and mental illness.[205] For example, PTSD often occurs together with depressive disorder, anxiety, panic attacks, alcohol and substance abuse, as well as personality disorder.[206] (T.J)

---

204. N. Isar, 'Undoing Forgetfulness: Chiasmus of Poetical Mind – A Cultural Paradigm of Archetypal Imagination', Europe's Journal Of Psychology, 1.3 (2005):
http://www.ejop.org/archives/2005/08/undoing_forgetf_1.html
205. M. B. First, 'Mutually Exclusive Versus Co-occurring Diagnostic Categories: The Challenge of Diagnostic Comorbidity', Psychopathology, 38.4 (2005): 206-210.
206. N. Long, C. MacDonald and K. Chamberlain, 'Prevalence of Posttraumatic Stress Disorder, Depression and Anxiety in Community Sample of New Zealand Vietnam War Veterans', Australian and New Zealand Journal of Psychiatry 30 (1996): 253-256; D. Kozari -Kovaèi , T. Ljubin and M. Grappe, 'Comorbidity of Posttraumatic Stress Disorder and Alcohol Dependence in Displaced Persons', Croatian Medical Journal 41 (2000): 173-178; A. Bleich, M. Koslowsky, A. Dolev and B. Lerer, 'Posttraumatic Stress Disorder and Depression: An Analysis of Comorbidity', The British Journal of Psychiatry 170 (1997): 479-482; D. Kozari -Kova i , D. K. Hercigonja and M. Grubiši -Ili , 'Posttraumatic Stress Disorder and Depression in Soldiers with Combat Experiences', Croatian Medical Journal, 42 (2001): 165-170; D. Kozari -Kova i and D. Kocijan-Hercigonja, 'Assessment of Posttraumatic Disorder and Comorbidity' Military Medicine 160 (2001): 677-680; D. Kozari -Kova i and A. Borove ki., 'Prevalence of Psychotic Comorbidity in Combat-Related Posttraumatic Stress Disorder', Military Medicine 170 (2005): 223-226.

Collective trauma

Collective trauma is a traumatic experience shared by a group of people or even an entire society. Various authors have investigated this phenomena and its in uence on society's dynamics and culture. It includes transgenerational transference of the trauma, experiences, and is can effect forming of individual or societal identity.

Hirst et al. investigated how social scientists locate collective memories in the social resources that shape them.[207] From one perspective, collective memories are explained as 'transcending individuals' or as being 'in the world'. Others think that individuals must remember collective as well as individual memories. They understand collective memories as shared individual memories. Hirst et al. tried to bridge these two approaches by making a difference between the design of social resources and memory practices.

Wessel et al. considered the concept of collective memory by making distinction between collective memories as a property of groups ('collectivistic memory') and on the other hand, memories that are a property of individuals who are an integral part of their social environment ('social memory').[208] They think that issues induced by collaborative remembering may be beneficial for recovery after the traumatic experience.

Bohleber et al. discuss that traumatic memories are not subject to transformation by the present when they are retrieved.[209] Those memories constitute one form of foreign body in the psychic-associative network and, therefore, they are not an exact replica of the traumatic experience but undergo specific remodellings. The process of psychotherapy requires remembrance and reconstruction of the traumatic events. Social discourse of historical truth for both the individual and society that is connected with disasters is defined as 'man-made'. Refusing to remember or understand often stems from the desire to avoid confrontation with the horrors and the victims' suffering. Especially with the Holocaust, the further problem is how to avoid its subjugation in historical description to categories that eliminate the horror and traumatic nature of the events. Remembering crimes unfolds a special set of dynamics. One example is their transgenerational effects on post-war German society.

Goren, investigated the nature of the attacks on September 11th, involvement of society as virtual eyewitnesses of these attacks, and traumatising impact on the cultural consciousness.[210] Psychological processes of identification, dissociation and splitting allowed idealisation at a safe distance when the collective tried to abort the mourning process and overcome the pain and helplessness of traumatic grief by going to war. (T.J.) See also: trauma, PTSD, collective unconscious

Collective guilt

Collective guilt in scientific research: a sense of responsibility for the acts of some other member of the group to which an individual belongs, even if this individual has not participated in the act. Schlesinger-Kipp, investigated generation of German psychoanalysts who were born between

---

207. W. H. and D. Manier, 'Towards a Psychology of Collective Memory', Memory 16.3 (2008): 183-200.
208. I. Wessel and M. Moulds, 'Collective Memory: A Perspective from (Experimental) Clinical Psychology', Memory 16.3 (2008): 288-304.
209. W. Bohleber, 'Remembrance, Trauma and Collective Memory: The Battle for Memory in Psychoanalysis', International Journal of Psychoanalysis 88.2 (2007): 329-352.
210. El. Goren, 'Society's Use of the Hero Following a National Trauma', American Journal of Psychoanalysis 67.1 (2007): 37-52.

1930 and 1945, and who grew up in a society that, due to the collective guilt of its adults, either superimposed general self-idealisation or self-acquittal with respect to those who were identified as perpetrators of this trauma, or would not address or process the trauma, at all.[211] These psychoanalysts, in their responses, perceived their own training analysts, part of the older generation, to have unconsciously, or perhaps even consciously, participated in the collective guilt or self-idealisation process.

Iyer examined emotions as predictors of opposition to policies and actions of one's country that are perceived to be illegitimate.[212] Two studies investigated the political implications of American and British citizens' anger, guilt, and shame responses to perceived harm caused by their countries' occupation of Iraq. In both studies, a manipulation of pervasive threat to the country's image increased participants' shame but not guilt. The emotions predicted political action intentions to advocate distinct opposition strategies. Shame predicted action intentions to advocate withdrawal from Iraq. Anger predicted action intentions to advocate compensation to Iraq, confrontation of agents responsible, and withdrawal from Iraq. Anger directed at different targets (ingroup, ingroup representative, and outgroup representative) predicted action intentions to support distinct strategies (Study 2). Guilt did not independently predict any political action intentions.

Tangney discusses that moral emotions represent a key element of human moral apparatus, influencing the link between moral standards and moral behavior.[213] He reviews current theory and research on moral emotions. Focus was first put on a triad of negatively valenced 'self-conscious' emotions-shame, guilt, and embarrassment. Tangney discusses current thinking on the distinction between shame and guilt, and the relative advantages and disadvantages of these two moral emotions. Several new areas of research are highlighted: research on the domain-specific phenomenon of body shame, styles of coping with shame, psychobiological aspects of shame, the link between childhood abuse and later proneness to shame, and the phenomena of vicarious or 'collective' experiences of shame and guilt. In recent years, the concept of moral emotions has been expanded to include several positive emotions-elevation, gratitude, and the sometimes morally relevant experience of pride.

McGarty investigated whether the Australian government should officially apologise to Indigenous Australians for past wrongs is hotly debated in Australia.[214] One study showed that group-based guilt was a good predictor of support for a government apology, as was the perception that non-Indigenous Australians were relatively advantaged. The second study found that group-based guilt was an excellent predictor of support for apology and was itself predicted by perceived non-Indigenous responsibility for harsh treatment of Indigenous people, and an absence of doubts about the legitimacy of group-based guilt. National identification was not a predictor of group-based guilt. The results of the two studies suggest that, just as individual emotions predict individual action tendencies, so group-based guilt predicts support for actions or decisions to be

211. G. Schlesinger-Kipp, 'Childhood in World War II: German Psychoanalysts Remember', American Academy of Psychoanalysis and Dynamic Psychiatry 35.4 (2007): 541-554.

212. A. Iyer, T. Schmader and B. Lickel, 'Why Individuals Protest the Perceived Transgressions of Their Country: the Role of Anger, Shame, and Guilt', Personality and Social Psychology Bulletin 33.4 (2007): 572-587.

213. J. P. Tangney, J. Stuewig and D. J. Mashek, 'Moral Emotions and Moral Behavior', Annual Review of Psychology 58 (2007): 345-372.

214. C. McGarty, A. Pedersen, C. W. Leach, T. Mansell, J. Waller and A. M. Bliuc, 'Group-based Guilt as a Predictor of Commitment to Apology', British Psychological Society 44.4 (2005): 659-680.

taken at the collective level.

Wohl examined how categorisation in uences victimised group members' responses to contemporary members of a historical perpetrator group.[215] Specifically, the authors tested whether increasing category inclusiveness − from the intergroup level to the maximally inclusive human level − leads to greater forgiveness of a historical perpetrator group and decreased collective guilt assignment for its harmdoing. Among Jewish North Americans (Experiments 1, 2, and 4) and Native Canadians (Experiment 3) human-level categorisation resulted in more positive responses toward Germans and White Canadians, respectively, by decreasing the uniqueness of their past harmful actions toward the in-group. Increasing the inclusiveness of categorisation led to greater forgiveness and lessened expectations that former out-group members should experience collective guilt compared with when categorisation was at the intergroup level. (T.J) See also: collective trauma, collective unconscious

Collective unconscious

Term introduced by Carl Gustav Jung. It consists of all humankind's common, shared mythological and symbolic past. It includes archetypes − representational images and configurations with universal symbolic meanings. Archetypal figures exist for the mother, father, child, and hero, among others. Archetypes contribute to complexes, feeling-toned ideas that develop as a result of personal experience interacting with archetypal imagery.[216] (T.J.) See also: collective guilt, collective trauma

Coping mechanism

Coping mechanisms are one group of coping skills. They are skills that a person uses for stress reduction. In psychological terms, these are consciously used skills. Unconscious counterpart of coping mechanism are defense mechanisms. Overuse of particularly coping or defense mechanisms may exacerbate individuals problem rather than remedy it.[217] (T.P)
See also: coping skills, coping strategies, stress

Coping skills

A coping skill is a behavioral tool which may be used by individuals to offset or overcome adversity, disadvantage, or disability without correcting or eliminating the underlying condition. All living beings routinely utilize coping skills in daily life.[218] Identifying our own type of coping skills, what we used to deal with specific problems, often helps. The range of successful coping skills varies

215. M. Wohl and N. Branscombe, 'Forgiveness and Collective Guilt Assignment to Historical Perpetrator Groups Depend on Level of Social Category Inclusiveness', Journal of Personality and Social Psychology, 88.2 (2005): 288-303.

216. H. Kaplan and B. Sadock, Kaplan & Sadock's Synopsis of Psychiatry, Ninth Edition, Philadelphia: Lippincott Williams & Wilkins, 2003. See also: C. G. Jung, The Archetypes and The Collective Unconscious, trans. R.F.C. Hull, London: Routledge, 1980.

217. R. S. Lazarus and S. Folkman, Stress, Appraisal, and Coping, New York: Springer, 1984; C. Aldwin and T. A. Revenson, 'Does Coping Help? A Reexamination of the Relation Between Coping and Mental Health', Journal of Personality and Social Psychology 53 (1987): 337-348.

218. Richard S. Lazarus and Susan Folkman, Stress, Appraisal, and Coping, New York: Springer, 1984; C. Aldwin and T. A. Revenson, 'Does Coping Help? A Reexamination of the Relation Between Coping and Mental Health', Journal of Personality and Social Psychology 53 (1987): 337-348.

widely with the problems to be overcome. However, the learning and practice of coping skills are generally regarded as very helpful to most individuals. Sharing of learned coping skills with others is often beneficial.[219]

Overuse of some coping methods may worsen individuals condition. The abuse of drugs or alcohol, substances is often used to escape from problems, and can lead to a wide variety of psychiatric symptoms and states as well to a greater health, social and economic problems.[220] (T.P) see also: coping mechanism, coping strategies, stress

Coping strategies

Coping strategies refer to the specific efforts, both behavioral and psychological, that people employ to master, tolerate, reduce, or minimise stressful events.[221] Two general coping strategies have been distinguished: problem-solving strategies and emotion-focused strategies. Problem-solving strategies are efforts to do something active to alleviate stressful circumstances. Emotion-focused coping strategies are efforts to regulate the emotional consequences of stressful or potentially stressful events. Research indicates that people use both types of strategies to combat most stressful events.[222] The predominance of one type of coping strategy over another is determined by personal style and by the type of stressful event.

Another distinction in coping strategies is between active and avoidant coping strategies. Active coping strategies are either behavioral or psychological responses designed to change the nature of the stressor itself or how one thinks about it, whereas avoidant coping strategies lead people into activities (such as alcohol use) or mental states (such as withdrawal) that keep them from directly addressing stressful events.[223] Active coping strategies (behavioral or emotional) are better ways to deal with stressful events than the avoidant coping strategies. Avoidant coping strategies are a psychological risk factor or marker for adverse responses to stressful life events. Broad distinctions, such as problem-solving versus emotion-focused, or active versus avoidant, have only limited utility for understanding coping, and so research on coping and its measurement has evolved to address a variety of more specific coping strategies, noted below in the measurement section[224]. (T.P) See also: Art as therapy or Art psychotherapy, coping skills, coping mechanisms, stress

219. C. J. Holahan and R. H. Moos, 'Risk, Resistance, and Psychological Distress: A Longitudinal Analysis with Adults and Children', Journal of Abnormal Psychology 96 (1987): 3-13.

220. R. D. Weiss, L. M. Najavits and S. M. Mirin, 'Substance Abuse and Psychiatric Disorders', in Richard Frances, Sheldon Miller and Avram H. Mack (eds) Clinical Textbook of Addictive Disorders, 2nd edition, London: The Guilford Press, 1998: 291-318.

221. C. Aldwin and T. A. Revenson, 'Does Coping Help? A Reexamination of the Relation Between Coping and Mental Health', Journal of Personality and Social Psychology 53 (1987): 337-348.

222. Adwin and Revenson, 'Does Coping Help?', 337-348.

223. C. S. Carver, M. F. Scheier and J. K. Weintraub, 'Assessing Coping Strategies: A Theoretically Based Approach', Journal of Personality and Social Psychology 56 (1989): 267-283.

224. S. Folkman and R. Lazarus, 'An Analysis of Coping in a Middle-aged Community Sample', Journal of Health and Social Behavior 21 (1980): 219-239; C. J. Holahan and R. H. Moos, 'Risk, Resistance, and Psychological Distress: A Longitudinal Analysis with Adults and Children', Journal of Abnormal Psychology 96 (1987): 3-13.

Denial

Avoiding the awareness of some painful aspect of reality by negating sensory data. Although repression defends against affects and drive derivatives, denial abolishes external reality. It may be used in both normal and pathological states.[225] (T.J.) See also Coping strategies

Dependence projective identification

The aim of dependence projective identification is to force 'the other' to help. Such persons usually look for someone else to offer help and support for themselves, even in situations that they have to decide themselves. Despite the innocent appearance of these calls for help, the underlying message on the covert communicative level is, "I cannot live without you". Such persons use expressions like, "what do you think?", "what should I do?", "can you help me?", and "I do not think that I can do it alone". Actually, most of the time they have the power to overcome all these problems and most of them are clever individuals. If these people cannot find 'the other' to receive their projective identification or their wishes to satisfy, their dependence needs are denied by the others and as their anxiety increases, crying attacks, hysterical crises, severe depressions, and even suicidal tendencies may be encountered. Regarding this aspect, the underlying mechanism in many cases of depression, agoraphobia, and conversion disorder is projective identification. There is a strengthening of the dependence of a child for the mother in the covert communication of mothers who use projective identification containing the message of, "the more you obey your mother's orders, the more your mother loves you". Thus, the determinative appearance in the mother-father-child relationship inhibits the initiative of the child by unnecessary advice and guidance.[226] (T.P.) See also: ingratiation projective identifications, power projective identification, projective identification, sexuality projective identification

Dissociation

Persons with dissociative disorders feel as though they have no identity, they are confused about who they are, or they experience multiple identities. What gives individuals their unique personalities – thoughts, feelings, and actions – is changed in such persons.[227] It is disruption in the usually integrated functions of consciousness, memory, identity, or perceptions of the environment.[228] Dissociation is a self-defense against trauma; it assists individuals to withdraw from trauma at the time it occurs, but it also delays the working through needed to place the trauma in perspective within their lives. Unlike the phenomenon of repression, in which material is transferred to the dynamic unconscious, dissociation creates a situation in which mental contents coexists in parallel unconsciousness.[229]

225. H. Kaplan and B. Sadock, Kaplan & Sadock's Synopsis of Psychiatry, Ninth Edition, Philadelphia: Lippincott Williams & Wilkins, 2003.
226. S. Cashdan, Object Relations Therapy: Using the Relationship, New York: W. W. Norton & Company, 1988, 53-78; E. Göka, F. V. Yüksel and F. Göral, 'Projective Identification In Human Relations', Turkish Journal Of Psychiatry, 17.1 (2006): 1-9.
227. H. Kaplan and B. Sadock, Kaplan & Sadock's Synopsis of Psychiatry, Ninth Edition, Philadelphia: Lippincott Williams & Wilkins, 2003.
228. American Psychiatric Association, Diagnostic and Statistical Manual of Mental Disorders, revised edition, Washington, DC: American Association Press, 1999.
229. H. Kaplan and B. Sadock, Kaplan & Sadock's Synopsis of Psychiatry, Ninth Edition, Philadelphia: Lippincott Williams & Wilkins, 2003.

Acute dissociation is one of the early predictors of developing PTSD.[230] Therefore, it would be important to address symptoms of dissociation during the acute post-traumatic phase, since dissociation may be one of the key markers of acutely traumatised people who will develop chronic PTSD. (T.J.) See also: amnesia, repression, PTSD

Empathy

An individual's objective and insightful awareness of the feelings and behaviour of another person. It should be distinguished from sympathy, which is usually non-objective and non-critical. It includes caring, which is the demonstration of an awareness of and a concern for the good of others. The imaginative projection of a subjective state into an object so that the object appears to be infused with it. The action of understanding, being aware of, being sensitive to, and vicariously experiencing the feelings, thoughts, and experience of another of either the past or present without having the feelings, thoughts, and experience fully communicated in an objectively explicit manner.[231] Empathy may be described as the ability to 'put oneself into another's shoes', or as a sort of emotional resonance. Heinz Kohut introduced this term in psychoanalysis.[232]

Some individuals do not have the ability to perceive the emotions of others (e.g. persons with autistic disorder). On the other hand, people with personality disorders can demonstrate empathy for others in a way that they are superficially charming, but regularly use this ability to manipulate others since they lack sympathy or compassion for others. Such lack of empathy may be seen in sadism.[233] (T.J.) See also: sadism, see masochism

Exhibitionism

Exhibitionism is one aspect of sexual behaviour for some persons, but others have this way of sexual behaviour simultaneously with sexual activities within their long-term relationships (although their urges become more prominent if any kind of interpersonal con icts appear). Excitement arises if the person that witnesses such behaviour seems shocked, scared or under impression. The definition of exhibitionism is an 'impulsive activity of displaying genitals in order to achieve sexual pleasure'. Genital exhibitionism occurs in mature men. It is connected with showing off in public places, in front of young or older women. Large numbers of pre-adolescent children are engaged in 'mutual genital games'. Exhibitionism is a complex defense mechanism

230. J. Briere, Catherine Scott and Frank Weathers, 'Peritraumatic and Persistent Dissociation in the Presumed Etiology of PTSD', American Journal of Psychiatry 165 (2005): 2295-2301; B. Marx and D. Sloan, 'Peritraumatic Dissociation and Experiental Avoidance as Predictors of Posttraumatic Stress Symptomatology', Behaviour Research and Therapy 43 (2005): 569-583; A. Shalev, T. Peri, L. Canetti and S. Schreiber, 'Predictors of PTSD in Injured Trauma Survivors: A Prospective Study', American Journal of Psychiatry 153 (1996): 219-225; P. Panasetis and R. Bryant, 'Peritraumatic versus Persistent Dissociation in Acute Stress Disorder', Journal of Traumatic Stress 16 (2003): 563-566; J. Murray, A. Ehlers and R. Mayou, 'Dissociation and Post-traumatic Stress Disorder: Two Prospective Studies of Road Accident Survivors', British Journal of Psychiatry 180 (2002): 363-368.
231. R. Rothenberg, The New American Medical Dictionary and Health Manual, 6th edition, New York: Signet, 1990; R. R. Greenson, 'Empathy and Its Vicissitudes', International Journal of Psychoanalysis 41 (1960): 418-424.
232. H. Kohut, How Does Analysis Cure?, Chicago: The University of Chicago Press, 1984, p. 82.
233. J. Morrison, DSM-IV Made Easy: The Clinician's Guide to Diagnosis, New York: The Guilford Press, 1995.

that leads to deviant personality traits. Freud explains exhibitionism in the view of the 'castration complex' because showing off encourages the person's belief of 'owning the penis'; and also through the aggression – because showing off scares other people through the symbolism of magical gesture, when an individual displays what he/she wants to see. Pure demonstration is not sufficient for achievement of orgasm. Exhibitionists have a strong sense of guilt, but mostly they are impotent and shy.[234] (T.J.)

Factitious disorder
According to the DSM-IV, Factitious Disorder is a intentional production or feigning of physical or psychological signs or symptoms. The motivation for the behavior is to assume the sick role. External incentives for the behavior (such as economic gain, avoiding legal responsibility, or improving physical well-being, as in malingering) are absent.[235]
It is the conscious awareness of the production of symptoms that differentiates factitious disorder from the somatoform disorders in which the patient unconsciously produces symptoms for an unconscious psychological benefit. It is the underlying motivation to produce symptoms that separates factitious disorders from malingering.[236] (T.P.) See also: malingering, somatoform disorders

Fetishism (redirect Fetish)
In the original sense, a fetish was an idol or other object that had magical siginificance. In the context of sexual activity, it refers to something that excites an individual's sexual fantasies or desires. Some of these objects include underwear, shoes, stockings, and other inanimate objects. The definition excludes cross-dressing that is not sexually exciting (as in Transvestic Fetishism) and objects designed for use during sex. Bras and panties are probably the most common objects used as fetishes. Some people collect great numbers of their preferred fetishes; some resort to stealing to get them. They may smell, rub, or handle these objects while masturbating, or they may ask sex partners to wear them. Without the fetish, such individuals may be unable to get an erection. The onset of Fetishism is usually in adolescence, but many patients report similar interests even in childhood. Although found to certain degree in women, nearly all fetishists are men. This disorder tends to be a chronic condition. With time, a person may use a fetish to replace human love objects.[237] (T.J.)

Flashback
Flashbacks are spontaneous, transitory recurrences. The episode usually lasts a few seconds to few minutes but can sometimes last longer. Most often, even in the presence of distinct perceptual disturbances, the person has insight into the pathological nature of the disturbance. Flashbacks can be triggered by emotional stress, sensory deprivation (such as monotonous driv-

234. J. Morrison, DSM-IV Made Easy, p. 474; World Health Organization, The ICD-10 Classification of Mental and Behavioural Disorders: Clinical Descriptions and Diagnostic Guidelines, Geneva: WHO, 1992; J. Laplanche and J. B. Pontalis, Rje nik psihoanalize, Naprijed, 1992.
235. A. Fleming and S. Eisendrath, 'Factitious Disorders', in Jerald Kay and Allan Tasman (eds) Essentials of Psychiatry, Hoboken, NJ: Wiley, 2006, 679-684.
236. J. Morrison, DSM-IV Made Easy: The Clinician's Guide to Diagnosis, New York: The Guilford Press, 1995, 311-315.
237. Morrison, DSM-IV Made Easy.

ing), or use of another psychoactive substance, such as alcohol or marijuana.[238] (T.J.) See also: reexoeriencing, PTSD, re-experiencing

Forgiveness

Barry et al.: the trait forgiveness is the disposition to forgive interpersonal transgressions over time and across situations.[239] By definition, forgiveness is the replacement of negative unforgiving emotions with positive, other-oriented emotions. Rumination may have an important role as a mediator between forgivingness and emotional outcomes; but authors hypothesised that the different content of rumination leads to different outcomes after transgressions. In one study, forgivingness was negatively correlated with trait anger, hostility, neuroticism, fear, and vengeful rumination and was positively correlated with agreeableness, extraversion, and trait empathy. Worthington et al. discuss the importance of forgiveness in healthcare since this is an almost unknown field of research.[240] Now it is known that there is psychology of forgiveness, but regarding the physiology, little is known. Forgiveness is a mark of compassion, love, and caring. Authors point out the importance of personal motive in forgiving, with the notion that altruistic motives have greater benefits than do self-interested motives. Other studies showed an absolute hierarchical status enhanced forgiveness and reconciliation, but in conditions of high procedural justice, but when perceptions of procedural justice were low, there was increased nedd for revenge.[241] (T.J.) See also: revenge

Grief

Grief without complications, is a normal response to loss. In the first phase, it is usually manifested as a state of shock, with expression of numbness or bewilderment. It lasts shortly, and it is usually followed by feelings of suffering, crying, as well with decreased appetite, weight loss, insomnia, problems with concentration, breathing, and feeling weak. Self-reproach is much more common in pathological grief.[242]
Phases of grief include: 1. shock and denial (minutes, days, weeks), 2. acute anguish (weeks, months), and 3. resolution (months, years).[243]
Individuals that manifest the 'survivor guilt' may believe that they should die. They might have problems in establishing new relationships. Process of denying the death of the lost one occurs during the bereavement period.[244]

238. H. Kaplan and B. Sadock, Kaplan & Sadock's Synopsis of Psychiatry, Ninth Edition, Philadelphia: Lippincott Williams & Wilkins, 2003.
239. J. W. Berry, E. L. Worthington Jr, L. E. O'Connor, L. Parrott III and N. G. Wade, 'Forgivingness, Vengeful Rumination, and Affective Traits', Journal of Personality 73.1 (2005): 183-225.
240. E. L. Worthington Jr, C. Vanoyen Witvliet, A. J. Lerner and M. Scherer, 'Forgiveness in Health Research and Medical Practice', EXPLORE: The Journal of Science and Healing 1.3 (2005): 169-176.
241. K. Aquino, T. Tripp and R. Bies, 'Getting Even or Moving On? Power, Procedural Justice, and Types of Offense as Predictors of Revenge, Forgiveness, Reconciliation, and Avoidance in Organizations', Journal of Applied Psychology 91.3 (2006): 653-68.
242. M. Viederman, 'Grief: Normal and Pathological Variants', American Journal of Psychiatry 152.1 (1995): 1-4.
243. H. Kaplan and B. Sadock, Kaplan & Sadock's Synopsis of Psychiatry, Ninth Edition, Philadelphia: Lippincott Williams & Wilkins, 2003.
244. Kaplan and Sadock, Kaplan & Sadock's Synopsis of Psychiatry.

Identification phenomena is when survivor accepts some qualities or characteristics of the deceased person. It can even be expressed in such a pathological level that the survivor develops physical symptoms similar to symptoms or illness of the deceased person.[245]
Anticipatory grief is expressed prior of the loss as opposed to grief that is expressed at or after certain loss. It should end when the anticipated loss occurs. If such grief is expanded, it might be difficult for the bereaved person to reestablish previous relationships. Sometimes it occurs with individuals who have been away for a long period of time, like those who were in a war or thought to be dead.[246]
Complicated, pathological, or abnormal grief refers to an abnormal course of grief. Grief can be absent or delayed or excessively intense and prolonged. An individual who is in such denial that they believe the deceased is still alive equates with a serious form of pathological grief.[247] (T.J.)
See also: denial, survivor guilt, anniversary reactions

Hyperarousal
Sadock stated: "The principal clinical features of PTSD are painful reexperiencing the event, a pattern of avoidance and emotional numbing, and fairly constant hyperarousal".[248]
According to DSM-IV, criteria symptoms of increased arousal include: 1) difficulty falling or staying asleep; 2) irritability or troubles with anger control; 3) difficulty concentrating; 4) hypervigilance; 5) exaggerated startle response.[249] (T.J.) See also: PTSD, reexperiencing, avoidance

Ingratiation projective identification
The person who uses ingratiation projective identification continuously shows self-denial in order to gain 'the other's' love. They ingratiates themselves to 'the other' by always putting themselves in a secondary position. However, in instances of disappointment, this usually transforms into telling off or calling 'the other' to account for what they have or have not done. Messages such as, "you did not appreciate the value of what I did for you!", and "I sacrificed myself for you!" are found in the covert communication. The individuals who are exposed to ingratiation projective identification, on the other hand, always feel that they are in a position in which they are obligated to feel grateful and express gratitude. Moreover, the aim of the person who uses this mechanism is to be appreciated. The covert communication message in ingratiation projective identification is, "you belong to me!" The message that they can be loved as long as they are useful was given to such individuals in their childhood. The child learns that he/she will be regarded as valuable and will be loved, and even will survive in such a case that he is useful and does things for 'the other', in this case the parent.[250] (T.J.) See also: dependence projective identification, power projective identification, sexuality projective identifications, projective identification

---

245. Kaplan and Sadock, Kaplan & Sadock's Synopsis of Psychiatry.
246. Kaplan and Sadock, Kaplan & Sadock's Synopsis of Psychiatry
247. Kaplan and Sadock, Kaplan & Sadock's Synopsis of Psychiatry.
248. H. Kaplan and B. Sadock, Kaplan & Sadock's Synopsis of Psychiatry, Ninth Edition, Philadelphia: Lippincott Williams & Wilkins, 2003.
249. American Psychiatric Association, Diagnostic and Statistical Manual of Mental Disorders, revised edition, Washington, DC: American Association Press, 1999.
250. S. Cashdan, Object Relations Therapy: Using the Relationship, New York: W. W. Norton & Company, 1988, 53-78; E. Göka, F. V. Yüksel and F. Göral, 'Projective Identification In Human Relations', Turkish Journal Of Psychiatry 17.1 (2006): 1-9.

Malingering

Malingering is the intentional faking of physical or psychological illness or symptoms. These symptoms are faked in order for some reason, such as gaining medication, getting disability payments, or missing work, i.e. malingering is intentional production of false or exaggerated symptoms motivated by external incentives, such as obtaining compensation or drugs, avoiding work or military duty, or evading criminal prosecution.[251] Malingering is not considered a mental illness. In the DSM-IV, malingering is the one of other conditions that may be a focus of clinical attention. Malingering behavior typically persists as long as the desire benefit outweighs the inconvenience or distress of seeking medical confirmation of the feigned illness. Malingering should be suspected in any of these situations: the patient has legal problems or the prospect of financial gain; the patient has Antisocial Personality Disorder; the patient tells story that does not accord with informants' accounts or with other known facts and the patient does not cooperate with the evaluation.[252] Malingerers tend to avoid symptoms such as those associated with more serious psychiatric disorders, because the pretense is very difficult to maintain and objective measures could detect the difference. On the other hand, to feign a sad mood, loss of interest in formerly enjoyed activities or a low energy may not be so difficult to demonstrate.[253]

Malingering is often confused with factitious disorder (in which the motive is not external gain but a wish to occupy the sick role) and the somatoform disorder (in which the symptoms are not intentionally produced at all).[254] (T.P.) See also: factitious disorder, somatoform disorder, malingering PTSD

Malingering PTSD

Malingering PTSD is a diagnosis particularly vulnerable to the malingering because it is characterised by a number of subjective symptoms and is commonly associated with reinforcing financial and personal gain (disability benefits).[255] Personal gain is always the motivation for malingering. During the past 20 years, research regarding the ability to detect malingering, the feigning of symptoms for secondary gain, in PTSD claimants has grown rapidly. PTSD is also characterised by a variable symptom profile and is highly comorbid with a variety of clinical and personality disorders, making detection of malingering a challenging endeavour.[256] (T.P.) See also: factitious disorder, malingering

---

251. J. Morrison, DSM-IV Made Easy: The Clinician's Guide to Diagnosis, New York: The Guilford Press, 1995.
252. W. H. Reid, 'Malingering', Journal of Psychiatry Practice 6 (2000): 226-228.
253. R. Rogers (ed.) Clinical Assessment of Malingering and Deception, 2nd edition, New York: Guilford Publications, 1997.
254. J. Morrison, DSM-IV Made Easy: The Clinician's Guide to Diagnosis, New York: The Guilford Press, 1995, p. 539.
255. E. Early, 'Imagined, Exaggerated and Malingered Post-Traumatic Stress Disorder', in C. Meek (ed.) Post-Traumatic Stress Disorder: Assessment, Differential Diagnosis and Forensic Evaluation, Sarasota, Florida: Professional Resource Exchange, 1990, 137-156.
256. J. Guriel and W. Fremouw, 'Assessing Malingered Posttraumatic Stress Disorder: A Critical Review', Clinical Psychology Review 23 (2003): 881-904.

Martyr

Today, it is expression most commonly used to describe someone who has been killed for his or her religious belief.

Some researchers have examined cases of martyrs in order to identify the basic issues of whether martyrdom can be viewed as altruistic suicide. They have identified several important issues: whom does the act have to benefit, does the act have to have its intended consequences or is the intent sufficient, does the martyr have to be thinking rationally, and whether execution by the State can be viewed as altruistic suicide.[257]

Other trends in research have focused on a historical comparison of ancient Greek and later Christian Greek Orthodox societies, noting that many people seemed to prefer death rather than apostasy.[258] The Greek Orthodox neo-martyrs were motivated by categories of martyrdom, having been accused of being political offenders or traitors or charged with being agitators since they advocated a better treatment for Christians. Such research insists that martyrdom cannot be explained in personality structures and psychological terms, but only in relation to Christian Orthodox faith, culture, history, and so on. Moreover, altruistic martyrdom by the neo-martyrs of the Christian Greek Orthodox Church is not defined as suicide.

When examining specific Islamic and psychological aspects of martyrdom (Istish'had) in the light of one example, several specialists in Islamic law (Shari'a), consider that martyrdom is legitimate and does not count as suicide of any kind.[259] (T.J.)

Masochism/sadism

Sexual Masochism and Sexual Sadism have a great deal in common besides the experience of pain during the sex act. Both conditions begin in childhood; both are usually chronic. Their methods include bondage, blindfolding, spanking, cutting, and humiliation (by defecation, urination, or forcing the submissive partner to imitate an animal). As time goes on, patients in both of these groups often need to increase the severity of the torture to produce the same degree of sexual satisfaction. In this sense, their behavior resembles an addiction (this part could be introduction for both masochism and sadism).[260]

Masochism was named after Hungarian writer Masochu.[261] It refers to an individual being fixated on the earliest phase in psychosexual development, and remaining at that level. It originates from early witnessing of the parent's intercourse (the primal scene). By choking, pricking, or shocking, some masochists in ict pain upon themselves. Perhaps 30% of them also participate in sadistic behavior at times. Although masochists derive sexual gratification from feeling pain or degradation, they do not necessarily surrender control. Many sadomasochistic relationships are carefully planned; often the partners agree upon a secret word by which the masochist can indicate that it really is the time to stop. (T.J.) See also: sadism, paraphilia, snuff movies

---

257. David Lester, 'Altruistic Suicide: A Look At Some Issues', Archives of Suicide Research 8.1 (2004): 37-42.

258. D. J. Constantelos, 'Altruistic Suicide or Altruistic Martyrdom? Christian Greek Orthodox Neo-Martyrs: A Case Study', Archives of Suicide Research 8.1 (2004): 57-71.

259. A. M. Abdel-Khalek, 'Neither Altruistic Suicide, nor Terrorism but Martyrdom: A Muslim Perspective', Archives of Suicide Research 8.1 (2004): 99-113.

260. J. Morrison, DSM-IV Made Easy: The Clinician's Guide to Diagnosis, New York: The Guilford Press, 1995, p. 374.

261. J. Laplanche and J. B. Pontalis, Rje nik psihoanalize, Naprijed, 1992.

Memorial
Memorial is an object which serves as a memory of something, usually a person (who has died) or an event. Popular forms of memorials include landmark objects such as statues or fountains (and even entire parks). The most common type of memorial is the gravestone. Also common are war memorials commemorating those who have died in wars. Memorials in the form of a cross are called intending crosses. Moroever, according to Wikipedia, "Internet Memorials and Tributes are becoming increasingly popular. Online tributes and memorials create a way for family and friends from various countries to interact and share memories and photographs. This is becoming more and more popular as it provides a private space that can be easily reected upon at any time".[262]

Mourning / bereavement
Bereavement, grief and mourning are terms that apply to the psychological reactions of those who survive a significant loss. The term grief is used to describe the subjective feeling that is precipitated by the death of a loved one. It is a synonym with the term mourning, although, mourning is the process of resolving the grief. It is expression for post-bereavement behavior. Bereavement literally means 'the state of being deprived of someone by death' and refers 'to being in the state of mourning'. The term grief comprises a wide range of emotions connected with cultural norms of a specific society as well as with the circumstances of the loss. "Grief work" is a "complex psychological process of withdrawing attachment and working through the pain of bereavement".[263] (T.J.) See also: grief, commemoration, anniversary reaction

Necrophilia
Obsession with obtaining sexual gratification from cadavers. Most persons with this disorder find corpses in morgues, but some have been known to rob graves or even to murder to satisfy their sexual urges. In the few cases studied, those with necrophilia believed that they were in icting the greatest conceivable humiliation on their lifeless victims.[264]
Necrophilia is a sexual deviation in which person has the sexual intercourse with dead bodies. It is manifested through oral activity, while body represents surrogate for mother or other lost object, in order to revive the moment of cognition about the death of beloved person. It is especially elaborated by Fromm which divides it into sexual and nonsexual. This deviation is often sublimated in the everyday situations – kissing and watching of death people, interest for everything rotten, converting everything living into non-living. It is also often manifested in dreams and conversations about accidents, death, crimes funerals.[265]
Kulenovic cites Joanne Bourke from her book An Intimate History of Killing where she explains how violence, destruction, and aggression with all its underlying basic traumas break out in war. War protagonists that were killing frequently enjoyed it. It was a truthful pleasure for them, so

262.
263. M. Viederman, 'Grief: Normal and Pathological Variants', American Journal of Psychiatry 152.1 (1995): 1-4.
264. H. Kaplan and Benjamin Sadock, Kaplan & Sadock's Synopsis of Psychiatry, Ninth Edition, Philadelphia: Lippincott Williams & Wilkins, 2003.
265. M. Kulenovi , Metapsihologija, nastranosti, osobitosti, Zagreb: Naprijed, 1986.

for all of them, killing among other things, also represented a sexual pleasure (the author cites letters, diaries and war reports from World War I and II, and from the Vietnam war).[266] (T.J.) Non-sexual necrophilia – the desire to touch a dead body, to be near it, to stare at it, and wish to mangle it. This is additionally related to the term and representation of necrophilic nonverbal comunication. Such necrophilic individuals enjoy when others see their crime perpetrated continuously in the same way. The typical example is Jack the Ripper.[267]

Intellectuals in war – it is generally the case that individuals with more education, with graduate degrees and other life achievements are involved in atrocities with sort of special seriousness that makes them feel content, satisfied and important. The most appropriate example is the perpetrator Radovan Karad i. In several examples, actors of horrible atrocities are individuals that are 'elite and graduated', while in some other examples individuals identify themselves with the group. Soldiers involved in war activities mostly originate from 'lower' and less educated milieu, specifically from rural and suburban environment, with low education, but mostly with moral preservation and with pragmatic orientation towards everyday life. Usually they did what was necessary to be alive and to survive, without perverse deviations from reality requests. Contact with war and its horror meant interruption with moral codes and standards of human relations and behavior.[268] (T.J.) See also: necrophobia or thanatophobia

Necrophobia

Necrophobia or Thanatophobia is a form of phobia. It is an extreme, exaggerated, specific, structured and irrational fear of death. It appears in childhood and continues to grow over the years, and in the old age it is accompanied with nosophobia and other mental disorders.[269]

Thanatophobia is derived from Thanatos (: 'death'), the personification of death. The usage differs, although in common speech the terms are used interchangeably. Thanatophobia is more specifically, but not limited to the fear of one's own death or dying.

Originally thanatophobia was strictly related to fear of being buried alive. Following early excavations of coffins and mausoleums bearing horrific scratch marks in icted by trapped victims, a new law was introduced in ancient Greece ordering all burials be delayed at least one hour, to assure that the 'deceased' were, in fact, dead. This gave way to the Greek term 'thanatophobia' for fear of a similar fate as these early victims.[270]

This phobia is rarely talked about. Most people think they are alone if they suffer from this problem. In reality this phobia poses little or no actual threat or danger.[271]

Death anxiety and more severe forms of thanatophobia are encountered frequently in the clinical population. However, approaches that allow behavioral solutions to these experiences are conspicuously absent in the literature. From an operant perspective, death anxiety arises from

---

266. M. Kulenovi , 'Necrophilia and Generals', Polemos: Journal of Interdisciplinary Research on War and Peace 2.03/04 (1999): 73-94.
267. Kulenovi , 'Necrophilia and Generals'.
268. Kulenovi , 'Necrophilia and Generals'
269. M. Novakovi , Danijela Tiosavljevi -Mari and Milan Gaji , 'Thanatophobia in the Patients on Dialysis', Vojnosanitetski pregled: Military-Medical and Pharmaceutical Review 63.4 (2006): 397-402.
270. See: http://en.wikipedia.org/wiki/Necrophobia
271. See: http://library.thinkquest.org/05aug/00415/thanatophobia.htm

repeated exposures to direct and implicit forms of the statement "I will die".[272]
Many necrophobics have trouble sleeping and often experience the urge to run out of their
beds at the slightest thought of death. Because of their fear, necrophobics tend to avoid situations where they may come into contact with the stimuli (funerals, hospitals, daily newspaper,
churchs).[273]
In psychotherapy is necessary to confront one's own mortality in order to grow or really be able
to live well.[274] (T.P.) See also: necrophilia, sacrifice

Paraphilias

Paraphilia (sexual deviations) means "abnormal or unnatural attraction". According to the definition (ICD-10), the sexual relationships of such people differ from normal with regard to their preferred sexual objects or in the ways they relate to those objects.[275] Their sexual activities revolve
around the themes of 1) objects or nonhuman animals; 2) humiliation or suffering of the patient
or partner; or 3) nonconsenting persons, including children. Mere desires or fantasies about
these sexual activities can upset some patients sufficiently to warrant a diagnosis, but far more
commonly patients act upon their desires. Paraphilic behavior may be present much of the time
or occasionally (e.g. when under the stress). Most fantasise sexual contact with their victims.[276]
(T.J.) See also: fetishism, voyeurism, necrophilia, sadis, masochism, exhibitionism

Passive Aggression

By definition, passive aggression is the expression of aggression to other persons but indirectly
in a form of passivity, masochism, or turning the aggression against the self. Some manifestations of such behavior are failure, procrastination, provocative behavior, self-demeaning clown-
ing, self-destructive acts, and illness that affect others more than the person themselves. Such
persons are inefficient, and often find excuses for delays. They are not direct about their needs
and wishes. In interpersonal relationships, they tend to put themselves in a position of dependence, but their behavior is experienced as punitive and manipulative.[277] Passive-aggression is a
defense mechanism that is mostly unconscious. The best way therapeudic treatment of passive-
aggressive behavior is to help the client to express the anger. (T.J.) See also masochism

Post-traumatic stress disorder

Post-traumatic stress disorder (PTSD) is one of the anxiety disorders that occur after a person
sees, is involved in, or hears an extreme traumatic stressor.[278]

272. M. A. Persimger, 'Death Anxiety as a Semantic Conditioned Suppression Paradigm', Perceptual and
     Motor Skills 60.3 (1985): 827-830.
273. Photiias and Photia Definitions: Necrophobia:: http://www.phobiaq.com/phobia/necrophobia209.html.
274. E. Kubler Ross, On Death and Dying, New York: Skribner, 1997.
275. World Health Organization, The ICD-10 Classification of Mental and Behavioural Disorders: Clinical
     Descriptions and Diagnostic Guidelines, Geneva: WHO, 1992.
276. J. Morrison, DSM-IV Made Easy: The Clinician's Guide to Diagnosis, New York: The Guilford Press,
     1995.
277. H. Kaplan and B. Sadock, Kaplan & Sadock's Synopsis of Psychiatry, Ninth Edition, Philadelphia: Lip-
     pincott Williams & Wilkins, 2003.
278. M. Maes, J. Myllee, L. Delmeireb and A. Jancaf, 'Pre and Post-disaster Negative Life Events in Relation
     to the Incidence and Severity of Post-traumatic Stress Disorder', Psychiatry Research 105 (2001): 1-12.

Traumatic experiences involve the potential for death or serious injury resulting in intense fear, helplessness, or horror. Traumatic events include combat or military exposure, sexual or physical abuse/assaults, serious accidents, natural disasters, domestic and family violence, etc.[279] While being exposed to this event, the affected person thinks that his/her life or other's lives are in danger. After exposure to such an event, the person may feel scared, confused, or angry.[280] If these reactions continue or get worse, PTSD can develop. Sometimes these reactions are delayed for a certain period of time. Most trauma survivors experience common stress reactions, but some of these reactions may last.

To make the diagnosis, the symptoms must last for more than a month after the event and must significantly affect important areas of life, such as family and work.[281]

History of PTSD

Reactions to traumatic events have been recognised for centuries. Descriptions of these reactions have changed over time. The diagnosis of PTSD was formally recognised as a psychiatric diagnosis in 1980.[282] Similar symptoms found in war veterans were described earlier as a 'cardiac neurosis', 'shell shock' or 'concentration camp syndrome' (7-9). In uence of personality traits is very important as a predictive factor for development of PTSD.[283]

Social awareness of the disorder, taking into account human rights, violence and disasters, has been increasing over the last 20 years.

Epidemiology of PTSD

The prevalence of the disorder differs depending on the population that is being investigated, as well as the use of various diagnostic criteria and scales. The lifetime prevalence of PTSD is estimated to be about 8 percent of the general population, although an additional 5 to 15 percent may experience subclinical forms of the disorder. Among high-risk groups whose members experienced traumatic events, the lifetime prevalence range from 5 to 75 percent.[284] In almost 80% of cases, PTSD occurs together with depressive disorder, anxiety, panic attacks, alcohol and

279. D. Kozaric–Kovacic and N. Pivac, 'Novel Approaches to the Treatment of Posttraumatic Stress Syndrome', in S Begeç (ed.) The Integration and Management of Traumatized People After Terrorist Attacks, Amsterdam: IOS Press, 2007, 13-40.
280. J. Morrison, DSM-IV Made Easy: The Clinician's Guide to Diagnosis, New York: The Guilford Press, 1995.
281. H. Kaplan and B. Sadock, Kaplan & Sadock's Synopsis of Psychiatry, Ninth Edition, Philadelphia: Lippincott Williams & Wilkins, 2003.
282. American Psychiatric Association, Diagnostic and Statistical Manual of Mental Disorders, 3rd edition, Washington, DC: American Association Press, 1980
283. American Psychiatric Association, Diagnostic and Statistical Manual of Mental Disorders, 1st edition, Washington, DC: American Association Press, 1952. See also: American Psychiatric Association, Diagnostic and Statistical Manual of Mental Disorders, 2nd edition, Washington, DC: American Association Press, 1968.
284. H. Kaplan and B. Sadock, Kaplan & Sadock's Synopsis of Psychiatry, Ninth Edition, Philadelphia: Lippincott Williams & Wilkins, 2003.

substance abuse, and personality disorders.[285]

Risk Factors for Development of PTSD

Most people exposed to traumatic events have some symptoms at the beginning, but not every-one will develop PTSD. The stressor alone is not sufficient to cause the disorder.[286] It is not yet clear why some people develop PTSD and others don't. Some people can develop acute stress reaction (ASR). Symptoms of acute stress reaction include: re-experiencing of the traumatic event, avoidance and hypersensitivity of autonomic nerve system (e.g. tachycardia, headache, diarrhea, sweating, etc.), as well as dissociative experiences soon after the traumatic event.[287] Dissociative defenses help persons remove themselves from trauma at the time that it occurs but also delay the working through needed to place the trauma in perspective within their lives.[288] This can sometimes lead to the development of PTSD.[289] There are also some people who will develop PTSD without previous ASR.

The main risk factors for developing PTSD are pre-traumatic factors (such as earlier psychiat-ric disorders, gender, personality traits, lower socioeconomic status, lower degree of education, ethnic minorities, previous trauma, and family history of psychiatric disorders); factors important during the traumatic event include severity of trauma, life-threating experiences, emotions con-nected with trauma, dissociation during and after the traumatic event, and post-traumatic factors include lack of social support and subsequent life stressors.[290]

Symptomatology of PTSD

In acute PTSD, the person develops symptoms within three months of the traumatic event. Symp-toms of chronic PTSD appear three months or later after the traumatic event. Delayed PTSD

---

285. N. Long, C. MacDonald and K. Chamberlain, 'Prevalence of Post-traumatic Stress Disorder, Depres-sion and Anxiety in Community Sample of New Zealand Vietnam War Veterans', Australian and New Zealand Journal of Psychiatry 30 (1996): 253-256; Dragica Kozari -Kova i , T. Ljubin and M. Grappe, 'Comorbidity of Posttraumatic Stress Disorder and Alcohol Dependence in Displaced Persons', Croatian Medical Journal 41 (2000): 173-178; A. Bleich, M. Koslowsky, A. Dolev and B. Lerer, 'Post-traumatic Stress Disorder and Depression: An Analysis of Comorbidity', The British Journal of Psychiatry 170 (1997): 479-482; D. Kozari -Kova i , D. K. Hercigonja and M. Grubiši -lli , 'Post-traumatic Stress Disorder and Depression in Soldiers with Combat Experiences', Croatian Medical Journal, 42 (2001): 165-170; D. Kozari -Kova i and D. Kocijan-Hercigonja, 'Assessment of Posttraumatic Disorder and Comorbidity' Military Medicine 160 (2001): 677-680; D. Kozari -Kova i and A. Borove ki., 'Prevalence of Psychotic Comorbidity in Combat-Related Posttraumatic Stress Disorder', Military Medicine 170 (2005): 223-226.
286. H. Kaplan and B. Sadock, Kaplan & Sadock's Synopsis of Psychiatry, Ninth Edition, Philadelphia: Lip-pincott Williams & Wilkins, 2003.
287. D. Kozari -Kova i and D. Kocijan-Hercigonja, 'Assessment of Post-traumatic Disorder and Comorbidity' Military Medicine 160 (2001): 677-680.
288. H. Kaplan and B. Sadock, Kaplan & Sadock's Synopsis of Psychiatry, Ninth Edition, Philadelphia: Lip-pincott Williams & Wilkins, 2003.
289. D. Kozari -Kova i and A. Borove ki, 'Prevalence of Psychotic Comorbidity in Combat-Related Post-Traumatic Stress Disorder', Military Medicine (170) 2005: 223-226
290. American Psychiatric Association, Diagnostic and Statistical Manual of Mental Disorders, 4th edition, Washington, DC: American Association Press, 1994; R. Yehuda and M. C. Wong, 'Pathogenesis of Post-traumatic Stress Disorder and Acute Stress Disorder' in D. J. Stein and E. Hollander (eds) Textbook of Anxiety Disorders, Washington, DC: American Psychiatric Publishing, 2002, 374-85.

occurs six months after the traumatic event (this form is very rare).

PTSD includes three main clusters of symptoms: 1. re-experiencing of the trauma; 2. persistent avoidance of stimuli associated with the trauma and numbing of general responses, and 3. persistent symptoms of increased arousal.[291]

Re-experiencing of the trauma (reliving the event) includes actual and intrusive disturbing memories, actual disturbing dreams, behaviour or emotions as if the traumatic event is being re-experienced, intensive psychological distress, and physiological reactivity.[292]

Persistent avoidance and numbing includes efforts to avoid thoughts, emotions, and conversation about situations that remind the person of an event, avoidance of trauma reminders, psychogenic amnesia (inability to recall an important aspect of the trauma), reduced interest in activities, feeling of detachment or estrangement from others, a restricted range of affect (e.g. unable to have loving feelings), and a sense of foreshortened future.[293]

Symptoms of hyperarousal include difficulty falling or staying asleep, irritability or outbursts of anger, difficulty concentrating, hypervigilance, and exaggerated startle response.[294]

Intrusive thoughts should be differentiated from ashbacks. With intrusive thoughts, the traumatic event is re-experienced in repeated thoughts (memories), in such a way that the person repeatedly experiences the traumatic event by remembering it through thoughts or images. The person does not have control over such symptoms as they appear at different intervals of time, and they are spontaneous. This can happen when some extrinsic stimulus (image, sound or scent) reminds the person of the traumatic event. Nightmares related to the traumatic event can also occur.[295]

Flashbacks occur when the traumatic event is re-experienced as an illusion, hallucination, and dissociative (' ashback') episode. The content of the ' ashback' is specifically related to trauma. It is transitory, occurs spontaneously, and it can be provoked by an extrinsic stimulus.[296]

When a person experiences ashbacks, they cannot differentiate the past from present events, and they relive the traumatic event. The person also experiences psychological disturbance usually manifested as fear, anger, and anxiety. When experiencing intrusive thoughts, the person is aware that it is a memory, although it is initiated as an unconscious process.[297]

The person with PTSD avoids all activities, stimuli, and situations that can be a reminder of the event, because they are afraid that it could provoke feelings of disturbance. Alcohol or substance abuse is often excessive in such people because they are used to block or 'blur' memories that

---

291. D. Kozari -Kova i and D. Kocijan-Hercigonja, 'Assessment of Posttraumatic Disorder and Comorbidity' Military Medicine 160 (2001): 677-680.

292. American Psychiatric Association, Diagnostic and Statistical Manual of Mental Disorders, 2nd edition, Washington, DC: American Association Press, 1968.

293. N. Long, C. MacDonald and K. Chamberlain, 'Prevalence of Post-traumatic Stress Disorder, Depression and Anxiety in Community Sample of New Zealand Vietnam War Veterans', Australian and New Zealand Journal of Psychiatry 30 (1996): 253-256.

294. American Psychiatric Association, Diagnostic and Statistical Manual of Mental Disorders, 2nd edition, Washington, DC: American Association Press, 1968.

295. H. Kaplan and B. Sadock, Kaplan & Sadock's Synopsis of Psychiatry, Ninth Edition, Philadelphia: Lippincott Williams & Wilkins, 2003.

296. Kaplan and Sadock, Kaplan & Sadock's Synopsis of Psychiatry.

297. R. Yehuda and M. C. Wong, 'Pathogenesis of Post-traumatic Stress Disorder and Acute Stress Disorder' in D. J. Stein and E. Hollander (eds) Textbook of Anxiety Disorders, Washington, DC: American Psychiatric Publishing, 2002, 374-85.

are reminders of the traumatic event. Some people have excessive activities, while others have extremely reduced interest in activities that used to be of a great importance to them. They feel detached from other people, think they are unable to experience love and joy, or feel that they are numb. They feel hopeless about the future, despairing, as if their life is over and that they have nothing to expect from life.[298]

Constant hyperarousal is manifested through difficulties with sleep (trouble with falling asleep or staying asleep). Sufferers often have fear of losing control over expressing anger or hostility, or they sometimes lose their control. They have difficulties with concentration and they are hyper-vigilant. It is very hard for them to adjust into society.[299]

Treatment of PTSD

The current methods for PTSD treatment include medications, psychotherapy and psychosocial treatment.[300]

Psychotherapy is preferred over medication, especially when symptoms are mild and when the disorder is presented as so-called 'uncomplicated PTSD' without without another simultaneous psychiatric disorder (comorbid disorders). In cases of moderate and heavy PTSD with comorbid disorders and post-traumatic personality disorders, psychopharmacology, psychotherapy and psychosocial treatment should be combined.

Prevention of PTSD

Although development of PTSD depends on various factors, correct and timely psychoeducation plays an important role after exposure to a traumatic event.[301] In that way, the psychotraumatised person has a higher level of knowledge about this disorder, its symptoms and behaviour patterns. The person should be encouraged to talk to family and friends about the experienced trauma, and it should be explained how important it is to share emotions with the people they trust. (T.J.) See also: traumatic event, stress, suicide and ptsd, witnessing and PTSD

Power projective identification

In power projective identification, there is the desire of being dominant and to control others by making 'the other' feel insufficient. Messages are like this: "do exactly what I say!", "obey me!" and "you cannot live without me!" are transferred to 'the other' as covert communication. There is the belief that 'the other' cannot do anything unless he/she behaves like the projector. Sexual discrimination may serve to supporting this projective identification. We encounter power projective identification in corporations as the dominant relationship type. The parents of individuals that use this projective identification, make the child feel that the parent cannot even give care, and actually it is the parent that needs to be cared for. Such cases are usually encountered in parents

298. American Psychiatric Association, Diagnostic and Statistical Manual of Mental Disorders, 2nd edition, Washington, DC: American Association Press, 1968.

299. American Psychiatric Association, Diagnostic and Statistical Manual of Mental Disorders, 2nd edition.

300. D. Kozari −Kova i and N. Pivac, 'Novel Approaches to the Treatment of Posttraumatic Stress Syndrome', in Suat Begeç (ed.) The Integration and Management of Traumatized People After Terrorist Attacks, Amsterdam: IOS Press, 2007, 13-40.

301. American Psychiatric Association, Diagnostic and Statistical Manual of Mental Disorders, 4th edition, Washington, DC: American Association Press, 1994.

who are physically or mentally handicapped, or who have chronic or malign diseases, or who are alcoholic. Children who have such parents see themselves as unwanted children and they are continuously in fear of being abandoned. A precocious type of child is encountered frequently with such parents. A child's personality is obliged to transform into an adult image. This projective identification can be obtained imaginatively. The infant who is afraid of being abandoned by his mother thinks, in his imagination, that he controls its mother's behaviors and with the help of dreams he/she lives as though he/she controls his mother. This, in turn, similarly leads to comprehension of projective identification. Dependence projective identification is frequent in females, while power projective identification is frequent in males.[302] (T.P.) See also: dependence projective identification, ingratiation projective identifications, sexuality projective identification, projective identification

Projective identification

The concept of 'projective identification' has grabbed the attention of many clinicians and theoreticians since its first description and various comments have been made about it. Projective identification is considered in three distinct ways within the 'Object Relations' approach.[303]

The first viewpoint regards projective identification as a defense mechanism observed in severe psychopathologies like 'borderline personality disorder'. Other pathologies that are seen in 'borderline' personality organisations, which were established by Kernberg, can be included in this group.[304] The second viewpoint defines projective identification as a mechanism, which arises in the transference and counter-transference transactions between the therapist and the patient during the psychoanalytic process. The third view claims that projective identification can be anything in human relations that a person has in his/her relationship with any other (person, association, group, or nation).[305]

Cashdan inserted the term projective identification into the communication concept by taking Ogden's model into account, and developing his own object relations therapy approach, which is based on the projective identification concept.[306]

According to Cashdan, the determinative factor which exist in projective identification is the induction of others to act in accordance with what is projected. A person inserts his/her own parts into 'the other', regarding the sensations and structures of his/her own psychological system, which are formed by experiences. The receiver of the projections is forced to accept and act in accordance with these parts.[307]

Cashdan described 4 basic types of projective identification, which come from pathological object relations in the early periods of life. These are dependence, power, sexuality, and ingratiation

---

302. S. Cashdan, Object Relations Therapy: Using the Relationship, New York: W. W. Norton & Company, 1988, 53-78; E. Göka, F. V. Yüksel and F. Göral, 'Projective Identification In Human Relations', Turkish Journal Of Psychiatry, 17.1 (2006): 1-9.

303. Göka, Yüksel and Göral, 'Projective Identification In Human Relations'.

304. O. Kernberg, 'Projection And Projective Identification: Developmental And Clinical Aspects', Journal of the American Psychonalaysis Association, (35)1987: 795-819.

305. E. Göka, F. V. Yüksel and F. Göral, 'Projective Identification In Human Relations', Turkish Journal Of Psychiatry, 17.1 (2006): 1-9.

306. Göka, Yüksel and Göral, 'Projective Identification In Human Relations'; Sheldon Cashdan, Object Relations Therapy: Using the Relationship, New York: W. W. Norton & Company, 1988, 53-78.

307. Cashdan, Object Relations Therapy.

projective identifications.[308]
There can be malign and destructive forms of projective identification that underlie many psychopathologies as well as benign forms that arise as a communication that is a necessity in human relationships.[309] The material, which is discarded during the projective identification process, may contain positive and negative aspects of the self. If the process of projective identification is followed by reality testing, this process can help the person to understand him/herself and 'the other'. To evaluate or reverse projective identifications is difficult when they are strong and demanding.[310]
Better understanding of the importance of projective identification in socialisation, in being human, in the processes of ego development, and in forms of having relationships that will contribute to the understanding of the nature of psychopathologies, the psychotherapeutic relationship, and psychotherapy, as well as the nature of many problems in normal human relations.[311] (T.P.)
See also: dependence projective identification, power projective identification, ingratiation projective identifications, sexuality projective identification

Reexperiencing
Sadock: "The principal clinical features of PTSD are painful reexperiencing the event, a pattern of avoidance and emotional numbing, and fairly constant hyperarousal".[312]
According to DSM-IV criteria, reexperiencing means that the traumatic event is persistently reexperienced in the following ways: 1) recurrent and intrusive distressing recollections of the event, including images, thoughts or perceptions; 2) recurrent distressing dreams of the event; 3) acting or feeling as if the traumatic event were recurring (this includes sense of reliving experience, hallucinations, and dissociative ashback episodes); 4) intense psychological distress at exposure to internal or external cues that symbolise or resemble an aspect of the traumatic event; 5) physiological reactivity on exposure to internal or external cues that symbolise or resemble an aspect of the traumatic event.[313] (T.J.) See also – PTSD, dissociation, asback, avoidance, hyperarousal

Regression
Attempt of a person to return to an earlier libidinal phase of functioning. Tendency is to avoid the tension and con ict evoked at the present level of development. It re ects the basic tendency to gain instinctual gratification at a less-developed period. It could be a normal phenomenon, since certain amount of regression is essential for relaxation, sleep, and orgasm in sexual intercourse. Regression is also an essential for creative process.[314] (T.J.)

---

308. Göka, Yüksel and Göral, 'Projective Identification In Human Relations'.
309. R. M. Young, 'Benign and Virulent Projective Identification in Groups and Institutions', European Conference of the Rowantree Foundation, 1992: http://human-nature.com/rmyoung/papers/paper3h.html
310. E. Göka, F. V. Yüksel and F. Göral, 'Projective Identification In Human Relations', Turkish Journal Of Psychiatry, 17.1 (2006): 1-9.
311. Göka, Yüksel and Göral, 'Projective Identification In Human Relations'.
312. H. Kaplan and B. Sadock, Kaplan & Sadock's Synopsis of Psychiatry, Ninth Edition, Philadelphia: Lippincott Williams & Wilkins, 2003.
313. American Psychiatric Association, Diagnostic and Statistical Manual of Mental Disorders, revised edition, Washington, DC: American Association Press, 1999.
314. H. Kaplan and B. Sadock, Kaplan & Sadock's Synopsis of Psychiatry, Ninth Edition, Philadelphia: Lippincott Williams & Wilkins, 2003.

Repression / Repressed

In repression, a person is expelling or withholding an idea or feeling from the consciousness. Primary repression is when ideas and feelings are restrained before they have reached consciousness. In secondary repression, what was once experienced at a conscious level is excluded from awareness. The repressed material is not forgotten, and it may be present in symbolic behavior. This defense mechanism differs from suppression since it effects conscious inhibition of impulses to the point of losing and not just postponing wished goals. In repression, conscious perception of instincts and feelings are blocked.[315] (T.J.) See also Flashback and re-experiencing

Revenge

Lane discusses that from developmental perspective, desires for revenge may have important adaptive functions in order to help the patient contain anxieties associated with developmental tasks that have not been mastered.[316]

Bishop and Lane explain how excessive entitlement can accompany a range of other problems in patients.[317] Roots of such problems can usually be found in emotional deprivation in childhood, especially when the child was narcissistic extension of the parents. This 'special' role becomes a learned attitude and behavior, but also a refuge and defense against the hurt, shame, and fear. Anger and vindictiveness provoked by this deprivation can have dangerous, murderous proportions, even with defensive entitlement that demands revenge

Bottom of Form

Possible connection of PTSD and revenge is a special issue. It is often thought that individuals with PTSD have strong feelings of revenge. Some investigations have shown that PTSD symptoms are associated with less openness to reconcilliation and more feelings of revenge.[318] Orth et al. investigated the relation between feelings of revenge and post-traumatic stress reactions.[319] Feelings of revenge were correlated with re-experiencing and hyperarousal, but not with avoidance. The retaliation motive implied in feelings of revenge was not shown to be significant for the relation between feelings of revenge and PTSD. But the relation has been moderated since victimisation. Therefore, feelings of revenge were presumably regarded as a maladaptive coping reaction to experienced injustice, but not in the first period after victimisation. (T.J.) See also – avoidance, hyperarousal, reexperiencing, PTSD, victim, forgiveness

Ritual and mourning

From the perspective of anthropologic and psychological phenomena, rituals have certain im-

---

315. Kaplan and Sadock, Kaplan & Sadock's Synopsis of Psychiatry.
316. R. Lane, 'The Revenge Motive: A Developmental Perspective on the Life Cycle and the Treatment Process', Psychoanalytic Review, 82.1 (1995): 41-64.
317. J. Bishop and R. C. Lane, 'The Dynamics and Dangers of Entitlement', Psychoanalytic Psychology 19 (2002): 739-58.
318. C. P. Bayer, F. Klasen and H. Adam, 'Association of Trauma and PTSD Symptoms with Openness to Reconciliation and Feelings of Revenge Among Former Ugandan and Congolese Child Soldiers', Journal of the American Medical Association 298.5 (2007): 555-559.
319. U. Orth, L. Montada and A. Maercker, 'Feelings of Revenge, Retaliation Motive and Posttraumatic Stress Reactions in Crime Victims', Journal of Interpersonal Violence 21.2 (2006): 229-243.

portance in processes of grief and mourning. George et al. describes that most headhunting traditions in the islands of Southeast Asia connect ritual violence to grief and mourning.[320] Some notions were made regarding rage and catharsis, debating intense emotions motivates individuals to take up cleansing acts of violence. Other research has been conducted in order to provide a more complex understanding of how ritual may be linked with processes of bereavement and violence. Ritualistic practices point out that the resolution of communal mourning is more significant than personal catharsis as a motivation for violence. Also that individual affect is remodelled collectively as 'political affect' and that different forms (vows, songs, noise, etc.) mediate the ways in which people resolve the grief.

Other findings indicate that individuals from different cultural backgrounds have a 'knowledge of grief' that was derived from their personal experiences almost in the same way as did the authors of the professional literature.[321] The findings also showed that cultural differences are perceived in mourning rituals, traditions and behavioural expressions of grief, without any specific differences in the individual, intrapersonal experiences of grief that can be linked with cultural heritage or ethnicity.

Lobar et al. described practices surrounding deceased ones by European, Asian, Caribbean, Central American, and South American families living in the United States.[322] A common theme of this research was that families of deceased individuals perform rituals and ceremonies in order to foster passage to God, the 'light', or another life. If their beliefs were stronger, they were more dedicated in performing such rituals and ceremonies according to their religion or culture.[323] (T.J.)
See also: grief, mourning, anniversary reactions

Sacrifice

It is erroneously believed that ritual murders are always motivated by religious belief. This may be true only some of the time. The key element which distinguished ritual sacrifice from signature/ritual murder is a religion. In the first instance, victims have to be killed as part of a religious ceremony.

According to the data from the Occult and Violent Ritual Crime Research Center there is some evidence that ancient religious rites in modern day terrorism were performances involving the murder of living beings.[324] The later domestication of sacrifice in evolved forms of religious practice, such as the Christian ritual of the Eucharist, masked the fact that most early forms of sacrifice involved a real animal or in some cases a human. They also mention the Book of Leviticus, which provides a detailed guide for preparing animals for sacrificial slaughter, and the Vedic Agnicayana ritual which is 3,000 years old (probably the most ancient ritual still performed today) involving the construction of an elaborate alter for sacrificial ritual. Some claim the ritual was

---

320. K. M. George, 'Violence, Solace, and Ritual: a Case Study from Island Southeast Asia', Culture, Medicine and Psychiatry 19.2 (1995): 225-60.
321. K. V. Cowles, 'Cultural Perspectives of Grief: An Expanded Concept Analysis', Journal of Advanced Nursing 23.2 (1996): 287-94.
322. S. L. Lobar, J. M. Youngblut and D. Brooten, 'Cross-Cultural Beliefs, Ceremonies, and Rituals Surrounding Death of a Loved One', Pediatric Nursing 32.1 (2006): 44-50.
323. M. B. Riddell, Ritual Abuse, Los Angeles: Ritual Abuse Task Force, Los Angeles County Commission for Women, 1989.
324. See: Occult and Violent Ritual Crima Research Centre: http://www.signatureprofilingassociates.com/ritualmurder.htm

originally based around a human sacrifice.

Historically, theologians proposed four different purposes of sacrifice: homage or praise in a form of pure adoration; thanksgiving for a favor granted; supplication or asking for anything from material goods to divine intervention; and expiating placating or requesting forgiveness or the removal or prevention of evil and misfortune.

Ritual or multimurders are a form of human sacrifice practised by some African tribes. The murder is carried out after body parts are removed while the victim is still alive.[325]

There are two forms of human sacrifice: blood sacrifice and burning sacrifice.

Blood Sacrifice is according to some Satanists usually reserved for those whose souls will be relinquished to Lucifer.[326] This soul, which has been martyred, will someday be reincarnated into the wasteland that is Earth and later occupy a revered place in hell. A blood sacrifice occurs in several of the ceremonies of Satanism. The sacrificial victim is usually cut from the upper part of the chest to above the pubic bone. The heart is often removed and mixed with blood, urine and feces to become an anthropophagous mixture. This victim's soul will go directly to Lucifer who will make a determination when it will be reunited with its body in a next life.

Burning sacrifice is considered a killing of vengeance or destruction.[327] This type of human execution is reserved for those who have done something against the coven or church as such they deserve to be killed. A victim burned to death can never be reincarnated, a vital concern to the Satanist. Moreover, the soul from the sacrifice goes directly to Lucifer making him stronger with each burned victim and each blood victim. (T.P.)

Sadism

Much of the behavior is complementary to that of of masochists; the difference is that sadists are the perpetrators rather than the recipients. In icting pain or humiliation is sexually stimulating to them; the suffering of others arouses them sexually. They experience fantasies of dominance and restraint. They usually limit themselves to only a few partners; most sadists have a willing partner. Sadists will sometimes use nonconsenting victims, and they may indulge in rape. When they do, it can be brutally different from ordinary rape – sadists will use even more force than is necessary.[328]   (T.J.) See also: masochism/sadism

Self-therapy

Self-therapy, self-help or self-improvement refers to self-guided improvement economically, intellectually, or emotionally – most frequently with a substantial psychological or spiritual basis. The basis for self-help is often self-reliance, publicly available information, or support groups where people with similar problems join together. From early exemplars in self-driven legal practice and home-spun advice, the connotations of the phrase have spread and often apply particularly to education, business, psychological or psychotherapeutic nostrums, purveyed through the popular genre of self-help books and through self-help personal-development movements. Some critics

---

325. H. J. Scholtza, V. M. Philliphs and G. J. Knobela, 'Muti or Ritual Murder', Forensic Science International, 87.2 (1997): 117-123.
326. See: Ritual Murder: http://www.signatureprofilingassociates.com/ritualmurder.htm
327. See: http://www.signatureprofilingassociates.com/ritualmurder.htm
328. J. Morrison, DSM-IV Made Easy: The Clinician's Guide to Diagnosis, New York: The Guilford Press, 1995.

have suggested that self-help books and programs offer 'easy answers' to difficult personal prob-lems. Commentators have criticised self-help books for containing pseudo-scientific assertions that tend to mislead the consumer, and many different authors have criticised self-help authors and claims.

From a therapeutic perspective, self-therapy may have a negative meaning. The term can also be used for patients willing to partake in the self-medication of their disorder.[329] (T.P.) See also self-monitoring

Self-monitoring

Self-monitoring is a technique of learning how to pay attention to problem behaviors or habits and to the stimuli that trigger that behaviour or habits into action. There are two types of self-monitoring techniques: qualitative and quantitative. Qualitative monitoring involves paying atten-tion to the quality of things that are happening and quantitative monitoring involves counting things that are happening.[330]

Self-monitoring works best when someone approaches it in a predominantly quantified way. That means, firstly, deciding what behaviors and habits will be monitored, and after that, figuring out a reasonable way to count or measure the occurrence of each behavior or habit and finally, count-ing the occurrence of each and every behavior using some measurement system.

Individuals need to have a system in place to self-monitor effectively. His/her system should de-scribe what will be monitored (behaviors/habits or triggers), how often and how the observations of monitoring will be recorded. (T.P.) See also: self-therapy, self-help, self-improvements

Self-victimisation

See: Dependence Projective Identification (T.P.)

Sexuality projective identification

The person who uses sexuality projective identification forces 'the other' to provide erotic reac-tions. Messages with sexual content are projected as covert communication. Differing from those that have normal sexual, relationships in which there is sexuality projective identification, sexual function does not arise spontaneously and is not impulsive, and sexuality overshadows all other aspects of the relationship. This means that when sexuality disappears, the relationship ends. Sexuality projective identification is unique in that it depends upon the behaviors being highly valued by the child, rather than the restriction of them and usually arises from a mother-child relationship in which the message of, "you are desired as long as you make me feel excited and stimulate me" is given. The child learns that his communications that are coy and irtatious, or that consist of sexuality are more valuable than the covert messages, which are not actually spelled.[331] (T.P.) See also: dependence projective identification, ingratiation projective identifica-tions, power projective identification, projective identification, sadism, masochism

---

329. J. Kay and A. Tasman, Essentials of Psychiatry, Hoboken, NJ: Wiley, 2006.
330. M. Snyder, 'Self Monitoring of Expressive Behavior', Journal of Personality and Social Psychology 30
    (1974): 526-537, http://ptsd.about.com/od/selfhelp/ht/selfmonitor.htm
331. S. Cashdan, Object Relations Therapy: Using the Relationship, New York: W. W. Norton & Company,
    1988, 53-78; E. Göka, F. V. Yüksel and F. Göral, 'Projective Identification In Human Relations', Turkish
    Journal Of Psychiatry, 17.1 (2006): 1-9.

Somatoform disorders

Somatoform disorder have emotional origins and include the following symptoms: excessive or chronic pain, conversion symptoms, chronic and multiple symptoms without adequate explanation, complaints that do not improve despite the use of treatments that help most patients and excessive concern with health or body appearance.[332] In contrast to malingering and factitious disorder, symptoms in somatoform disorders are not under voluntary control, that is, they are not intentionally produced or feigned.[333] (T.P.) See also: malingering, malingering ptsd, factitious disorder, somatoform disorder

Stockholm syndrome

This term was coined after the failed bank robbery in Stockholm in order to describe the positive emotional bond that a kidnapped victim may develop for their captor.[334] Namnyak et al. reviewed this phenomena in their article. But since, no validated diagnostic criteria have been described. Previous literature about this topic is of limited research value and it is not sufficient to support 'Stockholm syndrome' as a psychiatric diagnosis. Analysis of cases reported in the media reveals four common featured in victims of 'Stockholm syndrome'. It is as follows: each victim experienced direct threats, victims were kept in isolation, they had an opportunity to 'escape' during their period of captivity but failed to use the opportunity, and finally victims showed sympathy with their captors post-captivity. According to this, there is an identifiable pattern of experience and behaviour that may exist amongst victims. Synonyms for 'Stockholm syndrome' are: 'terror bonding' and 'traumatic bonding'.[335] (T.J.) See also: sadomasochism, dependence projective identification, masochism

Stress

The term stress is not a particularly useful term for scientists because it is such a highly subjective phenomenon that it defies definition. The term has been in use from 1936 when Hans Selye defined stress as "the non-specific response of the body to any demand for change". He had noted in numerous experiments that laboratory animals subjected to acute but different noxious physical and emotional stimuli all exhibited the same pathologic changes.[336] Seyle demonstrated that persistent stress could cause development of various diseases in animals similar to diseases in humans (heart attacks, stroke, kidney disease and rheumatoid arthritis). He also believed that most diseases were caused by specific but different pathogens.[337] The situation is actually the

332. J. Kay and Allan Tasman, Essentials of Psychiatry, Hoboken, NJ: Wiley, 2006.
333. J. Morrison, DSM-IV Made Easy: The Clinician's Guide to Diagnosis, New York: The Guilford Press, 1995: 287-310.
334. A. Favaro, D. Degortes, G. Colombo and P. Santonastaso, 'The Effects of Trauma Among Kidnap Victims in Sardinia, Italy', Psychological Medicine 30 (2000): 975-980.
335. D. L. Graham, E. I. Rawlings, K. Ihms, D. Latimer, J. Foliano, A. Thompson, K. Suttman, M. Farrington and R. Hacker, 'A Scale for Identifying 'Stockholm Syndrome' Reactions in Young Dating Women: Factor Structure, Reliability, and Validity', Violence and Victims 10.1 (1995): 3-22.
336. H. Seyle, 'A Syndrome Produced by Diverse Nocuous Agents', Journal of Neuropsychiatry and Clinical Neuroscience 10 (1998): 230-231.
337. R. S. Lazarus, 'From Psychological Stress to the Emotions: a History of Changing Outlooks' Annual Review of Psychology 44 (1993): 1-22.

opposite – many different insults could cause the same disease.

Soon after Selye's theory the term stress became popular but his original definition was completely ignored.

Today, in everyday language, the term 'stress' refers to an overbearing boss at work or some other
unpleasant situation an individual has been subjected to. Some people use the term to describe
their own reactions of some situation, while others use the term stress to refer to what they
perceive as the end result of these repeated responses. After many complains from scientists
regarding this confusion, one physician concluded in 1951 that "stress, in addition to being itself,
was also the cause of itself, and the result of itself".[338] (T.P) See also: coping mechanism, coping
skills, coping strategies, trauma, PTSD

Survivor guilt

Sadock: phenomena that is manifested in those who are relieved that someone else has died,
and not themselves.[339] Persons that survive may believe that they should die, and as a consequence, might have problems with establishing new relationships since they might have the feeling that they should betray the deceased person. Certain ways of denying the death of the lost
one occur during the bereavement period: in an effort to preserve the lost relationship, the person
treasures objects of the deceased or something that is a reminder of them ('linkage objects').
(T.J.) See also – grief, denial

Trauma

To understand what trauma is and how it can affect somebody's life, differences between stress,
crisis, and trauma should be explained. Yeager et al. gives a precise review of these differences.[340] They point out that some individuals find stress helpful in a way that when under stress they
work more efficiently. On the other hand, stress could be a burden in managing different tasks,
with all the physical and emotional consequences. The term crisis, may refer to anyone who is
experiencing something that is not going their way. Trauma reactions are significantly different
since they are precipitated by a random, sudden, and traumatic event (natural disasters, terrorism
and mass murders, violent sexual assaults, etc.)[341]

Individuals respond to stress in a different way. Responses are determined by an individual's
personality and character, temperament, another existing stressors, protective factors and coping
skills, adaptability to change, support system, as well as the intensity and duration of the stressor.
Therefore, what is simple stress for one individual may result in the onset of a crisis episode or
traumatic reaction for another.

Cocoran explaines that psychological trauma is defined by human reactions to traumatic stress,

338. See American Institute of Stress, http://www.stress.org/
339. H. Kaplan and B. Sadock, Kaplan & Sadock's Synopsis of Psychiatry, Ninth Edition, Philadelphia: Lip-
     pincott Williams & Wilkins, 2003.
340. Y. R. Yeager and A. R. Roberts, Differentiating Among Stress, Acute Stress Disorder, Crisis Episodes,
     Trauma, and PTSD: Paradigm and Treatment Goals, Oxford: Oxford University Press, 2003.
341. A. R. Roberts, 'An Overview of Crisis Theory and Crisis Intervention', in A. R. Roberts (ed.) Crisis
     Intervention Handbook: Assessment, Treatment and Research, 2nd edition, New York: Oxford University
     Press, 2000, 3–30; A. R. Roberts, 'Assessment, Crisis Intervention and Trauma Treatment: The integra-
     tive ACT Intervention Model', Brief Treatment and Crisis Intervention 2.1 (2002): 1–21.

violent crimes, infectious disease outbreaks, and other dangerous and life-threatening events.[342] Psychological trauma occurs when the individual's adaptive mechanisms are blocked because of the overexposure to stress hormones. Persistent hyperarousal mechanisms reoccur in continuum and they are amplified by traumatic recollections stored in the brain. The victims are constantly in alternation of their mental states from calm and peaceful ones to states of intense anxiety, agitation, anger, hypervigilance, and extreme arousal.[343]

Psychological trauma can happen soon after witnessing or being the victim of a traumatic event. It usually occurs in an acute stress disorder. Many times individuals have a delayed reaction to a traumatic event. Such delay after several weeks or several months usually surfaces in form of symptoms such as avoidance of familiar surroundings, intense fears, sudden breaking of appointments, social isolation, trance-like states, sleep disturbances and repeated nightmares, depressive episodes, and hyperarousal.[344]

A set of symptoms that develop after a person sees, is involved in, or hears of an extreme traumatic stressor is called 'post-traumatic stress disorder' (PTSD). According to DSM-IV, PTSD is an acute, chronic, delayed, debilitating, and complex mental disorder. It includes altered awareness, detachment, dissociative states, ego fragmentation, personality changes, paranoid ideation, trigger events, and vivid intrusive traumatic recollections.[345] PTSD is often comorbid with major depression, dysthymia, alcohol or substance abuse, and generalised anxiety disorder. The person reacts to this experience with fear and helplessness, sleep disturbances, hyperarousal and hypervigilance, persistently reliving the event through ashbacks and intrusive thoughts, and is unsuccessfully trying to avoid being reminded of it. The symptoms must last for more than a month and must significantly affect important areas of life.

Some stressors are so severe that almost anyone is susceptible for them. Such events are beyond the usual human, everyday experience. Such traumatic events comprise wars, torture, natural disasters, terrorism, rape, assault, or serious accidents. (T.J.) See also: PTSD, comorbidity, ashbacks

Trauma and media

Reisner discusses concept of 'trauma' not as a terrible experience but as a particular context for understanding and responding to a terrible experience.[346] In therapy, the media, and in international interventions, traumatised individuals are not only seen as people who suffer and who therefore deserve concern and aid, but also as people who suffer for others, and who are given special dispensation. They are treated with awe if they tell a certain kind of trauma story, but also ignored or vilified if they tell another. Trauma has become a story not only of pain and

342. J. Cocoran and A. R. Roberts, 'Research on Crisis Intervention and Recommendations for Further Research', in A. R. Roberts (ed.) Crisis Intervention Handbook: Assessment, Treatment and Research, 2nd edition, New York: Oxford University Press, 2000, 453–486.

343. A. R. Roberts, 'Assessment, Crisis Intervention and Trauma Treatment: The integrative ACT Intervention Model', Brief Treatment and Crisis Intervention 2.1 (2002): 1–21.

344. Y. R. Yeager and A. R. Roberts, Differentiating Among Stress, Acute Stress Disorder, Crisis Episodes, Trauma, and PTSD: Paradigm and Treatment Goals, Oxford: Oxford University Press, 2003.

345. American Psychiatric Association, Diagnostic and Statistical Manual of Mental Disorders, 4th edition revised, Washington, DC: American Association Press, 2002.

346. S. Reisner, 'Trauma: The Seductive Hypothesis', Journal of the American Psychoanalystic Association 51.2 (2003): 381-414.

its treatment, but a host of sub-stories involving the commodification of altruism, the justification of violence and revenge, and the place where voyeurism and witnessing intersect. Trauma has become not only the issue of suffering but of fantasy. The current view of trauma confers exceptional status of special privilege. and has in uenced the way how traumatised persons are presented in the media, how governments justify and carry out international responses to trauma. This response to trauma re ects an underlying belief system derived from narcissism. (T.J.) See also: Victim, Voyeurism, Witnessing,

Suicide and PTSD

According to epidemiological investigations between 1.1% and 4.6% of the population have a suicidal attempt at some point during their life.[347] But numerous studies have found strong link between suicide-related thoughts and behavior with trauma. Investigations have shown that PTSD patients (combat-related or civilian PTSD) are at higher risk for suicide.[348] Some studies have shown that higher risk was connected with high levels of impulsivity and poor social support.[349] Some point out that PTSD comorbid with depression enhances the risk for suicidal behavior.[350] Other factors that were strongly associated with suicide attempts were guilt about combat actions, survivor guilt, depression, anxiety and severe PTSD.[351] Suicide attemps are also higher among women who were sexually assaulted and raped.[352] (T.J.) See also PTSD, guilt (survivor guilt)

Torture

Torture represents the most severe form of trauma perpetrated by one human on another.[353]

---

347. R. C. Kessler, G. Borges and E. E. Walters, 'Prevalence of and Risk Factors for Lifetime Suicide Attempts in the National Comorbidity Survey', Archives of General Psychiatry 56 (1999): 617-26; S. R. Dube, R. F. Anda, V. J. Felitti, D. P. Chapman, D. F. Williamson and W. Giles, 'Childhood Abuse, Household Dysfunction and the Risk of Attempted Suicide Throughout the Life Span: Findings From the Adverse Childhood Experience Study', Journal of the American Medical Association 286 (2001): 3089-3096.
348. D. P. Adams, C. Barton, G. L. Mitchell, A. L. Moore and V. Einagel, 'Hearts and Minds: Suicide among United States Combat Troops in Vietnam', Social Science and Medicine 14.11 (1998): 1687-1694; N. Tarrier and L. Gregg, 'Suicide risk in civilian PTSD patients: predictors of suicidal ideation, planning and attempts', Social Psychiatry and Psychiatric Epidemiology 39 (2004): 655-661; M. Kotler, I. Iancu, R. Efroni and M. Amir, 'Anger, Impulsivity, Social Support and Suicide Risk in Patients with Posttraumatic Stress Disorder', Journal of Nervous & Mental Disease 189 (2001): 162-167.
349. Kotler, Iancu, Efroni and Amir, 'Anger, Impulsivity, Social Support and Suicide Risk in Patients with Posttraumatic Stress Disorder'.
350. M. Oquendo, D. A. Brent, B. Birmaher, L. Greenhill, D. Kolko, J. Zelazny, A. K. Burke, S. Firinciogullari, S. P. Ellis and J. J. Mann, 'Posttraumatic Stress Disorder Comorbid with Major Depression: Factors Mediating the Association with Suicidal Behavior', American Journal of Psychiatry 162.3 (2005): 560-566.
351. H. Hendin and A. P. Haas, 'Suicide and Guilt as Manifestations of PTSD in Vietnam Combat Veterans', American Journal of Psychiatry 148 (1991): 586-591.
352. R. T. Davidson, D. C. Hughes, L. K. George and D. G. Blazer. The Association of Sexual Assault and Attempted Suicide within the Community', Archives of General Psychiatry 53 (1996):550-555.
353. D. Silove, 'Torture and Refugee Trauma: Implications for Nosology an Treatment of Posttraumatic Syndromes', in F. L. Mak and C. C. Nadelson (eds) International Review of Psychiatry, Washington, DC: American Psychiatry Press (1996): 211-233.

According to Sadock, intentional physical and psychological torture can cause such emotional effects that may be worse than those in combat or other types of trauma.[354] The definition provided by the United Nations states that "torture is any deliberate in iction of severe mental pain or suffering, usually through cruel, inhuman, or degrading treatment or punishment". Recent approximations are that between 5 and 35 percent of the world's 14 million refugees have had at least one torture experience. Torture differs from other types of trauma since it is human in icted and intentional. Methods can be physical (beatings, burning of the skin, electric shock, or asphyxiation) or psychological (threats, humiliation, being forced to watch others, often loved ones, being tortured). It seems that the final purpose of torture is a psychological effect, because the torturer induces fear, helplessness, physical and mental weakness in the victim.

Certain elements of torture may especially impact the post-traumatic symptoms.[355] "The abuse is deliberate, and the perpetrators use methods that maximise fear, dread, and debility in the victim, the trauma is inescapable, uncontrollable, often repetitive, and conditions between torture sessions undermine the recovery capacity of the victim; feeling of shame, anger, betrayal, and humiliation, erode the victim's sense of security, integrity, and self-worth".[356]

Prevalence rates of PTSD among victims of torture are nearly 36 percent which is much higher than the average lifetime prevalence.[357] (T.J) See also PTSD, victim

Trauma from a distance

There are several investigations that have been conducted concerning the increased stress experienced by people living far from the mediation of certain events (e.g. terrorist attacks), particularly via television. Propper et al. investigated how the terrorist attacks of September 11, 2001, were traumatic for people living throughout the United States.[358] Their results showed that there is a direct association between television viewing and subsequent increases in stress and trauma. How viewing television coverage of a mass disaster could be connected with the development of PTSD is still poorly understood. Bernstein et al. assessed New York inhabitants a year after the September 11, 2001 attacks.[359] They found that 5.6% of participants had developed probable PTSD at the 1 year follow-up. Watching 12 or more hours of the September 11 attack anniversary

---

354. H. Kaplan and B.Sadock, Kaplan & Sadock's Synopsis of Psychiatry, Ninth Edition, Philadelphia: Lippincott Williams & Wilkins, 2003.

355. D. Silove, Z. Steel, P. McGorry, V. Miles and J. Drobny, 'The Impact of Torture on Posttraumatic Stress Symptoms in War-Affected Tamil Refugees and Immigrants', Comprehensive Psychiatry 43.1 (2002): 49-55.

356. A. E. Goldfeld, F. R. Mollica, B. H. Pesavento and S. V. Faraone, 'The Physical and Psychological Sequelae of Torture: Symptomatology and Diagnosis', Journal of the American Medical Association 259 (1998): 2725-2729; D. Silove, Z. Steel, P. McGorry, V. Miles and J. Drobny, 'The Impact of Torture on Posttraumatic Stress Symptoms in War-Affected Tamil Refugees and Immigrants', Comprehensive Psychiatry 43.1 (2002): 49-55.

357. H. Kaplan and B. Sadock, Kaplan & Sadock's Synopsis of Psychiatry, Ninth Edition, Philadelphia: Lippincott Williams & Wilkins, 2003.

358. R. E. Propper, R. Stickgold, R. Keeley and S. D. Christman, 'Is Television Traumatic? Dreams, Stress, and Media Exposure in the Aftermath of September 11, 2001', Psychological Science 18.4 (2007): 334-340.

359. K. T. Bernstein, J. Ahern, M. Tracy, J. A. Boscarino, D. Vlahov and S. Galea, 'Television Watching and the Risk of Incident Probable Posttraumatic Stress Disorder: a Prospective Evaluation', Journal of Nervous and Mental Disorders 195.1 (2007): 41-47.

news coverage was associated with a 3.4-fold increased risk of new-onset probable PTSD. Other authors also found a positive association between the hours of watching TV news related to the attack and distress, and a small positive association between hostility toward the perpetrators, TV watching, and distress.[360]
Previous thought has linked the risk of exposure to trauma to specific occupational groups, including military, firefighters, and law enforcement. The most recent events in North America have expanded the scope of trauma to innocent bystanders, as demonstrated following the terrorist attack in New York City and sniper attacks in Rockville, Maryland, and northern Virginia.[361] (T.J.)
See: trauma

Victim

In different disciplines, the term victims has different meanings. The term is most often used in criminology, religion, psychotherapy and New Age contexts. In criminology, the term victim refers to the victim of some. In religious studies, it refers to animal or human sacrifice. In the context of psychotherapy, the term refers to a posited role in the Karpman drama triangle model of transactional analysis and in the New Age context, it refers on an undesirable inferred psychological type or state. (T.P.) See also: projective identification, victim role/posited role

Victim role or posited role playing

Eric Berne described different positions people can take in life. One of them is so called 'victim role'.[362] This tactic involves portraying oneself as an innocent victim of circumstances or someone else's behavior in order to gain sympathy, evoke compassion and thereby get something from another. Whenever a person refuses to take responsibility for themselves, they are unconsciously choosing to react as a victim.
Victimhood can be defined by the three positions outlined in a diagram developed by a psychiatrist, and teacher of Transactional Analysis, Stephen Karpman. He calls it the 'Drama Triangle'. The three roles on the Drama Triangle are Persecutor, Rescuer and Victim. Karpman placed these three roles on an inverted triangle and described them as being the three aspects, or faces of victim. No matter where the person may start out on the triangle, victim is where they end up, therefore no matter what role he/she is in on the triangle, the person is in a position of victimhood.
Rescuers see themselves as 'helpers' and 'caretakers'. They need someone to rescue (victim) in order to feel vital and important. It's difficult for rescuer to recognise themselves as ever being in a victim position – they're the ones with the answers after all.
Persecutors identify themselves primarily as victims. They are usually in complete denial about their blaming tactics. When it is pointed out to them, they argue that attack is warranted and necessary for self protection. The Rescuer and the Persecutor are the two opposite extremes of the victim. (T.J.) See also: victim

---

360. E. Cardeña, J. M. Dennis, M. Winkel and L. J. Skitka, 'A Snapshot of Terror: Acute Posttraumatic Responses to the September 11 Attack', Journal of Trauma Dissociation 6.2 (2005): 69-84.
361. K. R. Yeager and A. R. Roberts, Differentiating Among Stress, Acute Stress Disorder, Crisis Episodes, Trauma, and PTSD: Paradigm and Treatment Goals, Oxford: Oxford University Press, 2003.
362. E. Berne, Games People Play, New York: Growe Press, 1964.

Vicarious trauma

According to Way, the term vicarious traumatisation was first used by McCann and Pearlman in 1990 to describe pervasive changes that occur within clinicians over time as a result of working with clients who have experienced sexual trauma.[363] These include changes in the clinician's sense of self, spirituality, worldview, interpersonal relationships, and behavior.[364] Other terms for vicarious traumatization are compassion fatigue or secondary traumatic stress, countertransference, and burnout.

Figley suggested compassion fatigue as the most appropriate term to describe secondary traumatic stress effects.[365] He suggested that clinicians who treat traumatized clients are particularly vulnerable to developing compassion fatigue as a result of empathic engagement with clients and exposure to their traumatic material. Countertransference refers to a clinician's unconscious and conscious affective, behavioral, and cognitive response to a particular client's transference (not specific to trauma clients) within the treatment relationship . Burnout refers to a generalized emotional exhaustion that helping professionals may develop over time related to various work-related stressors.[366]

An ethical concern is that vicarious trauma may interfere with clinicians' ability to work effectively with clients.[367] (T.J.) See: vicarious retribution

Vicarious retribution

Lickel provided a new framework for understanding one aspect of aggressive con ict between groups, which is referred to as vicarious retribution.[368] Vicarious retribution occurs when a member of a group commits an act of aggression toward the members of an outgroup for an assault

---

363. I. Way, K. M. Vandeusen, G. Martin, B. Applegate and D. Jandle, 'Vicarious Trauma: A Comparison of Clinicians Who Treat Survivors of Sexual Abuse and Sexual Offenders', Journal of interpersonal Violence 91.4 (2004): 49-71; I. L. McCann and L. A. Pearlman, 'Vicarious Traumatization: A Framework for Understanding the Psychological Effects of Working with Victims' Journal of Traumatic Stress 3.1 (1990): 131-149.

364. K. R. Chrestman, 'Secondary Exposure to Trauma and Self Reported Distress Among Therapists', in B. H. Stamm (ed.) Secondary Traumatic Stress: Self Care Issues for Clinicians, Researchers and Educators, 2nd edition, Lutherville, MD: Sidran Press, 1999, 37-47; R. E. Freeman-Longo, 'Introduction: A Personal and Professional Perspective on Burnout', in S. B. Edmunds (ed.) Impact: Working with Sexual Abusers, Brandon, VT: Safer Society Press, 1997, 51-60; N. Kassam-Adams, 'The Risks of Treating Sexual Trauma: Stress and Secondary Trauma in Psychotherapists', in B. H. Stamm (ed.) Secondary Traumatic Stress: Self Care Issues for Clinicians, Researchers and Educators, 2nd edition, Lutherville, MD: Sidran Press, 1999, 37-47.

365. C. R. Figley, 'Compassion Fatigue as Secondary Traumatic Stress Disorder: An Overview', in C. R. Figley (ed.) Coping with Secondary Traumatic Stress Disorders in Those Who Treat the Traumatized, New York: Brunner/Mazel Publishers, 1999, 1-20.

366. C. R. Figley, 'Compassion Fatigue: Toward a New Understanding of the Cost of Caring', in B. H. Stamm (ed.) Secondary Traumatic Stress: Self Care Issues for Clinicians, Researchers and Educators, 2nd edition, Lutherville, MD: Sidran Press, 1999, 3-28.

367. L. A. Pearlman and K. W. Saakvitne, Trauma and the Therapist: Countertransference and Vicarious Traumatization in Psychotherapy with Incest Survivors, New York: W.W. Norton, 1995.

368. B. Lickel, N. Miller, D. M. Stenstrom, T. F. Denson and T. Schmader, 'Vicarious Retribution: The Role of Collective Blame in Intergroup Aggression', Personality and Social Psychology Review 10.4 (2006): 372-90.

or provocation that had no personal consequences for him or her but which did harm a fellow in-group member. Furthermore, retribution is often directed at outgroup members who, themselves, were not the direct causal agents in the original attack against the person's ingroup. Thus, retribution is vicarious in that neither the agent of retaliation nor the target of retribution were directly involved in the original event that precipitated the intergroup conflict. It is described how ingroup identification, outgroup entitativity, and other variables, such as group power, influence vicarious retribution. (T.J.) See: vicarious trauma

Vietnam syndrome
According to Sadock, the psychiatric morbidity associated with Vietnam War veterans that finally brought the concept of post-traumatic stress disorder, as it is currently known, to fruition.[369] (T.J.)

Voyeurism
Watching people engaged in private activities is sexually arousing to voyeurs. This is even true for people who do not have paraphilia, such as those who enjoy pornographic films. The difference is that a voyeurs' gratification derives from viewing ordinary people who do not realise they are being watched and would probably would not permit it if they did. The victims are almost always strangers. Most voyeurs will usually masturbate while they are watching. Afterwards, they may fantasize having sex with the target, though activity with the target is rarely sought. Some voyeurs prefer this method of sexual gratification, but most have normal sex otherwise. They take precautions to avoid detection. Nearly all of these patients are men. They usually begin with this activities in their teens – almost always by the age of 15. Once begun, this tends to be a chronic disorder.[370] (T.J.) See also: sadomasochism, voayerism, paraphilias

Witness
Witness is someone who has firsthand knowledge about a crime or dramatic event through their senses (e.g. seeing, hearing, smelling, touching) and can help certify important considerations to the crime or event. A witness who has seen the event firsthand is known as an eyewitness. Witnesses are often called before a court of law to testify in trials.

Witnessing and PTSD
There are many different opinions if a victim could be a reliable witness. Especially if the witness suffers from PTSD, and how could this symptoms influence his/her memory.
Sparr in his reviews about PTSD and witnessing gives variety of studies that have shown a relationship between PTSD and deficits in explicit memory function.[371] Trauma victims often, either willingly or unwillingly, take part in legal matters, therefore it is not surprising that considerable importance is attached to their recollections of the traumatic event. One of such example is

369. H. Kaplan and B. Sadock, Kaplan & Sadock's Synopsis of Psychiatry, Ninth Edition, Philadelphia: Lippincott Williams & Wilkins, 2003.
370. J. Morrison, DSM-IV Made Easy: The Clinician's Guide to Diagnosis, New York: The Guilford Press, 1995.
371. L. F. Sparr and J. D. Bremner, 'Post-traumatic Stress Disorder and Memory: Prescient Medicolegal Testimony at the International War Crimes Tribunal?', Journal of the American Academy of Psychiatry Law 33.1 (2005): 71-8.

the trial at the International War Crimes Tribunal in The Hague in 1998, where for the first time psychiatric experts were invited to give their opinions about the nature and accuracy of explicit memory after experiencing trauma in individuals with PTSD.[372]
The trial turned on the witness's memory of her traumatic experiences (which were not in question) and her recollections with regard to the persons (especially the defendant) who were present during the trauma. The victim and principal witness had been diagnosed with PTSD. The defendant's lawyers suggested that the victim's memory had been adversely affected by traumatic experiences.
Most professionals divide memory functions into explicit and implicit memory.[373] Explicit memory comprises material that can easily be brought to consciousness, such as facts or lists of words. Implicit memory refers to material that cannot be easily brought to consciousness, such as how to ride a bicycle or play a piano. Patients with lesions of the hippocampus have specific deficits in explicit (declarative) memory, sometimes referred to as neurological amnesia. Another type of amnesia, dissociative amnesia, differs from neurological amnesia (a consistent deficit in ability to learn new information). Dissociative amnesia is seen primarily in trauma victims.
Disturbances of memory, including intrusive memories and dissociative amnesia, are a part of the clinical presentation of PTSD. Stress is associated with damage of one part of the brain (hippocampus) and associated problems with new learning and memory.[374] Stress also inhibits the growth of neurons, or neurogenesis, in the hippocampus.[375]
Patients with PTSD have deficits in verbal declarative memory (known to be mediated at least in part by the hippocampus), including learning lists of words or similar material.[376]
These memory deficits are different from the disturbances of memory listed as symptoms of PTSD, including dissociative amnesia and intrusive memories, and similar to the deficits in patients with neurological amnesia who have known hippocampal damage. Consistent with the hypothesis that stress induced hippocampal damage is responsible for the verbal declarative memory deficits of PTSD are findings of smaller hippocampal volume in PTSD.[377]
The wide range of memory disturbances associated with PTSD can lead to fragmentation and distortion of traumatic memories. On a biological level, stress hormones such as cortisol and

---

372. Prosecutor v. Anto Furund ija, ICTY Case No. IT-95-17/1-T. Available at www.un.org\icty (accessed May 10, 2004)
373. S. M. Zola-Morgan and L. R. Squire, 'The Primate Hippocampal Formation: Evidence for a Time-Limited Role in Memory Storage', Science 250 (1990): 288-90.
374. R. M. Sapolsky, 'Why Stress is Bad For Your Brain', Science 273 (1996): 749-750.
375. R. S. Duman, J. E. Malberg and S. Nakagawa, 'Regulation of Adult Neurogenesis by Psychotropic Drugs and Stress', Journal of Pharmacology and Experimental Therapeutics 299 (2001): 401-407; E. Vermetten, M. Vythilingam, S. M. Southwick, et al, 'Long-Term Treatment with Paroxetine Increases Verbal Declarative Memory and Hippocampal Volume in Posttraumatic Stress Disorder', Biological Psychiatry 54 (2003): 693-702.
376. J. D. Bremner, T. M. Scott, R. C. Delaney, et al, 'Deficits in Short-Term Memory in Post-Traumatic Stress Disorder', American Journal of Psychiatry 150 (1993): 1015-1019; M. W. Gilbertson, T. V. Gurvits, N. B. Lasko, et al, 'Multivariate Assessment of Explicit Memory Function in Combat Veterans with Posttraumatic Stress Disorder', Journal of Traumatic Stress 14 (2001): 413-420.
377. J. D. Bremner, P. R. Randall, T. M. Scott, et al, 'MRI-based Measurement of Hippocampal Volume in Posttraumatic Stress Disorder', American Journal of Psychiatry 152 (1995): 973-981; J. D. Bremner, Does Stress Damage the Brain? Understanding Trauma-Related Disorders from a Mind-Body Perspective. New York: W. W. Norton, 2002.

norepinephrine act at the level of the hippocampus and other brain regions to both inhibit and strengthen memory formation.

The time course of release of these hormones can in uence the formation of the traumatic memory, leading to both strengthening and weakening of memory. Traumatic memories are memories for events related to a trauma. Such memories are different from neutral memories, involving an event in a person's life that was not associated with exposure to a trauma, although both are autobiographical in nature.

Some researchers have questioned whether there are fundamental differences between neutral and traumatic memories.[378]

Another factor contributing to the political culture surrounding legal aspects of the trauma and memory debate is the controversy about the accuracy of delayed recall of traumatic events. There are at least two studies in patients with PTSD showing an increase in memory distortion on so-called 'false memory tasks'.[379]

No study directly addresses the relationship between traumatic memories and recall accuracy. More recently a prospective investigation of human eyewitness memory for highly stressful events indicates that under conditions of extreme stress, human memory is extremely poor.[380]

One study showed that memories of traumatic events in Persian Gulf War veterans changed over time. Southwick et al. conducted a set of studies demonstrating that memory of traumatic events is subject to considerable alteration over time.[381] In the first study, Gulf War veterans were interviewed one month, two years, and six years after returning from the war. When requestioned the first time, combat veterans changed their answers to specific questions about their trauma exposure. The veterans were more likely to say, after being interviewed at a two-year point, that they had seen more trauma than originally described. Although there was alteration in memory in nearly all subjects, the greatest changes were seen in veterans suffering from PTSD, and the more PTSD symptoms subjects had, the more they changed their answers. In the six-year follow-up study, alterations in memory (increase or decrease) were also significantly related to PTSD symptomatology. All subjects were absolutely convinced that their answers were right, even though they changed their answers each time and were sure that each answer was correct. The answers provided by the subjects were considered 'inconsistent' rather than 'inaccurate', because the research team had no way of knowing which accounts were true. Separate studies by Roemer et al. and by North et al. have shown that many individuals with PTSD symptoms on

---

378. J. F. Kihlstrom, 'The Trauma-Memory Argument', Consciousness and Cognition 4.1 (1995): 63-67.
379. J. D. Bremner, K. K. Shobe and J. F. Kihlstrom, 'False Memories in Women with Self-Reported Child-hood Sexual Abuse: An Empirical Study', Psychological Science 11.4 (2000): 333-337; S. A. Clancy, D. L. Schacter, R. J. McNally, et al, 'False Recognition in Women Reporting Recovered Memories of Sexual Abuse', Psychological Science 11.4 (2000): 26-31.
380. C. A. Morgan, G. Hazlett, A. Doran, et al, 'Accuracy of Eyewitness Memory for Persons Encountered During Exposure to Highly Stressful Personally Relevant Events', International Journal of Law Psychiatry 27 (2004): 265-79.
381. S. M. Southwick, C. A. Morgan, A. Darnell, et al, 'Trauma-Related Symptoms in Veterans of Operation Desert Storm: A 2-Year Followup', American Journal of Psychiatry 152 (1995): 1150-1155.

one-year follow-up may deny symptoms they had previously endorsed.[382] Roemer et al. reported that, while Gulf War veterans with and without PTSD were inconsistent when reporting trauma exposure, veterans with PTSD provided significantly more inconsistencies than people without PTSD.[383] Studies by Foa et al. and van der Kolk and Fisler also show that female rape victims may change their story to a significant degree and that memory in people who have highly stressful, life-threatening experiences may be 'unorganised'.[384]

In the final judgment of this case, the Trial Chamber accepted defense testimony about inconsistencies of memory in individuals with PTSD, but that victim's primary memory provides compelling affirmation that the event has occurred, and other inconsistencies do not diminish credibility (ICTY Case 2004). (T.J.) See also PTSD, amnesia, dissociation, ashbacks, trauma

---

382. C. S. North, E. M. Smith and E. L. Spitznagel, 'One-Year Follow-Up of Survivors of a Mass Shooting', American Journal of Psychiatry 154 (1997): 1696-1702; L. Roemer, B. Litz, S. M. Orsillo, et al, 'Increases in Retrospective Accounts of War-zone Exposure Over Time: The Role of PTSD Symptom Severity', Journal of Traumatic Stress 11 (1998): 597-605.

383. L. Roemer, B. Litz, S. M. Orsillo, et al: 'Increases in Retrospective Accounts of War-zone Exposure Over Time: The Role of PTSD Symptom Severity', Journal of Traumatic Stress 11 (1998): 597-605.

384. E. B. Foa, C. Molnar and L. Cashman, 'Change in Rape Narratives During Exposure Therapy for Post-traumatic Stress Disorder', Journal of Traumatic Stress 8 (1995): 675-690; B. A. van der Kolk and R. E. Fisler, 'Dissociation and the Fragmentary Nature of Traumatic Memories: Overview and Exploratory Study', Journal of Traumatic Stress 8 (1995): 505-525.

LIST OF ILLUSTRATIONS

WORKS CITED

Abdel-Khalek, A. M. (2004): 'Neither Altruistic Suicide, nor Terrorism but Martyrdom: A Muslim Perspective', Archives of Suicide Research 8(1); 99-113.

Adams, D. P., Barton, C., et.al. (1998), 'Hearts and Minds: Suicide among United States Combat Troops in Vietnam', Social Science and Medicine 14(11): 1687-1694

Adilkno (1998): The Media Archive, New York: Autonomedia.

Agamben, G. (1999): Remnants of Auschwitz, trans. Daniel Heller-Roazen, New York: Zone Books.

Aldwin, C. and T. A. Revenson (1987), 'Does Coping Help? A Reexamination of the Relation Be tween Coping and Mental Health', Journal of Personality and Social Psychology 53: 337-348.

American Psychiatric Association (1952): Diagnostic and Statistical Manual of Mental Disorders, 1st edition, Washington, DC: American Association Press,

American Psychiatric Association (1968): Diagnostic and Statistical Manual of Mental Disorders, 2nd edition, Washington, DC: American Association Press.

American Psychiatric Association (1980): Diagnostic and Statistical Manual of Mental Disoders, 3rd edition, Washington, DC: American Association Press.

American Psychiatric Association (1994): Diagnostic and Statistical Manual of Mental Disorders, 4th edition, Washington, DC: American Association Press.

American Psychiatric Association (1999): Diagnostic and Statistical Manual of Mental Disorders, revised edition, Washington, DC: American Association Press.

American Psychiatric Association (2002): Diagnostic and Statistical Manual of Mental Disorders, 4th edition revised, Washington, DC: American Association Press

Aquino, K., Tripp, T., et.al. (2006): 'Getting Even or Moving On? Power, Procedural Justice, and Types of Offense as Predictors of Revenge, Forgiveness, Reconciliation, and Avoidance in Organizations', Journal of Applied Psychology 91.(3): 653-68.

Barthes, R. (1991): 'The Photographic Message', A Barthes Reader, New York: Hill and Wang, pp. 15-31.

Bataille, G. (1988): The Accursed Share: An Essay on General Economy, trans. Robert Hurley, New York: Zone.

Bataille, G.: (1989) The Tears of Eros, trans. by Peter Connor, San Francisco: City Lights Books,

Bayer, C. P., Klasen, F., et.al. (2007), 'Association of Trauma and PTSD Symptoms with Open ness to Reconciliation and Feelings of Revenge Among Former Ugandan and Congolese Child Soldiers', Journal of the American Medical Association 298(5): 555-559.

Beauvoir, S. (1953): The Second Sex, trans. H.M. Parshley, London: Jonathan Cape.

Bennett, J. (2005): Emphatic Vision: Affect, Trauma and Contemporary Art, Stanford: Stanford University Press.

Berne, E. (1964): Games People Play, New York: Growe Press.

Bernstein, J. M. (2004): 'Bare Life, Bearing Witness', Parallax 10(1): 2-16

Bernstein, K. T. Ahern, J. et.al. (2007): 'Television Watching and the Risk of Incident Probable Posttraumatic Stress Disorder: a Prospective Evaluation', Journal of Nervous and Mental Disorders 195(1): 41-47.

Berry, J. W. Worthington E. L. Jr, et.al.(2005): 'Forgivingness, Vengeful Rumination, and Affective

Traits', Journal of Personality 73(1): 183-225

Bhabha, H. (1994): The Location of Culture, London: Routledge, 1994.

Bishop, J. and Lane, R. C. (2002): 'The Dynamics and Dangers of Entitlement', Psychoanalytic Psychology 19: 739-58

Bleich, A., Koslowsky, M. , et.al, (1997): 'Post-traumatic Stress Disorder and Depression: An Analysis of Comorbidity', The British Journal of Psychiatry 170: 479-482

Bohleber, W. (2007): 'Remembrance, Trauma and Collective Memory: The Battle for Memory in Psychoanalysis', International Journal of Psychoanalysis 88(2): 329-352

Böll, H (1976): Group Portrait with Lady, trans. Leila Vennewitz, Harmondsworth: Penguin

Borowski, T (1967): 'Auschwitz, Our Home (A Letter)', in This Way for the Gas, Ladies and Gentlemen, trans. by Barbara Vedder, Harmondsworth: Penguin.

Boyd, d.: 'erosion of youth privacy - the local panopticon', apophenia, http://www.zephoria.org/thoughts/archives/2006/05/20/erosion_of_yout.html.

Bremner, J. D., Randall, P. R. , et.al. (1995): T. M. Scott, et al, 'MRI-based Measurement of Hippocampal Volume in Posttraumatic Stress Disorder', American Journal of Psychiatry 152: 973-981

Bremner, J. D., Shobe, K. K., et.al. (2000): 'False Memories in Women with Self-Reported Child hood Sexual Abuse: An Empirical Study', Psychological Science 11(4): 333-337

Briere, J., Scott, C., et.al. (2005), 'Peritraumatic and Persistent Dissociation in the Presumed Etiology of PTSD', American Journal of Psychiatry 165: 2295-2301 Cardeña, E., Dennis, J. M., et.al. (2005), 'A Snapshot of Terror: Acute Posttraumatic Responses to the September 11 Attack', Journal of Trauma Dissociation 6(2): 69-84

Caruth, C. (1995): 'Trauma and Experience: Introduction', in Cathy Caruth (ed.) Trauma: Explora tions in Memory, London: John Hopkins University Press.

_____. (1996) Unclaimed Experience: Trauma, Narrative and History, Baltimore: The Johns Hopkins University Press, 1996

Carver, C. S., Scheier, M. F, et.al. (1989), 'Assessing Coping Strategies: A Theoretically Based Approach', Journal of Personality and Social Psychology 56: 267-283

Cashdan, S. (1988): Object Relations Therapy: Using the Relationship, New York: W. W. Norton & Company, 1988: 53-78

Celan, P. (2000): Gesammelte Werke, Vol. 3, Frankfurt am Main: Suhrkamp.

_____. (2003) 'Reply to a Questionnaire from the Flinker Bookstore, Paris, 1958', in Collected Prose, trans. Rosmarie Waldrop, New York: Routledge.

_____. (2005): Paul Celan: Selections, Berkeley: University of California Press

Charny, I. W. (1994): 'Toward a Generic Definition of Genocide', in G. J. Andreopoulos (ed.) Genocide: Conceptual and Historical Dimensions, Philadelphia: University of Pennsylvania Press.

Cologne, A.d: Virtual Memorial http://www.a-virtual-memorial.org/

Chrestman, K. R. (1999): 'Secondary Exposure to Trauma and Self Reported Distress Among Therapists', in B. H. Stamm (ed.) Secondary Traumatic Stress: Self Care Issues for Clini cians, Researchers and Educators, 2nd edition, Lutherville, MD: Sidran Press: 37-47

Clancy, S. A. Schacter, D. L. Et.al. (2000): 'False Recognition in Women Reporting Recovered Memories of Sexual Abuse', Psychological Science 11(4): 26-31

Cocoran, J. and Roberts, A. R. (2000): 'Research on Crisis Intervention and Recommendations for Further Research', in A. R. Roberts (ed.) Crisis Intervention Handbook: Assessment,

Treatment and Research, 2nd edition, New York: Oxford University Press: 453–486

Cohen-Liebman, M. S. (2002): 'Art Therapy', in Michel Hersen and William Sledge (eds) Ency
    clopedia of Psychotherapy, New York: Elsevier Science, 2002.

Constantelos, D. J. (2004) 'Altruistic Suicide or Altruistic Martyrdom? Christian Greek Orthodox
    Neo-Martyrs: A Case Study', Archives of Suicide Research 8(1): 57-71

Cowles, K. V. (1996): 'Cultural Perspectives of Grief: An Expanded Concept Analysis', Journal of
    Advanced Nursing 23(2): 287-94.

Davidson, R. T. Hughes, D. C., et.al. (1996). The Association of Sexual Assault and Attempted
    Suicide within the Community', Archives of General Psychiatry 53: 550-555

Deleuze, G. and Guattari, F. (1996): 'The First Positive Task of Schizoanalysis', in Gary Genosko
    (ed.) A Guattari Reader, Cambridge: Blackwell Publishers, 77-95

Derrida, J. (2005): 'Language Is Never Owned: An Interview', in Thomas Dutoit and Outi
    Pasanen (eds) Sovereignties in Question: The Poetics of Paul Celan, New York: Fordham
    University Press

(2001) On Cosmopolitanism and Forgiveness, trans. Mark Dooley and Michael Hughes,
    London: Routledge.

Delaney, R. C., et. al. (1993): 'Deficits in Short-Term Memory in Post-Traumatic Stress Disorder',
    American Journal of Psychiatry 150: 1015-1019

Dick, P. K. (1979): Vulcan's Hammer, London, Arrow Books.

Dolar, M. (2006): A Voice and Nothing More, Cambridge: MIT Press.

Dube, S. R., Anda, R. F., et.al. (2001): 'Childhood Abuse, Household Dysfunction and the Risk of
    Attempted Suicide Throughout the Life Span: Findings From the Adverse Childhood Experi
    ence Study', Journal of the American Medical Association 286: 3089-3096

Duman, R. S., Malberg, J. E., et.al. (2001): 'Regulation of Adult Neurogenesis by Psychotropic
    Drugs
    and Stress', Journal of Pharmacology and Experimental Therapeutics 299.: 401-407

Early, E. (1990): 'Imagined, Exaggerated and Malingered Post-Traumatic Stress Disorder', in
    C. Meek (ed.) Post-Traumatic Stress Disorder: Assessment, Differential Diagnosis and
    Forensic Evaluation, Sarasota, Florida: Professional Resource Exchange: 137-156

Elias Sanbar, E. (2004) : Les Palestiniens: Images d'une terre et de son peuple de 1839 à nos
    jours. Paris: Editions Hazan

Favaro, A., Degortes, D., et.al (2000) 'The Effects of Trauma Among Kidnap Victims in Sardinia,
    Italy', Psychological Medicine 30: 975-980

Felman, S. (1992): 'The Return of the Voice: Claude Lanzmann's Shoah' in Shoshana Felman
    and Dori Laub (eds) Testimony: Crises of Witnessing in Literature, Psychoanalysis, and His
    tory, New York and London: Routledge, 1992.

Felman, S. (1999) 'Benjamin's Silence', Critical Inquiry 25(2) 201-234

Figley, C. R. (1999) 'Compassion Fatigue: Toward a New Understanding of the Cost of Caring',
    in B. H. Stamm (ed.) Secondary Traumatic Stress: Self Care Issues for Clinicians, Research
    ers and Educators, 2nd edition, Lutherville, MD: Sidran Press: 3-28

Figley, C. R. (1999): 'Compassion Fatigue as Secondary Traumatic Stress Disorder: An Over
    view', in C. R. Figley (ed.) Coping with Secondary Traumatic Stress Disorders in Those Who
    Treat the Traumatized, New York: Brunner/Mazel Publishers: 1-20

First, B. M. (2005): 'Mutually Exclusive Versus Co-occurring Diagnostic Categories: The Chal
    lenge of Diagnostic Comorbidity', Psychopathology, 38(4).: 206-210

Fleming, A. and Eisendrath, (2006): 'S. Factitious Disorders', in Jerald Kay and Allan Tasman (eds) Essentials of Psychiatry, Hoboken, NJ: Wiley: 679-684

Foa, E. B., Molnar, C. Et.al (1995): 'Change in Rape Narratives During Exposure Therapy for Posttraumatic Stress Disorder', Journal of Traumatic Stress 8.: 675-690

Folkman, S. and Lazarus, R. (1980): 'An Analysis of Coping in a Middle-aged Community Sample', Journal of Health and Social Behavior 21: 219-239

Foucault, M. (1977). Discipline and Punish : the Birth of the Prison. London, Allen Lane.

_____. (1979). The History of Sexuality. London, Penguin : Viking : Pantheon.

Freeman-Longo, R. E. (1997): 'Introduction: A Personal and Professional Perspective on Burn out', in S. B. Edmunds (ed.) Impact: Working with Sexual Abusers, Brandon, VT: Safer Soci ety Press: 51-60

Freud, S. (1950) Totem and Taboo: Some Points of Agreement Between the Mental Lives of Savages and Neurotics, trans. James Strachey, London: Routledge and Kegan Paul,

_____. (1953-74): 'Remembering, Repeating and Working Through', Standard Edition of the Complete Psychological Works of Sigmund Freud, London: Hogarth, Vol. 12

_____. (1953-74): 'The Interpretation of Dreams' in Standard Edition of the Complete Psycho logical Works of Sigmund Freud, London: Hogarth, Vol. 5

George, K.M (1995): 'Violence, Solace, and Ritual: a Case Study from Island Southeast Asia', Culture, Medicine and Psychiatry 19(2): 225-60

Gilbertson, M. W., Gurvits, T. V. , et.al. (2001): N. B. Lasko, et al, 'Multivariate Assessment of Explicit Memory Function in Combat Veterans with Posttraumatic Stress Disorder', Journal of Traumatic Stress 14: 413-420

Göka, E. and Göral, Fs (1988): Projective Identification In Human Relations'; Sheldon Cashdan, Object Relations Therapy: Using the Relationship, New York: W. W. Norton & Company: 1-9.

Göka, E., Yüksel, F. V., et.al. (2006), 'Projective Identification In Human Relations', Turkish Jour nal Of Psychiatry, 17(1): 53-78.

Goldfeld, A. E. Mollica, F. R., et. al. (1998): 'The Physical and Psychological Sequelae of Torture: Symptomatology and Diagnosis', Journal of the American Medical Association 259: 2725-2729

Golding, S. (1997) The Eight Technologies of Otherness, London: Routledge,

_____. (1999): Honour, London: Taylor Francis

Goren, E. (2007): 'Society's Use of the Hero Following a National Trauma', American Journal of Psychoanalysis 67(1): 37-52

Graham, D. L., Rawlings, E. I.,, et.al. (1995): 'A Scale for Identifying 'Stockholm Syndrome' Reac tions in Young Dating Women: Factor Structure, Reliability, and Validity', Violence and Vic tims 10(1): 3-22

Greenson, R. R. (1960): 'Empathy and Its Vicissitudes', International Journal of Psychoanalysis 41: 418-424

Guriel, J. and Fremouw, W. (2003): 'Assessing Malingered Posttraumatic Stress Disorder: A Critical Review', Clinical Psychology Review 23: 881-904

Heinz Kohut, How Does Analysis Cure?, Chicago: The University of Chicago Press, 1984

Hendin, H. and Haas, A. P. (1991): 'Suicide and Guilt as Manifestations of PTSD in Vietnam Combat Veterans', American Journal of Psychiatry 148: 586-591

Herman, E.S. and Chomsky, N. (1988): Manufacturing Consent: The Political Economy of the Mass

Media, New York: Pantheon Books.

Hirst, W. and Manier, D. (2008): 'Towards a Psychology of Collective Memory', Memory 16(3)

Hobbes, T. (2006): Leviathan. Mineola, N.Y., Dover ; Newton Abbot.

Holahan, C. J. and Moos, R. H. (1987): 'Risk, Resistance, and Psychological Distress: A Longi
tudinal Analysis with Adults and Children', Journal of Abnormal Psychology 96: 3-13

Huppert, H. (1988: '»Spirituell«: Gespräch mit Paul Celan', in Werner Hamacher and Winfried
Menninghaus (eds) Paul Celan, Frankfurt am Main: Suhrkamp.

Illouz, E. (2007): Cold Intimacies: the Making of Emotional Capitalism, Cambridge: Polity Press.

Isar, N. (2005): 'Undoing Forgetfulness: Chiasmus of Poetical Mind – A Cultural Paradigm of
Archetypal Imagination', Europe's Journal Of Psychology, 1(3):   http://www.ejop.org/
archives/2005/08/undoing_forgetf_1.html

Iyer, A, Schmader, T et.al. (2007): 'Why Individuals Protest the Perceived Transgressions of Their
Country: the Role of Anger, Shame, and Guilt', Personality and Social Psychology Bulletin
33(4): 572-587

Bremner, J. D. (2002). Does Stress Damage the Brain? Understanding Trauma-Related Disor
ders from a Mind-Body Perspective. New York: W. W. Norton, 2002.

Laplanche, J. and J. B. Pontalis (1992): Rje nik psihoanalize, Naprijed.

Jabès, E. (1990): La mémoire des mots, trans. Pierre Joris, Paris: Fourbis

Jerald Kay and Allan Tasman, Essentials of Psychiatry, Hoboken, NJ: Wiley, 2006.

Jung, C. G. (1980): The Archetypes and The Collective Unconscious, trans. R.F.C. Hull, London:
Routledge.

Kaplan, H. and Sadock, B.(2003): Kaplan & Sadock's Synopsis of Psychiatry, Ninth Edition,
Philadelphia: Lippincott Williams & Wilkins.

Kassam-Adams, 'N. (1999): The Risks of Treating Sexual Trauma: Stress and Secondary Trauma
in Psychotherapists', in B. H. Stamm (ed.) Secondary Traumatic Stress: Self Care Issues for
Clinicians, Researchers and Educators, 2nd edition, Lutherville, MD: Sidran Press: 37-47

Kay, J. and Tasman, A. (2006): Essentials of Psychiatry, Hoboken, NJ: Wiley.

Kernberg, O. (1987): 'Projection And Projective Identification: Developmental And Clinical
Aspects',

Journal of the American Psychonalaysis Association, 35: 795-819

Kessler, R. C., Borges, G., et.al (1999): 'Prevalence of and Risk Factors for Lifetime Suicide At
tempts in the National Comorbidity Survey', Archives of General Psychiatry 56: 617-26

Khalil Sakakini Cultural Center: Nakba: http://www.alnakba.org

Kihlstrom, J. F. (1995): 'The Trauma-Memory Argument', Consciousness and Cognition 4(1)

Kline, D., and Burstein, D (2005): blog!, New York: CDS Books: 63-67

Kolk, van der B. A. and Fisler, R. E. (1995) 'Dissociation and the Fragmentary Nature of Trau
matic Memories: Overview and Exploratory Study', Journal of Traumatic Stress 8: 505-525

Kotler, M. Iancu, I., et.al. (2001): 'Anger, Impulsivity, Social Support and Suicide Risk in Patients
with Posttraumatic Stress Disorder', Journal of Nervous & Mental Disease 189: 162-167

Kozari -Kova i , D and Pivac, N (2007): 'Novel Approaches to the Treatment of Post-traumatic
Stress Syndrome', in Suat Begeç (ed.) The Integration and Management of Traumatized
People After Terrorist Attacks, Amsterdam: IOS Press: 13-40

Kozari -Kova i , D. and Kocijan-Hercigonja, D. (2001): 'Assessment of Post-traumatic Disorder
and Comorbidity' Military Medicine 160: 677-680

Kozari -Kova i , D. and Borove ki, A. (2005): 'Prevalence of Psychotic Comorbidity in Combat-

Related Post-Traumatic Stress Disorder', Military Medicine 170: 223-226
Kozari -Kova i , D. Hercigonja, D.K. et.al. (2001) 'Post-traumatic Stress Disorder and Depression in Soldiers with Combat Experiences', Croatian Medical Journal, 42: 165-170
Kozari -Kova i , D., Ljubin, T., et.al (2000): 'Comorbidity of Posttraumatic Stress Disorder and Alcohol Dependence in Displaced Persons', Croatian Medical Journal 41: 173-178
Kristeva, J (1982) Powers of Horror: An Essay on Abjection, trans. by Leon S. Roudiez, New York: Columbia University Press,
Kubler Ross, E. (1997): On Death and Dying, New York: Skribner.
Kulenovi , M. (1986).; Metapsihologija, nastranosti, osobitosti, Zagreb: Naprijed.
_____. (1999) 'Necrophilia and Generals', Polemos: Journal of Interdisciplinary Research on War and Peace, 2(03/04): 73-94
Lacan, J.(1981): Ecrits: A Selection, New York: Norton. 1981
Lacan, J.(1997): The Ethics of Psychoanalysis 1959-1960: The Seminar of Jacques Lacan: Book VII, trans. Dennis Porter, edited by Jacques Alain-Miller, New York and London: W.W. Norton & Company.
Lane, R. (1995): 'The Revenge Motive: A Developmental Perspective on the Life Cycle and the Treatment Process', Psychoanalytic Review, 82.1 (1995): 41-64
Lanzmann, C. (1985): Shoah: The Complete Text of the Acclaimed Holocaust Film, New York: Da Capo Press.
Laplanche, J. and Pontalis, J. B. (1992): Rje nik psihoanalize, Naprijed.
de Lappe, J.: Iraqi Memorial http://www.Iraqimemorial.org
Laub, L. (1992): 'An Event Without a Witness: Truth, Testimony and Survival', in Shoshana Fel man and Dori Laub (eds) Testimony: Crises of Witnessing in Literature, Psychoanalysis, and History, New York and London: Routledge: 75-92
Lazarus, R. S. (1993) 'From Psychological Stress to the Emotions: a History of Changing Out looks' Annual Review of Psychology 44.: 1-22
Lazarus, R. S. and Folkman, S. (1987): Stress, Appraisal, and Coping, New York: Springer.
Lester, D. (2004): 'Altruistic Suicide: A Look At Some Issues', Archives of Suicide Research 8(1): 37-42
Levi, P. (1984): The Periodic Table, trans. Raymond Rosenthal, New York: Schocken Books
_____. (1987) If This is a Man and The Truce, trans. Stuart Woolf, London: Abacus.
_____. (1988) The Drowned and the Saved, trans. Raymond Rosenthal, New York: Summit Books.
_____. (1989) Other People's Trades, trans. Raymond Rosenthal, New York: Summit Books
_____. (1992) Collected Poems, trans. Ruth Feldman and Brian Swann, London: Faber & Faber
_____. (1993) Survival in Auschwitz: The Nazi Assault on Humanity, trans. Stuart Woolf, New York: Collier.
Lickel, B., Miller, N., et. al. (2006): 'Vicarious Retribution: The Role of Collective Blame in Inter group Aggression', Personality and Social Psychology Review 10(4): 372-90
Lobar, S. L., Youngblut, J. M., et.al.(2006): 'Cross-Cultural Beliefs, Ceremonies, and Rituals Surrounding Death of a Loved One', Pediatric Nursing 32(1): 44-50
Long, N., Carol MacDonald, C., et.al. (1996): 'Prevalence of Post-traumatic Stress Disorder, Depression and Anxiety in Community Sample of New Zealand Vietnam War Veterans', Australian and New Zealand Journal of Psychiatry 30: 253-256
Lyotard, J. F. (1990) Heidegger and "the jews", trans. Andreas Michel and Mark S. Roberts,

Minneapolis, University of Minnesota Press

Maes, M., Myllee, J.;, et.al. (2001): 'Pre and Post-disaster Negative Life Events in Relation to the Incidence and Severity of Post-traumatic Stress Disorder', Psychiatry Research 105: 1-12

Mallon, T. (1984): A Book of One's Own, New York: Ticknor & Fields.

Manier D. (2008): 'Towards a Psychology of Collective Memory', Memory 16(3): 183-200

Marx, B. and Sloan, D. (2005): 'Peritraumatic Dissociation and Experiental Avoidance as Predictors of Posttraumatic Stress Symptomatology', Behaviour Research and Therapy 43: 569-583

McCann, I. L. and Pearlman, L. A. (1990): 'Vicarious Traumatization: A Framework for Understanding the Psychological Effects of Working with Victims' Journal of Traumatic Stress 3(1): 131-149

McGarty, C., Pedersen, A., et.al. (2005): 'Group-based Guilt as a Predictor of Commitment to Apology', British Psychological Society 44(4): 659-680

Mirbeau, O. (1931): Torture Garden, trans. Alvah C. Bessie, New York: Claude Kendall

Morgan, C. A., Hazlett, G. et al (2004): , 'Accuracy of Eyewitness Memory for Persons Encountered During Exposure to Highly Stressful Personally Relevant Events', International Journal of Law Psychiatry 27: 265-79

Morrison, J. (1995): DSM-IV Made Easy, The Clinician's Guide to Diagnosis, New York: The Guilford Press.

Murray, J., Ehlers, A., et. al. (2002):'Dissociation and Post-traumatic Stress Disorder: Two Prospective Studies of Road Accident Survivors', British Journal of Psychiatry 180: 363-368

Naggar, C. (2003): George Rodger: An Adventure in Photography – 1908-1995, Syracuse, New York: Syracuse University Press

North, C. S., Smith, E. M., et. al. (1997): 'One-Year Follow-Up of Survivors of a Mass Shooting', American Journal of Psychiatry 154: 1696-1702

Novakovi , M., Tiosavljevi -Mari , D., et.al.: (2006): 'Thanatophobia in the Patients on Dialysis', Vojnosanitetski pregled: Military-Medical and Pharmaceutical Review 63(4): 397-402

Oquendo, M. , Brent, D. A., et. al. (2005): 'Posttraumatic Stress Disorder Comorbid with Major Depression: Factors Mediating the Association with Suicidal Behavior', American Journal of Psychiatry 162(3): 560-566

Orth, U., Montada, L., et. al. (2006): 'Feelings of Revenge, Retaliation Motive and Posttraumatic Stress Reactions in Crime Victims', Journal of Interpersonal Violence 21(2): 229-243

Osaka Human Rights Museum: Shaheed: http://www.shaheed.jp.

Ozick, C. (1989) Metaphor and Memory: Essays, New York: Alfred Knopf

Paech, J. (2003): 'Ent/setzte Erinnerung', in Sven Kramer (ed.) Die Shoah im Bild. München: Boorberg.

Panasetis, P. and Bryant, R. (2003): 'Peritraumatic versus Persistent Dissociation in Acute Stress Disorder', Journal of Traumatic Stress 16: 563-566

Pearlman, L. A. and Saakvitne, K. W. (1995): Trauma and the Therapist: Countertransference and Vicarious Traumatization in Psychotherapy with Incest Survivors, New York: W.W. Norton.

Persimger, M. A. (1985): 'Death Anxiety as a Semantic Conditioned Suppression Paradigm', Perceptual and Motor Skills 60(3); 827-830

Propper, R. E. Stickgold, R., et. al. (2007): 'Is Television Traumatic? Dreams, Stress, and Media

Exposure in the Aftermath of September 11, 2001', Psychological Science 18(4): 334-340

Reid, W. H. (2000) 'Malingering', Journal of Psychiatry Practice 6: 226-228

Reisner, (2003) 'Trauma: The Seductive Hypothesis', Journal of the American Psychoanalystic Association 51(2): 381-414.

Riddell, M. B. (1989): Ritual Abuse, Los Angeles: Ritual Abuse Task Force, Los Angeles County Commission for Women.

Roberts, A. R. (2000): 'An Overview of Crisis Theory and Crisis Intervention', in A. R. Roberts (ed.) Crisis Intervention Handbook: Assessment, Treatment and Research, 2nd edition, New York: Oxford University Press: 3–30

Roberts, A. R. (2002): 'Assessment, Crisis Intervention and Trauma Treatment: The integrative ACT Intervention Model', Brief Treatment and Crisis Intervention 2(1): 1–21

Roemer, L., Litz, B. , et. al. (1998): 'Increases in Retrospective Accounts of War-zone Exposure Over Time: The Role of PTSD Symptom Severity', Journal of Traumatic Stress 11: 597-605

Rogers, R. (ed.) (1997): Clinical Assessment of Malingering and Deception, 2nd edition, New York: Guilford Publications.

Roth, P. (1986): 'A Man Saved By His Skills', The New York Times Book Review, October 12.

Rothenberg, R. (1960), The New American Medical Dictionary and Health Manual, 6th edition, New York: Signet

Ryn, Z. and Klodzinski, S. 'An der Grenze zwischen Leben und Tod. Ein Studie über die Erschei nung des „Muselmann" in Konzentrationslager [At the Borderline between Life and Death: A Study of the phenomenon of the Muselmann in the Concentration Camp]', in Auschwitz-Hefte, Vol. 1.

Reisner, S. (2003): 'Trauma: The Seductive Hypothesis', Journal of the American Psychoana lystic Association 51(2)

Sapolsky, R. M.: (1996) 'Why Stress is Bad For Your Brain', Science 273: 749-750

Schlesinger-Kipp, G. (2007) 'Childhood in World War II: German Psychoanalysts Remember', American Academy of Psychoanalysis and Dynamic Psychiatry 35(4): 541-554

Scholtza, H. J. ,Philliphs, V. M. (1887): 'Muti or Ritual Murder', Forensic Science International, 87(2)

Sekula, A. (1986): 'The Body and the Archive', October 39: 117-123

Seyle, H. (1998): 'A Syndrome Produced by Diverse Nocuous Agents', Journal of Neuropsychia try and Clinical Neuroscience 10: 230-231

Shalev, A. T. Peri, L., et. al. (1996): 'Predictors of PTSD in Injured Trauma Survivors: A Prospec tive Study', American Journal of Psychiatry 153: 219-225

Silove, D., Steel, Z. et. al., (2002): 'The Impact of Torture on Posttraumatic Stress Symptoms in War-Affected Tamil Refugees and Immigrants', Comprehensive Psychiatry 43(1): 49-55

Silove, D. (1996): 'Torture and Refugee Trauma: Implications for Nosology an Treatment of Posttraumatic Syndromes', in F. L. Mak and C. C. Nadelson (eds) International Review of Psychiatry, Washingon, DC: American Psychiatry Press: 211-233

Snyder, M. (1974): 'Self Monitoring of Expressive Behavior', Journal of Personality and Social Psychology 30.

Sontag, S. (2003): Regarding the Pain of Others, New York: Farrar, Straus and Giroux

Sophocles (1987): Antigone, trans. Andrew Brown, Wiltshire: Aris and Phillips.

Southwick, S. M. Morgan, C. A., et. al.(1995), 'Trauma-Related Symptoms in Veterans of Opera tion Desert Storm: A 2-Year Followup', American Journal of Psychiatry 152: 1150-1155

Sparr, L. F. and Bremner, J. D. (2005): 'Post-traumatic Stress Disorder and Memory: Prescient Medicolegal Testimony at the International War Crimes Tribunal?', Journal of the American Academy of Psychiatry Law 33(1): 71-8

Struk, J. (2004): Photographing the Holocaust: Interpretations of the Evidence, London and New York: I. B. Tauris.

Szondi, P. (2003): Celan Studies, Stanford: Stanford University Press, 2003

Tangney, J. P. Stuewig, J. et. al. (2007): 'Moral Emotions and Moral Behavior', Annual Review of Psychology 58: 345-372

Tarrier, N. and Gregg, L. (2004): 'Suicide risk in civilian PTSD patients: predictors of suicidal ideation, planning and attempts', Social Psychiatry and Psychiatric Epidemiology 39: 655-661

Timms, D. 'Identity, Community and the Internet', http://www.odeluce.stir.ac.uk/docs/Identitypaper26Aug.pdf

Vermetten, E., Vythilingam, S. M., et. al., (2003) 'Long-Term Treatment with Paroxetine Increases Verbal Declarative Memory and Hippocampal Volume in Posttraumatic Stress Disorder', Biologi cal Psychiatry 54: 693-702

Viederman, M. (1985): 'Grief: Normal and Pathological Variants', American Journal of Psychiatry 152(1): 226-228

Way, I. , Vandeusen, K. M. et. al. (2004): 'Vicarious Trauma: A Comparison of Clinicians Who Treat Survivors of Sexual Abuse and Sexual Offenders', Journal of interpersonal Violence 91(4): 49-71

Weiss, R. D., Najavitis, L. M., et. al. (1998): 'Substance Abuse and Psychiatric Disorders', in Richard Frances, Sheldon Miller and Avram H. Mack (eds) Clinical Textbook of Addictive Disorders, 2nd edition, London: The Guilford Press: 291-318

Wessel, I. and Moulds, M. (2008): 'Collective Memory: A Perspective from (Experimental) Clini cal Psychology', Memory 16(3): 288-304

Winer, D. 'Scripting News', http://www.scripting.com/2007/01/01.html.

Women: Memory and Repression in Argentina: http://argentina.engad.org/

Wohl, M. and Branscombe, N. (2005): 'Forgiveness and Collective Guilt Assignment to Histori cal Perpetrator Groups Depend on Level of Social Category Inclusiveness', Journal of Per sonality and Social Psychology, 88(2): 288-303

World Health Organization (1992): The ICD-10 Classification of Mental and Behavioural Disor ders: Clinical Descriptions and Diagnostic Guidelines, Geneva: WHO.

Worthington, E. L. Vanoyen, Jr. C., et. al. (2005): 'Forgiveness in Health Research and Medical Practice', EXPLORE: The Journal of Science and Healing 1(3): 169-176

Yeager, K. R. and Roberts, A. R. (2003): Differentiating Among Stress, Acute Stress Disorder, Crisis Episodes, Trauma, and PTSD: Paradigm and Treatment Goals, Oxford: Oxford Univer sity Press.

Yehuda, R. and Wong, M. C. (2002): 'Pathogenesis of Post-traumatic Stress Disorder and Acute Stress Disorder' in D. J. Stein and E. Hollander (eds) Textbook of Anxiety Disorders, Washington, DC: American Psychiatric Publishing: 374-85

Young, R. M. (1992): 'Benign and Virulent Projective Identification in Groups and Institutions', European Conference of the Rowantree Foundation, http://human-nature.com/rmyoung/papers/paper3h.html

i ek, S. (1989) The Sublime Object of Ideology, Verso, London.
_____. (2006) 'Freud Lives!', London Review of Books, May 25,
    http://www.lrb.co.uk/v28/n10/zize01_.html
Zola-Morgan, S. M. and Squire, L. R. (1990) 'The Primate Hippocampal Formation: Evidence for
    a Time-Limited Role in Memory Storage', Science 250: 288-90.
Zolghadr, T. (2006): 'Them and Us', Frieze 96

AUTHORS BIOGRAPHIES

Mauricio Arango is a Colombian-born artist and educator who lives and works in New York. His art practice alludes to the current dynamics of media, temporality, memory and forgetting. His work is an attempt to examine dominant narratives and assess what is lost within them: i.e. the disregard for – and reshaping of – world cartographies; the exclusion of minorities from national subjectivities; and the elimination of peripheries from the making of history. Arango's work has appeared at diverse venues, including: Artists Space in New York; Stills Gallery, Edinburgh, Scotland; the Sydney Opera House, Sydney, Australia; the International Society for Electronic Art at the San Jose Museum of Art, US; The Sao Paolo Museum of Contemporary Art, Brazil; The Colombian Biennial of Electronic Art, Bogota, Colombia. He has also received grants and commissions from the Sao Paulo Museum of Contemporary Art (Sao Paulo, Brazil), Forecast Public Artworks (Saint Paul, US), The Minnesota State Arts Board (US), the Kulturfonds der Stadt Salzburg (Salzburg, Austria), and from Low-Fi, The Net Art Locator (London, UK) among others. Recently he participated in the prestigious Independent Study Program at the Whitney Museum of American Art in New York. http://www.mauricioarango.net/

Sezgin Boynik completed his graduate studies in Mimar Sinan University Sociology Department with a thesis on Situationist International in 2003. He prepared the book Nationalism and Contemporary Art with Minna Henriksson and History of Punk and Underground Resources in Turkey 1978-1999 with Tolga Güldallý in 2007. Currently living in Pristina, Kosovo he lectures at the Faculty of Philology at the University of Priština.

Adila Laïdi-Hanieh is Algerian-Palestinian. She teaches modern Arab intellectual history and Palestinian contemporary art at Bir Zeit University, and writes on arts and cultural practice. She ran the Khalil Sakakini Cultural Centre in Ramallah from its establishment in 1996 to 2005 where she curated among other exhibitions the 100 Shaheed 100 Lives touring exhibition in 2001. She received an MA in Arab Studies from Georgetown University in the US, and studied painting with Fahr el Nissa Zeid.

Tihana Jendricko, M.D. is a working psychiatrist at Department of Psychiatry, Regional Center for Psychotrauma Zagreb, University Hospital of Dubrava. Her research has been centered on stress-related disorders and PTSD, the area in which she has published six scientific articles and about 20 abstracts.

Andreja Kuluncic lives in Zagreb, Croatia. Her artistic practice is characterised by an exploration of new models of sociability and communication situations, an interest in socially engaged themes, a confrontation with different audiences, and a collaboration on collective projects. She sets up her own interdisciplinary networks, regarding artistic work as a research in progress, a process of cooperation (co-creation) and self-organisation. She often asks the audience to actively participate and 'finish' the work. Kuluncic's work has been featured in exhibitions such as documenta 11, Manifesta4, Istanbul Biennial, as well as in the Whitney Museum and in PS1. http://www.andreja.org.

Geert Lovink is a media theorist, Internet critic and author of various publications including Dark Fiber, Uncanny Networks, My First Recession and Zero Comments. He worked on various media projects in Eastern Europe and India and earned his PhD from the University of Melbourne, Australia. In 2003, he worked as a post-doctoral researcher at the Centre for Critical and Cultural Studies, University of Queensland. He is co-founder of projects that combine meetings, publications and online debates such as The Digital City, Nettime, Fibreculture, Incommunicado, MyCreativity and VideoVortex. In 2004, Lovink founded the Institute of Network Cultures within the Interactive Media School at Amsterdam Polytechnic (HvA) and was appointed Associate Professor at the Media & Culture Department, University of Amsterdam. His blog can be found at http://www.networkcultures.org/geert.

Ana Peraica (Split, Croatia) Raised as the third generation in a family of photographers, she started working with 'technical images', becoming a curator of photography, film/video and new media. Her essays in the domains of visual studies, media theory and political analysis focusing on contemporary cultural products have been published in magazines such as Springerin (Vienna), Issues in Contemporary Arts and Culture (Maastricht), Pavilion (Bucharest), Afterimage (Rochester) and many others.... She is an editor of the reader ena na raskrizju ideologija (Split, HULU/Governmental Office for the Equality of Rights, Split, 2007) after the project Woman at the Crossroad of Ideologies (alternate title). A selection of her essays entitled Sub/verzije is in print with Revolver Publishing/Vice Versa. She is currently writing a new book Photography as the Evidence. She teaches Visual Culture, Media Arts and Propaganda Systems in Media at the Department of Cultural Studies, Faculty of Philosophy at the University of Rijeka. Peraica is a member of IKT, AICA and ISAST.

Tina Peraica is a working psychotherapist at Department of Psychiatry, Regional Centre for Psychotrauma Zagreb, University Hospital Dubrava. She is educated in Integrative Psychotherapy and Psychosocial Treatment of Domestic Violence Perpetrator. She is a Secretary of the Croatian Association of Integrative Psychotherapy and Coordinator and psychotherapist at the Government Counselling Centre for Child and Adult Domestic Violence Victims. She has published four scientific articles and the same number of book chapters and about 30 abstracts, mostly in regard to stress related disorders.

Marko Peljhan founded the arts organisation Projekt Atol in 1992 and its technological branch, PACT SYSTEMS, which was started by creating an online satellite navigation urban interface project, the UCOG-144. In 1995 he co-founded LJUDMILA (Ljubljana Digital Media Lab). In 1999, the Projekt Atol Flight Operations was founded, serving as the organisational branch for ight and space ight related projects. Since 1999, Peljhan works as the ight director of the parabolic art/science ights with the Yuri Gagarin Cosmonaut Training Centre in Moscow and the MIR – Microgravity Interdisciplinary Research Consortium – which brings together artists and scientists to work within the aerospace field in an integrated way. From 2001 to 2004, he served in the Government of Slovenia's Strategic Council for Information Society as a representative of new media based and technology development NGOs. He is also one of the most acclaimed Slovenian contemporary conceptual artists, working at the intersection of media, technology and arts. In 2006, the new initiative, which is the continuation of the Makrolab project, I-TASC, was endorsed by the International Polar Year. His work has appeared at major international exhibitions and venues such as Documenta X (Kassel, Germany); the Second Johannesburg Biennale (South Africa); Ars Electronica (Linz, Austria); Media City (Seoul, Korea), Gwangju Biennale (Korea); Manifesta; Venice Biennale (Italy); International Symposium of Electronic Art (ISEA); Dutch Electronic Art Festival (DEAF) (Rotterdam, the Netherlands); Transmediale (Berlin, Germany) and others. Among the prizes for his work, he received the Medienkunst prize at the ZKM (Karlsruhe, Germany) in 2000; in 2001, he received the Golden Nica, together with Carsten Nicolai for their work Polar; in 2004, he was given the UNESCO Digital Media Art Award for Makrolab, and in 2007, was awarded the Preseren Foundation Prize, also for Makrolab.

Martha Rosler's work is centred on everyday life and the public sphere, often with an eye to women's experience. Recurrent concerns are the media and war, as well as architecture and the built environment, from housing and homelessness to systems of transport. Her work has been seen in the Venice Biennale of 2003; the Liverpool Biennial and the Taipei Biennial (both 2004); as well as many major international survey shows, including the Documenta exhibition in Kassel, Germany, and several Whitney Biennials. She has had numerous solo exhibitions. A retrospective of her work, 'Positions in the Life World' (1998-2000), was shown in five European cities and, concurrently, at the International Center of Photography and the New Museum of Contemporary Art (both in New York). Her solo show, 'London Garage Sale', was held at the Institute of Contemporary Arts in London in June 2005, revisiting a series of exhibitions she has held since 1973 that centre on the American garage sale. E- ux sponsored 'The Martha Rosler Library', which made over 7,500 volumes from her private collection available as a public resource from November 2005; the collection then travelled to the Frankfurter Kunstverein in Germany and to Antwerp's Muhka (Museum of Contemporary Art) in conjunction with NICC, an artist-run space. She serves in an advisory capacity to the departments of education at the Whitney Museum of American Art and the Museum of Modern Art, the Buell Center for the Study of American Architecture at Columbia University, and the Center for Urban Pedagogy (all in New York City).

Marko Stamenkovicic is an art historian, critic, and curator based in Belgrade (Serbia). Appointed curator at the O3ONE Art Space in Belgrade since April 2006. BA in Art History at the University of Belgrade, Faculty of Humanities (Art History Department, 2003). MA in Cultural Policy and Cultural Management at the University of Arts in Belgrade (UNESCO Chair for Cultural Management and Cultural Policy in the Balkans, 2005). Since 2001, active in various international programs (Artists Space Gallery, New York; Guggenheim Collection, Venice; SKC Gallery, Belgrade). His research interests range from interdisciplinary analyses of contemporary visual arts and curatorial studies to institutional cultural organisation, art management, and political, social and economic aspects of aesthetic discourses. His current engagement, within the self-organised working platform art-e-conomy, revolves around the intersection of contemporary art, economy, and business, where the new global markets and their proper logic are seen as a site of social and cultural events, which are globally determined by the social and cultural behavior of participants/consumers. He is focused on themes that posit social campaigning, economic awareness and corporate (political) citizenship as the dominant social forms of organisation. His current research, based on the post-Marxist thought, revolves around the issue of contemporary art curatorship, focusing on themes such as: the status of curatorial practices in the post-socialist condition, cultural implications of EU enlargement, methodologies in terms of organising exhibitions in the context of globalisation, critical positioning within the global sphere of art production, and discursive projects dealing explicitly with political, social, and economic features of contemporary art and art system. Beside exhibition-making and curatorial criticism, he is writing on issues of contemporary art and collaborates with artists, collectives, institutions and organisations that strategically examine corporate system developments in the global art world.

Stevan Vukovic graduated from the Faculty of Philosophy at the University of Belgrade. He continued his postgraduate studies at Jan Van Eyck Akademie in Maastricht, the Netherlands and Bauhaus Dessau in Germany. He is currently working on a PhD thesis at the Fine Art Academy at the University of Art in Belgrade. He holds teaching positions as a lecturer in Art in Public Space at the Faculty of Fine Art in Osijek, Croatia, and at the Faculty of Architecture, at the Univesity of Belgrade (http://www.publicart-publicspace.org/). He also works as a coordinator for visual art at the SKC Belgrade, editor for digital arts at the O3ONE project space in Belgrade, as well as being editor for culture at the Forum Magazine of the Union of Architects of Serbia.

Dot.Bomb and Boo Hoo

It is an ironic detail that the dotcon ur-parable, Michael Wolff's *Burn Rate*, already appeared in 1998, way before the phenomenon got its 'dotcom' label. Wolff, a "leader of an industry without income" describes the 1994-1997 period which his New York new media publishing company turned out to be an 'Internet venture', attracting venture capital. Michael Wolff was the creator of the best-selling *NetGuide*, one of the first books to introduce the Internet to the general public. Being one of the first movers he quickly turned his company into a 'leading' content provider. With a 'burn rate' of half a million a month Wolf New Media LLC subsequently got dumped by VCs. Michael Wolff explains the hype logic under which he operated:

> The Internet, because it is a new industry making itself up as it goes along, is particularly susceptible to the art of the spin. Those of us in the industry want the world to think the best of us, Optimism is our bank account; fantasy is our product; press releases are our good name.[385]

The company operated under Rosetto's law, named after *Wired* founder Louis Rosetto that says that content, not technology, is king. Early Internet entrepreneurs with a media and publishing background such as Rosetto and Wolf had the utopian believe that technology would become a transparent and low-priced commodity. Revenue streams would come from marketing partnerships, advertisement, direct sales and most of all, content replication, not from technology-related businesses. Views diverted as to whether or not consumers were willing to pay for content. So far Internet users would only pay for hardware, access and, to a certain level, for software. "On the West coast, the Wired disciples believed information wanted to be free; here in New York they blissfully believed information wanted to be paid for".[386] Neither model worked. Users were mistaken for customers. Around the same time Michael Wolff left the scene, the nearly bankrupt *Wired*, after two failed IPOs, in early 1998 was sold to the 'old media' publishing giant Condé Nast. Wolff: "My early belief that the Internet was a new kind of manufacturing and distribution economics, was replaced".(p. 328).

The dotcoms became victims of their own speed religion. The dromo-Darwinist belief in the 'survival of the fastest' (you are either one or zero, with nothing in between) dominated all other considerations. The 'amazing over-the-horizon radar' capacity (John Doerr) broke down almost immediately after first signs of a recession set in. The hyper growth dogma and drive towards the dominance of a not yet existing e-commerce sector overshadowed the economic common sense, fuelled by the presumption of something, very big, out there, an opportunity, as blank and beautiful as a virgin, waiting to be snatched.

The dotcom could be defined by its business model, not by its technology focus. There was hardly any emphasis on research ('too slow'). The domination of high-risk finance capital over the dotcom business model remains an uncontested truth. Dot companies were depending on capital markets, not on their customer base. Michael Wolff sums up what was going to be a dotcom mantra:

385.Michael Wolff, Burn Rate, London: Orion Books, 1999, p. XII.
386.Michael Wolff, p. 63. In Burn Rate there is, in my view, an accurate description of Louis Rosetto's Amsterdam-based magazine Electric Word and the climate in the early nineties which let to their move to San Francisco (not New York) in order to found Wired (described in the chapter 'How it got to be a wired world' pp. 26-51).

The hierarchy, the aristocracy, depends on being first. Land, as in most aristocracies, is the measure. Not trade. Who has the resources to claim the most valuable property – occupy space through the promotion of brands, the building of name recognition, the creation of an identity – is the name of the game. Conquer first, reap later.[387]

David Kuo's *Dot.Bomb* is perhaps the most accessible dotcom story in the genre thus far. Unlike Michael Wolff with his investigative new journalism style, Kuo lacks the critical ambition and just wrote down what he experienced. The book tells the story from an employee perspective about the rise and rise and sudden fall of the retail portal Value America.[388] Craig Winn, a rightwing Christian with political ambitions who already had gone through an earlier bankruptcy case with Dynasty Lighting, founded the retail portal in 1996. Comparable to mail order, the basic idea behind Value America was to eliminate the middlemen and ship products directly from manufacturers to consumers. Winn got powerful financial backing but the portal didn't quite work and attracted only few customers, offering poor service to its clients. In the face of rising expenditure, the board of directors forced Winn to resign not long before the company was liquidated in August 2000.[389]

Value America is a perfect example of a dotcom scheme which had the coward mentality of messing up, knowing that someone else would deal with the carnage. As David Kuo writes of the underlying logic: "We were supposed to do the Internet shuf e—get in, change the world, get rich, and get out".[390] The New Economy could only function under the presumption that in the end the 'old economy', in one way or another, was going to pay the bill; either in another round of venture capital financing, investments of pension funds or institutional investors, banks, employees or day traders. Somebody was going to bleed. In dotcom newspeak this scheme was better known as 'prosper'. Akin to pyramid schemes everyone was going to 'prosper'. Not from the profitability of e-commerce but from large sums of money that would change hands quickly, in a perfectly legal way, covered up by official auditing reports, way before the world would find out about the true nature of the New Economy.

Towards the end of his account, David Kuo wonders why events didn't turn out the way they were meant to: "We discovered that the prevailing wisdom was awed. The Internet is a tremendous force for change, but the industry chews up more folks than it blesses". (p. 305) As a true Darwinist of his age, Kuo admits that chances of getting rich that quick and easy weren't really that high. While in Las Vegas, looking at an IMAX movie about the Alaska gold rush of the 1890s, he muses:

---

387. Michael Wolff, p. 8.
388.http://web.archive.org/web/20000619022736/http://www.valueamerica.com/ (this is the URL of
    Value America as kept alive inside one of the worlds biggest web archives).
389.Value America's downfall from $74.25 a share on April 8, 1999 to $2 one year later made VA one of
    the first in a long series of dotcom crashes. John A. Byrne in Business Week Online, May 1, 2000 wrote
    a stunning reconstruction of Value America's doings.
390.David Kuo, Inside an Internet Goliath – from Lunatic Optimism to Panic and Crash, London: Little,
    Brown and Company, 2001, p. 305.

More than hundred thousand people ventured near the Arctic Circle in search of their chunk of gold. Of those only a handful ever found anything of any worth. A few thousand covered the cost of their trip. Most came back cold and penniless. Thousand froze to death.[391]

And then comes the revelation:

The truth hit me over the head like a gold miner's shovel. Despite the hype, headlines, and hysteria, this was just a gold rush we were in, not a gold mine we found. We might look like hip, chic, cutting-edge, new economy workers, but in fact, a lot of us were kin to those poor, freezing fools, who had staked everything on turning up a glittering of gold. [392]

The comparison with the 1890's gold rush might be attractive explanation for those involved. The gold rush narrative reinterprets business as lottery. There were no concepts or decisions, just chance statistics. The right historical parallels would perhaps be tulipomania (Amsterdam, 1636), the South Sea bubble (UK, 1720), railway stocks in 19th century UK or the boom of the Roaring Twenties that ended in the 1929 stock market crash. Compared to the Alaskan Gold rush there was no hardship during Dotcommania. Long hours were voluntary and compensated by parties and stock options. Besides some social pressure to comply there was no physical endurance to speak of. All participants are still in an ecstatic mood and would go for it again, if they could. None of the dotcommers froze to dead. It was good fun. As the now famous quote of a boo.com analyst says:

For the first nine months of its existence, the company was run on the economic rule of the three C's—champagne, caviar and the Concorde. It's not often you get to spend $130 million. It was the best fun.[393]

Boo.com, a fashion, sports and lifestyle venture, is another case of the pursuit of arrogance. Sold as entrepreneurial courage, it got into the fortunate position to fool around with investors' money while aunting all existing economic laws. Boo.com was destined to be become a global e-tailor empire. Way before a single item was sold it was valued at $390 million. Founded by two Swedes, Ernst Malmsten and Kajsa Leander in early 1998, when the New Economy craze picked up in Europe, boo was supposed to become the first global online retailer of sports and designer cloths, "using only the most cutting-edge technology". *Boo Hoo* is Ernst Malmsten's stunning hubris-laden account that tells of the excitement of how easy it was to collect millions for an over-hyped business plan, assisted by of ine 3D demo design and the right buzzwords. London- based boo.com got backing of the Bennetton family, a small British investment firm called Eden Capital, the luxury-goods magnate Bernard Arnault and a number of Middle Eastern investors. Despite, or thanks to, all the money boo.com turned out to be a management nightmare. As a Swedish report analysed the company:

---

391. Kuo, p. 306.
392. Kuo, p. 306.
393. London Telegraph, May 19, 2000. Richard Barbook, in a private email, remarks: "It was *4* Cs in the joke about Boo.com. Being an up-tight Tory newspaper, The Daily Telegraph had to leave out the C which can make you feel very self-confident about everything: cocaine. Don't forget that the English consume more illegal chemicals per head than any other nation in the EU".

Ericsson was no good at systems integration. Hill and Knowlton did not know how to sell the story to the media. JP Morgan was not bringing in investors fast enough. The chief technology officer was not up to his job. Even Patrik Hedelin, a fellow founder, was too much of an individual to be a good chief financial officer.[394]

The Boo dream imploded, only six months after its launch. After having burned $130 million Boo. com folded less than a month after the NASDAQ crash in April 2000.

Retrospectively, Ernst Malmsten is ready to admit that the core of the problem at boo.com was speed, the belief that Rome could be built in a day.

Instead of focusing single-mindedly on just getting the website up and running, I had tried to implement an immensely complex and ambitious vision in its entirety. Our online magazine, the rollout of overseas offices, and the development of new product lines to sell on our site—these were all things that could have waited until the site was in operation. But I had wanted to build utopia instantly. It had taken eleven Apollo missions to land on the moon; I had wanted to do it all in one.[395]

Those who taught Kuo and Malmsten & Co. these New Economy truisms remain un- named. George Gilder, Kevin Kelly or Tom Peters do not show up in these chronicles. As in a psychedelic rush the dotcom actors got caught in events and moments later were dropped into the garbage bin of history, left behind with nothing but question marks. Ernst Malmsten:

In my head I see images of all boo's employees, who worked day and night with such enthusiasm; and the investors who were so confident of our future that they had put $130 million into the company. Two years' work, five overseas offices, 350 staff. All these people trusted me and now I have failed. What have I done? How could things have gone so wrong?[396]

As instructed by 'leadership' gurus, Ernst and Kajsa wasted a lot of time and resources creating a brand for their not-yet-existing business. The company image got turned into a *Gesamtkunst-werk* (total art work). The founders showed total devotion. "We determined that every aspect of our business, from the look of our website to the design of our business cards, should send a clear message who we were and what we stood for".[397] The launch of the (empty) boo brand throughout 1999, fuelled by press releases, demo designs and parties, all of which created the risk of media over-exposure at a time when the web portal itself was nowhere near finished. On the technology front, Ericsson, responsible for the e-commerce platform, turned out to do a lousy job. As Malmsten explains it:

---

394. Incompetence backed by less expert investors, 4 December 2001. Reviewer: A reader from Stockholm, Sweden (found on thewww.amazon.com.uk site).
395. Ernst Malmsten, together with Erik Portanger and Charles Drazin, Boo Hoo, a dotcom story from concept to catastrophe, London: Random House, 2001, p. 233.
396. Malmsten, p. 4.
397. Malmsten, p. 106.

The breaking point had come when its 30-page feasibility study landed on my desk... The first thing that struck me how imsy it seemed. Then I got the bill. At $500.000, it was roughly five times more than I'd expected. As we had been having considerable doubts about working with Ericsson, I saw no reason why I should accept it.[398]

This left Boo without a master plan, thereby creating a delay of many months:

There was one thing guaranteed to bring us back down to earth again. Technology. As we began to pull together the different parts of the platform, more and more bugs seemed to pop up. So many in fact that no one had any clear notion when the launch date would actually be.[399]

Still, "technology felt more like a pip in the tooth than something we really had to worry about. It barely dented that summer's mood of bullish self-confidence". (p. 215-216) In early August 1999, only weeks before launching the boo.com site, Malmsten discovers that pretty much nothing works.

Systems architecture, the user interface, product data, the application development process— there were problems in pretty much all these areas. Our overall project management was a disaster too. We were now working with eighteen different technology companies who were scattered around the world. What they needed was a central architect.[400]

Boo didn't have any version control. A central system of management should have been in place to track versions and create a central code base.

In the case of Boo and Value America it is significant that there was no executive technologist on board in an early stage of the venture. The lesson Malmsten learned from all these disasters is a surprising one. Instead of scaling down at a crucial moment, thereby giving technology more time to develop and give technologists a greater say in the overall project planning, Malmsten retrospectively suggests outsourcing. "We should never have tried to manage the development of the technology platform ourselves". (p. 308) However, in e-commerce there were—and still are—no out-of-the-box solutions. Unaware of the imperfect nature of technology the dotcom founders showing off a regressive understanding of the Internet. Instead of entering deeper into the complexities and the ever-changing standards, they simply instrumentalized technology as a tool, which was supposed to do the job—just like the ads said.

Surprisingly, both Kuo and Malmsten admit they hadn't used Internet before they got involved in their dotcom venture and do not even particularly like the medium. Internet entrepreneur Malmsten confesses he doesn't particularly like computers and hadn't used the Internet before September 1996. In both stories technology is portrayed as an 'obstacle,' not the core and pride of the business. As technological outsiders Kuo and Malmsten have visibly been irritated about the imperfect nature of technology. The permanent state of instability is a source of eternal enjoyment for geeks—and should be permanent worry for those who are in it for the business.

398.Malmsten, p. 108.
399.Malmsten, p. 215.
400.Malmsten, p. 231.

Victims' Symptom (PTSD and Culture)

Victims' Symptom is a collection of interviews, essays, artists' statements and glossary definitions, which was originally launched as a Web project (http://victims.labforculture.org). Produced in 2007, the project brought together cases related to past and current sites of conflict such as Srebrenica, Palestine, and Kosovo reporting from different (and sometimes conflicting) international viewpoints. The Victims Symptom Reader collects critical concepts in media victimology and addresses the representation of victims in economies of war.

Contributions by: Mauricio Arango, Sezgin Boynik, Alejandro Duque, Andreja Kuluncic, Adila Laïdi-Hanieh, Geert Lovink, Marko Peljhan, Martha Rosler and Stevan Vukovic.

Edited by Ana Peraica, writer and curator of media arts, photography, film and new media, based in Split, Croatia.

Printed on Demand
ISBN: 978-90-78146-11-7

www.ingramcontent.com/pod-product-compliance
Lightning Source LLC
LaVergne TN
LVHW012330060326
832902LV00011B/1815